Praise for *It's Not a Rehearsal*:

'It's a brave, honest and funny book, complete with an eccentric, pushy mother, drink, drugs, mental breakdown and even a seven-year threesome' *Sunday Mirror*

'A colourful life which will make for a potentially explosive read' *Daily Express*

'It is an unflinchingly frank story – but also a brave and deeply touching one, coloured by Amanda's hilarious sense of humour' *Daily Mail*

'Unconventional and utterly engrossing . . . Amanda Barrie's story is the very stuff of an original and indeed courageous life' *Gay Times*

'Her book is a moving account by a brave, vibrant and beguiling actress' Lynda Lee-Potter, *Daily Mail*

'Her autobiography reveals the personality of a hardworking actress who comes across as amusing and downright nice' *Manchester Evening News*

Amanda Barrie was born Shirley Broadbent in Ashton-under-Lyne near Manchester. By the age of thirteen she was working as a chorus girl and in 1956 became a regular at London's famous Winston's Club.

Following smaller film parts, she played the eponymous lead in *Carry on Cleo* in 1963 and her West End roles have included *Oh Kay!*, *Noises Off*, *Stepping Out* and *Any Wednesday*.

Amanda became a regular on *Coronation Street* in 1989 and her departure in 2001 was marked by a controversial cancer story line. After leaving the soap Amanda returned to the stage before her new television role in ITV's *Bad Girls*.

IT'S NOT A REHEARSAL

THE AUTOBIOGRAPHY

AMANDA BARRIE

WITH HILARY BONNER

headline

First published in 2002
by HEADLINE BOOK PUBLISHING

First published in paperback in 2003
by HEADLINE BOOK PUBLISHING

10 9 8 7 6 5 4 3 2 1

ISBN 0 7553 1123 X

Typeset in Granjon by Avon DataSet Ltd, Bidford-on-Avon, Warwickshire

Printed and bound in Great Britain by
Clays Ltd, St Ives plc
Text design by Jane Coney

HEADLINE BOOK PUBLISHING
A division of Hodder Headline
338 Euston Road,
London NW1 3BH

www.headline.co.uk
www.hodderheadline.com

For my mother.

ACKNOWLEDGEMENTS

Thanks, in alphabetical order because I did not know how else to arrange them, are particularly due to the following for their help during the writing of this book: Annie, Barry, Beryl, Caroline, Catherine, Chris and Edna, Heather, Rachel and Maggi.

As a dyslexic I could not even write a postcard unaided, let alone a book. And if I had attempted to do so readers would have had to purchase their own personal code-breaking machine the size of the famous Enigma. So I turned to my writer friend Hilary Bonner, who is much the same size, to decipher my outpourings – which, to my gratitude and relief, she has done so faithfully that I have almost begun to believe that I did write down every word myself.

PROLOGUE

✌

hen I was a little girl I dreamed of being a great ballerina, but as I always seemed to be the swan at the end pulling faces at the audience to make them laugh, it didn't quite work out.

I am told that my life story may surprise those who know me only from afar, and probably best of all as Alma in *Coronation Street*. Actually, as related in the pages of this book, it has also surprised me somewhat. Living it is not quite the same as seeing it in print.

I made my professional theatre début when I was four. I ran away to become a Soho showgirl when I was thirteen. I first fell in love when I was eleven. And I mean 'in love'. It was no schoolgirl crush, but instead a deeply emotional experience which has coloured everything

1

that has happened to me since. Years later, I asked one of my former headmistresses what sort of child I had been.

'You were never a child,' she replied.

Well, I may not have been then, but I have frequently turned into one since. If I had to describe myself in one sentence I would say that I am a mixture of hopeful innocence and weary worldliness.

From my home town of Ashton-under-Lyne to the West End; from being expelled from two schools thanks largely to my dyslexia to somehow learning to play Shakespeare; from ballet school and panto in my grandfather's theatre to *Coronation Street*'s Weatherfield; from that first schoolgirl love through all the diverse relationships in which I have found myself immersed; my life has at least been full and varied, much more so than I realised until putting this book together.

It has also, I am told, been an unusual one. I don't know. I have nothing to compare it with.

I do know that it has been a fairly spectacular roller-coaster ride. I know that periods of it have been quite thrilling. I know that on occasions I have reached for the stars while on others I have fallen to the ground in despair. Literally.

Yet I have always been able to laugh, and indeed laughter has very often been my salvation.

I was blessed with a certain ability as a performer, and I had the good fortune to discover at an early age that the theatre was where I belonged. But so much else has eluded me. I have never been able to achieve a proper homelife the way it seems to me almost everybody else does. The theatre has always been my only real home, which I know sounds a bit trite but it is the truth, as is everything you will read on these pages.

I have been lucky enough to have been pretty successful in my career, despite my battles with health problems, including a nervous breakdown and dyslexia. I have worked, over the years, with the very best in show business. I can name-drop for England. I have made a number of films, appeared in countless television shows, and played most theatres in the country including almost all those in the West End, where I took the lead in shows like *Oh, Kay!*, the musical written for my all-time heroine Gertrude Lawrence, Alan Ayckbourn's *Absurd Person Singular*, Michael Frayn's *Noises Off*, and Richard Harris's *Stepping Out*. And I am grateful to the British public for remembering. I still receive as many fan letters for *Carry On Cleo*, released in 1964, as I do for *Coronation Street*, from which I departed last year amid much emotional turmoil when my long-time character Alma died of cancer.

Throughout it all, until now, I have been a very private person, guarding my personal life with the ferocity of an angry Rottweiler.

Often I have been protecting others as well as myself. The world, thankfully, has changed since I was growing up and starting out into it. As a young woman I felt that I had to be like everyone else in order to survive, and I deeply desired to be so. However, I was all too aware that I wasn't like everyone else. I felt I didn't quite belong – except, of course, in the theatre. I never dared let people know what I was feeling deep inside because I actually believed that the truth would destroy me.

I always knew that I would tell the truth one day, and I find it a great relief now to be open and frank about everything that I am. I have never had secrets from family and close friends, but it has taken me this long to be able to cope with the idea of the rest of the world knowing all about me.

I have decided to be honest in this book about every aspect of my life, including my sexuality, partly because I don't want to hide what I am from anyone any more, and partly because I am sick to death with being forced to defend myself when I don't see why I should have to.

I am frequently chased by paparazzi photographers, particularly if I am in the company of someone they think they may be able to link me with romantically. I recently asked one such young man if he would pursue his grandmother through the streets of Soho. He merely looked bewildered. In January this year I was astonished to find the *News of the World* camped outside my hotel in Bradford where I was appearing in pantomime. They were apparently investigating my love life. I am sixty-seven years old. I have a bus pass. I do not know whether to be appalled or flattered. I am definitely staggered, and – on a good day – more than a little amused.

There is no need for any further investigation. The truth – all of it – is within these pages. I could not see the point in producing an autobiography unless I told the truth.

I have changed the names of certain people in order to continue to protect them. I have no desire to put anyone in a position of having aspects of their lives that they have always kept private revealed against their wishes. I know all too well what the fear of that is like.

But as far as my life goes – this is it.

And by God, it wasn't a rehearsal!

CHAPTER ONE

❧

I was born one stormy Saturday night in the old Lancashire mill-town of Ashton-under-Lyne, my arrival heralded by a violent cloud-burst over the bleak moorland nearby. I had no idea, of course, as I bellowed my way indignantly into the world in the little back bedroom above my grandmother's tailor's shop, that the weather raging outside might prove an omen of things to come.

It seems, however, that I began my life in much the same way that I was to proceed, at least through my childhood – stubbornly, and with more than my share of belligerence directed at forces, people and events contriving to take control of me without my say-so.

The traumas of my birth, which apparently took an inordinately long time, were vividly and somewhat gruesomely described to me on an annual basis by my mother, Connie, from before I even understood

5

what she was talking about, until her death. Every year, on my birthday, 14 September, I was re-born.

'I was just going into labour now,' she would begin early in the morning. Features contorted, eyes rolling, arms waving, she would act it all out for me. Throughout the day I would be given a highly dramatic almost minute-by-minute account of her agony and my reluctance to emerge.

'You were an extremely lazy baby,' she told me. 'You just couldn't be bothered to be born.'

Although my mother was never a professional performer she was one of the most theatrical people I ever encountered. And she was very beautiful. She had lovely chestnut hair, soft brown eyes and always dressed as glamorously as possible. Every man she met seemed to fall for her, and she could always bend them to her will. She was a terrifyingly determined woman. You crossed Connie Broadbent at your peril. Yet she could also be utterly beguiling. More often than not she got her own way without anyone fully realising what had happened.

There was a telling early indication of her extraordinary ambition for me, an ambition which was to dominate both our lives, in the name she chose for me. I was christened Shirley Anne Broadbent – after Shirley Temple.

My very first memory, going right back to when I was a baby, is of chewing the blue paint off my cot, although I have no idea why, or even how, as I didn't have any teeth at the time. My next memory at around the age of two, and one of the most vivid of my childhood, is of not being able to sleep because I had rags tied into my hair and I couldn't put my head on the pillow. My mother, of course, had decided that I should have curly hair just like my child-star namesake. So almost every night of my childhood, from when I was a toddler, it was Curly-Top and rags for me.

Connie invariably did things differently to other people. I was born in my grandparents' home above their tailor's shop because she refused to go into hospital, but fortunately at least recognised that she should have someone like my Grandmother Pike around. In fact, I think it was only my grandmother who persuaded her that a doctor might also be a good idea.

At the time my parents had quite a grand house in Mottram, nearer the moors, which I don't really remember because we only lived there for the first two years of my life before moving into the centre of Ashton to a house in Richmond Street, close to my grandparents. I think my mother was happier there. She always had fantasies about being out in far away places, but in fact she was a complete townie. She liked the idea of living in ridiculously remote locations miles from anywhere, but when she got there and found she couldn't nip to whatever was the nearest Ashton had to Harvey Nics in the thirties, the reality didn't suit her at all.

My father, Hubert, an accountant, was a nice, gentle, quiet person who probably wanted nothing more than a nice, gentle, quiet sort of life – something he was never likely to get with my mother. He had a lovely sense of humour, played the piano, and, albeit only for his own amusement, wrote comic monologues. Nonetheless, he always seemed to me to be quite ordinary compared with Mother and was totally over-shadowed by her. But then, almost everybody was.

Even my parents' wedding, orchestrated, of course, by Connie, was extraordinary. The Broadbents and the Pikes considered themselves to be among the foremost families in the town, and my mother made sure that her wedding lived up to all expectations. She even arranged for a flock of doves to be released above Ashton Parish Church as the wedding party emerged after the ceremony. God knows what happened to those doves, poor things. They probably developed a severe bout of bronchitis on their way to Oldham.

Hubert wore morning dress while Connie was resplendent in white satin with a train several feet long. There were no less than eight bridesmaids, plus two 'dainty attendants' as they were known – a little boy and girl dressed as pages.

The local paper devoted almost an entire broadsheet page to this over-the-top event, including publishing a list not only of the wedding guests but also of their gifts. Quite an encouragement to generosity, I should imagine.

> At one o'clock, half an hour before the ceremony, the footpath along Stamford-street, between Old-square and St Michael's-square were crowded with people anxious to catch a glimpse of the bride and her bridesmaids, and of the guests as they arrived.
>
> Over five hundred people crowded into the courtyard in front of the church, and a special detachment of police was necessary to control the crowds and regulate the traffic.
>
> As the bride and groom left the church after the ceremony, the police had great difficulty in maintaining a passage for them to the street, and the bride was nearly swept off her feet, so eager were the crowd to get a glimpse of her. It was only by forming a circle round the bride and bridegroom that they were able to reach their car in safety.
>
> *Ashton Reporter*, 30 September 1933.

My mother always knew how to attract attention. I suspect that, had he been given a choice, my father would have preferred a much quieter, more private wedding.

Hubert had become an accountant against his will, rather strangely forced into the profession by my grandfather who, although an accountant too, was also a very colourful character, an idiosyncratic entrepreneur. Grandfather Broadbent had a rather unlikely past. As a young man he had worked for the railways and been a bit of a revolutionary, certainly an ardent trade-union activist. He loved the theatre and eventually came to run the Theatre Royal in Ashton, helping to start the show-business careers of The Crazy Gang and Jack Hilton, among others.

Grandfather Broadbent was almost as ambitious for me to succeed in a show-business career as my mother – and that was going some! Mummy wanted me to dance, so I danced. Aided and abetted by Grandfather Broadbent, she sent me to dancing class when I was two and a half. It never occurred to me to say 'no'. At that age you go where your parents take you, don't you? And at that age even I did what I was told.

My mother made Gypsy Rose Lee seem like Mother Teresa – shy, modest and retiring. From when I was just a toddler, every night I would be made to dance and sing for her and she would say to me, 'Use your eyes,' and all those other hideous things stage mothers come out with. Then from the moment I started to appear in theatre she was in the wings shouting, 'Sing up, baby. Smile. SMILE!' She would also be organising everybody else while making her bitter hatred of all the other mothers and their children perfectly clear.

My father thought the whole thing was ridiculous. I still have this vision of him being told to sit in a corner of the living room while my mother rolled back the carpet and I was made to perform. That happened virtually every night. It seems crazy now to think that my parents would both only have been in their late twenties at the time (my mother was twenty-two and my father twenty-four when I was born) and that I was already an old pro.

I was always anxious when I performed. Not surprising when you think about what went on. Almost all the mothers were awful, relentlessly pushing their kids on in competitions and auditions.

My first theatrical tragedy was watching a little girl at some talent contest being zipped into a costume, and it just zipped up her skin. Nobody seemed to notice until it was too late. I remember thinking, 'Oh, dear. Now it's got to be unzipped and all that skin will come out the other side.' Unsurprisingly the poor girl screamed the place down.

Even family holidays were not allowed to be merely holidays for me. The clue came when Mummy packed. She always took my dance costumes, my tap shoes and my music. The bucket and spade came last, not that I had much time for them. We entered every seaside competition going and I remember only too well the lengths to which she would go.

We went on holiday to Llandudno when I was three. It was towards the end of that long eerie summer of 1939 during which everybody seemed to be trying to forget the threat of a war they knew was fast approaching. In some ways it was just like any typical British family seaside holiday at the time. Fat, grown-up relatives, wearing about six overcoats, sat around in deck chairs, watching me trying to get into a freezing cold sea and yelling, 'It'll be all right when you get your shoulders under.'

I remember getting into trouble for collecting used Durex off the beach and trying to blow them up thinking they were balloons. I remember being rubbed down while covered in sand so that it felt as if I was being sandpapered, and finally being given hot tea to drink to thaw me out. Pretty normal stuff really before the days of package holidays in the sunshine. But for me there was always another side.

IT'S NOT A REHEARSAL

In Llandudno there was a crisis when Mummy discovered that she had forgotten to take my sheet music for 'I Am Just a Little Girl Who's Looking For a Little Boy to Love', the Gershwin song, which was my current party piece. She soon found a solution though. She simply walked into the middle of a full orchestra rehearsal on the pier and stopped it. There were hundreds of musicians there. I believe the orchestra was the Welsh Philharmonic but that did not faze my mother one little bit. She just strode up to the conductor (whom I later learned was John Morarva, who was quite well known then) and said, 'Excuse me. I have a terrible problem. My daughter hasn't got her music. Could you help, please?'

He was so astonished that he did. He sat me on the piano, on the stage, and asked me to sing the song to him, then he jotted the notes down on a piece of sheet music, and underneath he wrote 'I Am Just a Little Girl'. He scribbled it all down and instructed my mother to tell whoever would be accompanying me to play the chords underneath. So up she pranced to the musicians in the talent competition I was in and they did precisely that. I won it too. I think all concerned were probably afraid of what might happen if I lost.

Many years later my mother gave me a scrapbook of childhood photographs, which included a snapshot of me that day. Underneath it she had written in her big sprawling handwriting, rather typically using gold ink, 'You were wonderful, darling.'

That holiday in Llandudno was a landmark in my early life for another rather more important reason about which I knew little or nothing at the time. It retains a certain unreality. We were there, freezing on the beach with me struggling to win inconsequential talent competitions, when Britain declared war on Germany on 3 September 1939. Although the outbreak of war was beyond my comprehension, I never forgot the day it happened because that was when I was given

Loppy, my toy rabbit, who has been glued to my side ever since.

The whole family was there for that final holiday before the war, including my grandparents Broadbent and Pike, and my Uncle Graeme, my mother's younger brother, who was joining the army. He wanted to buy me a present for my birthday eleven days later and announced that, as war had broken out, I could choose absolutely anything I wanted. I was duly marched along to Lumley's, *the* toy shop in Llandudno.

The attrition of wartime had yet to bite and the shelves of Lumley's were stocked with every possible toy a child could wish for. But I had eyes for nothing but my Loppy. I spotted her almost at once in a huge glass case along with a lot of other soft toys. I just homed in on her. It was as if I had found my soulmate.

My mother, of course, was dismayed. Loppy was an extremely modest choice. The families Broadbent and Pike were gathered in order to buy me a big, big present. But I only wanted Loppy. My mother took me to look at a rather advanced toy car you could sit in and drive with pedals, and she was particularly disappointed when I showed absolutely no interest whatsoever in a huge walking doll with curls which may or may not have resembled Shirley Temple. I had fixed on Loppy, an ordinary, light brown, five inches or so tall, stuffed rabbit with no distinguishing features to recommend her. It was as if my life depended on acquiring the creature. In my head I named her even before she was mine. My mother had been reading *Peter Rabbit* to me. Flopsy, Mopsy, Cotton-tail and Peter were extremely dear to my heart, and Loppy was the nearest name to Flopsy that I could get my tongue around, I think. It also suited her because of her big floppy ears.

Uncle Graeme duly bought Loppy for me, and the following Christmas my mother, who occasionally, albeit only occasionally, knew when even she was beaten, tucked into the top of my stocking another, slightly smaller but equally plain, rabbit whom I called Lena and grew to love every bit as much as Loppy. I have always been devoted to both my rabbits. From the moment I was given them I could never be separated from them. It made me ill – or maybe I made myself ill, who knows – to be apart from them.

When, as a very small child, I went into hospital to have my tonsils removed, I came round from the operation to find Loppy and Lena were no longer in my bed where I had left them. I immediately had a terrible panic attack. My temperature shot through the roof, and apparently I came close to departing this life. It transpired that the nursing staff had taken my rabbits out of the ward to be fumigated because there was a scarlet-fever scare. As soon as they were returned to me I recovered. Almost exactly the same thing happened again when Loppy and Lena were inadvertently shut in a trunk in our hotel room on holiday.

Another time, when I was still a very little girl, my mother was unwise enough to use the removal of Loppy as some kind of threat when I had misbehaved. I promptly threw a telephone directory straight through a window. And, yes, the window was closed at the time. Mummy also told me, 'The only reason you love those rabbits so much is because they can't tell you what they think of you.' This could well have been true! But love them I did, and still do.

Many, many years later I was on tour with a revue and my suitcase containing my rabbits went missing on a train. My then agent Alec Graham travelled miles back from where we were in the north of England to Crewe to collect it because he realised I would simply not be able to go on without knowing that Loppy and Lena were safe.

Indeed, and I'm sorry if this sounds barking mad, but to this day it would destroy me to lose them. They have been a constant factor through a life that has had depressingly little continuity. They are bashed and battered and have lost most of their tufted woollen fur and I periodically patch them up with bits of cotton wool and old nylon stockings. They look a bit like bank robbers, actually.

I clung to them in air-raid shelters during the war. They were always with me whenever I performed as a child. Throughout my life I have clung to them whenever I have been unhappy, and I cling to them still.

It was in Grandfather Broadbent's theatre that I made my professional stage début at the age of four. I was introduced to theatre at the deep end – doing eight shows a week in *A Christmas Carol*. In the thirties no one controlled the hours small children worked in show business, and my mother certainly had no wish to.

I can clearly recall being carried, in my pink flowered dressing gown, which I hated, past the queue at the stage door. My mother might have wanted me to be Shirley Temple, but I was never the sort of child who liked ribbons and bows or anything pretty-pretty any more than I liked having my hair curled. I was half asleep most of the time because I couldn't sleep at night. My mother was always saying, 'Go to sleep. You've got two shows tomorrow.'

Indeed, that remained my kind of schedule until I went into *Coronation Street*. But, whatever the next day held, how could anybody with their head full of the most ridiculous bits of old cloth, tied tightly into knots and pulling the roots out of their scalp, be expected to sleep?

In many ways my childhood was taken over by this other world of show business, but I didn't think about it like that at the time. After all, I didn't know any better. Yet I did feel anxious about it. I also had a distinct feeling of *déjà vu* when I went on stage. It may have been the sense of belonging that I have always had in the theatre, although I actually believe it was more than that. From the first moment I ever went on stage I felt as if I had done it before.

In *A Christmas Carol*, I had to appear suddenly from the bottom of a Christmas tree. In order for this to happen the scene needed to be pre-set, with me shut in a box, curled up into a little ball until my moment came. At some point quite late into rehearsals, it was realised that I would actually have to stay in this box through two long scenes. There was considerable panic about this. After all, I was only four and most kids of my age would have been terrified. Indeed, the first time I had to do it I could hear people going absolutely bananas. My mother was on one side of the stage hissing, 'Are you all right? Stay where you are! You'll be all right.' Meanwhile, my dancing teacher was on the other side doing the same.

The extraordinary thing was that I didn't mind being put in the box. I just took it for granted like everything else about performing and the theatre. I crouched there in the dark wishing they would all shut up. Then when I finally heard my music cue and I opened the little door, climbed out and saw the audience, through a haze of cigarette and cigar smoke, I just thought: 'Oh, my God, I've done it again.' It really was as if I'd been there before. I felt no fear, only a slight sense of tiredness. And, as I well know now, if you ask any actor going on stage what they feel they will always reply, 'Tired.' I've never heard one say, 'Great, I feel great. I really want to do the show today.'

For me, from the start, it was always laughter that got me going, made it all work. Before *A Christmas Carol* opened we had to do a photocall. I sat on Father Christmas's knee wearing a crinoline dress, which naturally I hated as I was always very opinionated about clothes – and the skirt went over my head which really upset me. But everybody laughed, and I found that I rather liked that. Then in the show there was a very tall demon who did a hands-knees-and-bumpsydaisy routine with me. He found it extremely amusing to bump me so hard that I bounced straight off stage into the wings. I didn't like that either, but as I went flying I heard the audience laugh. Now that was different. I thought, 'I see. This is how you do it . . .'

I learned fast. From then on I made a big performance of being knocked off stage.

At the end of the show everyone was given flowers, and a big tea chest full of toys and sweets was brought on stage for me. It was quite nauseating really, but they'd all gone 'ooh, ahh' about my performance and this was my reward, which was a huge treat, as the war had begun and these things were already getting to be in short supply. Then Grandfather Broadbent, who, as an old trade-union man, an alderman and a former town mayor, would make a speech at the opening of a fridge, led me forward and announced, 'This is my granddaughter, who is going to be a star.'

I didn't know what he was talking about. But I do remember him saying it. It was Grandfather Broadbent who would take me to the theatre every Saturday night, sit me in a box, point at some unfortunate on stage, and tell me, 'Now that's how you don't do it.'

He was show-business mad. Once when I was going back to my boarding school he actually pulled me off a train and rushed me to The Queen's Hotel, Manchester, to meet Buster Keaton.

'Now never forget that hand has shaken the hand of Buster Keaton,' he told me solemnly.

For my other great supporter, my mother, part of the process of putting her daughter on the stage was taking me to all the pantomimes going every year. She was very particular about the seats she booked – always the stalls and never in the middle of the row. At the Palace Theatre, Manchester, she liked the end seats three or four rows back because they gave you a clear run to the steps leading on stage. Then the minute the kids were invited on stage she would catapult me forward.

I never enjoyed pantomime because my heart used to be thumping down my nose at the prospect of what was to come.

However, I have to admit that when I actually got up there it was all right. I have always felt all right on stage, and that has never changed. It's like a kind of protected place to me, about the only place where I don't care what I look like – which I realise is ridiculously paradoxical but it is the truth.

One of the occasions when I felt that sense of *déjà vu* particularly strongly was when I was booted up onto the stage and came face to face with an extremely famous pantomime dame called G. S. Melvin. As usual I was kept on when the others went off stage, probably because I was the youngest, so I was left alone with this great sweaty face covered in make-up looking down at me. I clearly remember thinking, 'He's tired,' and I kind of understood. G. S. Melvin didn't look a bit the way he did on the other side of the footlights. He was a big, big star, a pantomime genius really, yet you could see so much weariness in his eyes. I think I recognised him for what he was as well as what he did.

The Second World War changed so much, as it did in every family throughout the country. My father was never called up although his brothers were. It was always believed that Grandfather Broadbent had done a deal with someone, which is just the sort of thing he would have done, and instead Hubert became a fireman. It was through the war years that he changed from being a warm, rather funny man, reasonably content with his lot, into a kind of Captain Mainwaring figure.

My main memories of the war are of spending one half of it in a bread bin – with Loppy and Lena of course – and the other half performing to frequently bemused audiences.

My mother had a big tin bread bin which she used to sit me in down in the cellar whenever there was an air raid. The only time my life was ever in peril during the war was when two shelves carrying Mummy's entire supply of black-market Batchelor's peas collapsed on my head just as I was climbing out of my bin.

The performances, predictably enough, were usually my mother's idea. I think I was her war effort. Anyway, it was thanks to her that during my *Coronation Street* years I could never pass through Manchester's Piccadilly Station without the vision of me singing 'Roll Out the Barrel' by the ticket barrier, having been dragged there by my mother to see our boys off to war. I suspect they were far keener to get to Hitler once they'd witnessed the hideous sight of this Shirley Temple lookalike singing to them while being poked in the side by a mad woman issuing frantic instructions. 'Sing louder. Smile! SMILE! Use your eyes!'

I always hated the dresses my mother put me in. I can still remember them in every ghastly frilly detail as well as the bows she insisted on tying in my hair. The embarrassment of it makes me cringe to this day.

Our poor boys didn't get to escape me even after they'd come back from war, at least not if they were wounded. Mother used to take me round the hospitals singing. It was always the Brahms Lullaby, not a song you would associate with me really, but presumably considered suitable for the sick.

On one occasion the sick really got more than they deserved, poor souls. The pianist asked me how many choruses there were in the lullaby, and although I was programmed to sing it I had absolutely no idea what a chorus was. I said four, perhaps because it sounded like a good number or perhaps because it was my age. So he played four of them and as I was singing I thought, 'Oh, he means these things does he, but there are only two of them. OK. I'll sing the second one again and then I'll sing the first one again.' It may have been the longest rendition of the Brahms Lullaby ever. Men who had survived Dunkirk were probably dying of boredom in their beds.

I also used to perform in my maternal grandfather's air-raid shelter. Now that wasn't so bad. Both my grandfathers were true eccentrics and I absolutely adored them.

Grandfather Pike, who looked very much like Charles Laughton, was a tailor and very fussy about his appearance. As a soldier during the First World War he had apparently contrived to make himself a special uniform because he couldn't stand the roughness of army cloth nor the ill-fitting cut of the trousers. By the time I was born he had taken to wearing a hand-stitched white suit about the place, which was quite something in a northern industrial town in the thirties.

Naturally, Grandfather Pike's air-raid shelter was rather different to most. He created an escape world in his basement. He turned it into a kind of south of France theatre set. There was this very pretty sort of *trompe l'œil* seascape complete with a sandpit for me to play in. He had tables laid up with umbrellas above them, and as soon as the air-raid siren went off he would dress up as a French waiter and pop a load of potatoes in the oven to bake. Then he would come downstairs, put a French singer's record on the gramophone and serve the baked potatoes to the entire family gathered in his basement.

One wartime Christmas he dressed up in drag and pretended to be our long-lost Aunty Doris. He wore this huge hat with a veil and full make-up. He was so good that some of the family actually fell for it. I remember knowing it was him all right but also that I didn't think it was at all odd for my grandfather to dress as a woman.

I don't know whether my performances were a plus or a minus, but word got round about Grandfather Pike's extraordinary air-raid shelter and ultimately half of Ashton seemed to be packed into his basement every time the siren went off.

After a bit it began to occur to me that I might be able to turn this performing thing rather more to my advantage. I rounded up any of the neighbourhood kids I could find who played 'round the back' as we described it, and press-ganged them into becoming performers. We used to climb up onto the flat roof of the shed of our house, which was in an alleyway a bit like the one behind Coronation Street, and we'd put on a show, which at least made a change from looking for German spies or collecting shrapnel. I was extremely precocious when it came to performing. I used to set the whole thing up and tell the others what to do. People would come and watch and I'd go around with a box afterwards and collect money from them – the grand sum of a halfpenny was the norm I think – on the pretext that it was going to the war effort. Actually it was usually being spent on the comics *Dandy* and *Beano* of which I was rather fond.

Throughout the war, indeed throughout my early childhood, it was my father who got me out of bed in the mornings, dressed me, gave me my breakfast, and sent me off to school. My lunch, invariably bacon sandwiches, was always packed into my gas-mask case. The whole family gave me their bacon rations because I was such a sickly child. Bacon sandwiches, with very well-done crispy bacon, quickly became, and have remained to this day, absolutely my favourite food. Should gas masks ever have been called for during the war I would have had to stick bacon sandwiches up my nostrils.

My mother was never involved in any of this because she never got up in the mornings, although naturally she conducted the proceedings from her bed, looking rather like Rita Hayworth. I just took it for granted that this was the way things were, that mothers didn't get up until mid morning, and that this was what fathers normally did – although it most certainly was not in those days.

There were other strange things too. Apart from when I was away from home, I slept in the same bed as my mother from when I was born until I was thirteen. My father was banished to the room next door. I suppose he must have returned to the marital bed occasionally. After all, I have a brother, Chris, who is seven years younger than me. However, my memory is entirely of me being in bed with my mother, something it never occurred to me to question until many years later. Indeed, I never had a bedroom of my own until I was almost thirty, when I acquired the Covent Garden flat that is still my home.

Even though it was my father who basically looked after me when I was little, I always felt quite distanced from him and as I grew up he became a more and more remote and shadowy figure. Indeed, after my brother was born, my father had very little to do with me at all.

Although my mother and I were so close, and she was always very possessive of me, it wasn't the normal mother–daughter relationship. We slept in the same bed but I never remember her even giving me a cuddle. Not a lot of cuddling went on in our house. Only my Grandfather Pike ever hugged me, and, perhaps because I wasn't used to it, I didn't like it. I would make myself go stiff and sort of slide down onto the floor out of his arms. It was a long time before I was ever comfortable with any sort of physical contact.

From the beginning my mother treated me as a friend rather than as a daughter. And as a grown-up friend, too. It would be all too easy to treat her merely as a typical stage mum, but she was much more complex than that, as was our relationship. It was just that she wanted the best for me. I don't think you can successfully push a child through a door it doesn't want to go through. But she spotted in me the one thing I was good at, which was dancing, and she nurtured it. Perhaps that is partly why there was such a special bond between us. We remained close in spite of everything. We were always up to something together.

Mummy's priorities were inclined to be different from other people's. She loved all that was beautiful in life and didn't like to be distracted by tedious practicalities. When she was supposed to be paying the butcher's bill she would spend the money on an antique Georgian wine cooler instead. I spent much of my formative years zigzagging along the streets of Ashton in order to avoid irate shopkeepers, and limboing along the pavements beneath their windows so that they couldn't see me. My mother could be quite outrageous, but she made everything we did seem so much fun.

We had our own special little world and I was always trying to please her. Although I didn't want curly hair, I knew she wanted that for me, so one night I decided to help her out by pouring a whole bottle of Curly-Top over my head. It turned out to be viral malt – a thick brown substance commonly used as a tonic in those days – and the mess was dreadful.

I always wanted to be like my mother, too. I used to watch her stop the ladders in her stockings with nail varnish, so I copied her. The only thing was that I wasn't wearing stockings, of course, so I just painted my legs. And as we didn't have any nail-varnish remover I had red legs for ages.

I also usually had a red face. As a very little kid I started to blush whenever I thought anyone was looking at me. The really strange thing is that, from the beginning, the only time I didn't care about people looking at me or what I looked like was when I was on stage.

By the time I was five I was a seasoned performer and I was really quite old already. I think I knew, even then, that the theatre was my natural habitat, and that maybe I would always be more at home in the world of make-believe than in real life.

CHAPTER TWO

꙳

The trouble really began when I was seven and my brother was born. Later in life Chris and I were to become best friends, but when he was born he was quite simply an intrusion. He just got in my way. My life was shattered by this horrible blue wrinkled thing.

When I was supposed to be introduced to him, shortly after his birth, I locked myself in the outside lavatory at my Grandfather Pike's house and refused to come out. I sat on the pan looking at the bits of newspaper and magazine, good quality ones like the *Tailoring Weekly*, which we used for lavatory paper, all tied up with string and hanging from the wall. It was just like a scene out of *Billy Elliot*. I just sat there sulking, although I was not usually a sulker, and very wickedly praying that my new brother would die before I got upstairs to see him.

My mother had already written little letters to me, allegedly from this dear unborn child, but that merely convinced me in advance that his arrival was going to be seriously bad news. It was a bit like getting letters from the Inland Revenue, really.

When he was a baby Chris hated me too. I was never in any doubt about that. He used to bite me and once he bit right through my finger. My life with my mother was never the same after his arrival and my father seemed to transfer his affections to him entirely.

Of course most of this was probably just coincidence, because it was around then that my parents' marriage began to fall apart.

I remember my mother actually telling me, when I was still very little, that my father was having an affair. Once I came home from primary school to find a large pregnant lady on our door-step. She was screaming at my mother, 'You will not be in this house next week and nor will your children.'

Strangely enough I can't recall how my mother responded to that, but I remember my reaction well enough. I flew at this woman, kicking at her legs with all my might – which was not inconsiderable as I already had dancer's muscles. She'd threatened my home and my instinct was to fight. It was the first time I remember being overcome by such rage – although my mother always told me that the first word I ever uttered was an angrily shouted 'No!' which came out like 'Naaaahhhh!' – but it was to be far from the last.

My father, meanwhile, did not move from the kitchen table where I can still see him clearly as he sat there sobbing with his head in his hands.

They must have sorted it out somehow, because I never saw the pregnant woman again. But from then on I was aware of an atmosphere in the house. That was when the terrible rows began and my father began to cut off from me.

Then at one point, when Chris was just a toddler, Mummy walked out, taking him with her. I have no idea where she went. She left me behind like a kind of deposit. I think she wanted to make sure she could come back if she wanted to. Sure enough, after a few weeks she returned.

I felt totally bewildered and rejected, but she never even told me she was sorry. Maybe she wasn't able to. That was Connie. She always did exactly what she wanted. Meanwhile, I continued to associate this terrible disruption with the arrival of my dear brother.

Throughout all of this my mother continued to dress me up as Shirley Temple or whatever whim took her fancy, while my father constantly complained about her obsession with turning me into a child star. I was only about nine when I was invited to a Masonic party where everybody else looked like the kids that they were, and I was dressed up in a strapless black velvet top with a long black net skirt. My mother had stuffed cotton wool down the front to give me a bosom, pinned a red rose in the middle to conceal my lack of cleavage and put my hair up like Margaret Lockwood's. I was hugely embarrassed and felt really conspicuous. I do remember, however, that two of the boys at the party had a stand-up fight over me!

With my mother appearances were everything. She never asked how I got on with people, or told me to be nice to someone, or any of the things that I was aware of other mothers doing. It was always how I looked that mattered. To Connie Broadbent that was the passport to getting places.

My mother and father developed a kind of double-act routine where she would build me up and he would slap me down. She would tell people I was about to meet how beautiful I was, while my father, curiously perhaps as by this time he and my mother were getting on so badly, would introduce me by saying, 'This is my daughter. She will never be as attractive as her mother.'

I do think my father's low opinion of the way I looked was the start of me never having any confidence in my appearance, which I always believe to be a mess and that has stayed with me throughout my life. I know actresses always say that, but in my case it really is true.

Meanwhile, my mother, totally unabashed, would announce, 'My daughter is far more beautiful than Elizabeth Taylor.' Then I would arrive and be convinced they were all going, 'Oh Christ, look at that.' I felt I was a big let-down.

Looking back, my mother spent her whole life trying to turn me into a creature that I could never be. However, it was then that I began to learn to make fun of myself before anybody else did, something else that has stayed with me, and that I still do.

It was also around then that I began to say these fervent prayers because I realised already that I was going to be a dancer, and nobody built like my mother could ever become one. Connie Broadbent made Dolly Parton look like Twiggy. My mother had enormous tits, as indeed did most of the women in my family, and I really didn't want them. I would peer over the bedclothes at her as she was getting ready for bed and pray and pray and pray, telling my body, 'You are *not* having those things, because if you did a pirouette with those, you'd fall flat on your face.'

My prayers were answered. I never did grow any boobs worth mentioning. Indeed, there were later to be occasions when I wished that I had not prayed quite so hard.

The strain between my parents was horribly apparent to me. I knew something very wrong was going on. But I still was not remotely prepared for what eventually happened.

When I was just nine they sent me to boarding school. I thought I was going to die.

There have been many tough times in my life, but I have never since experienced absolute despair like I did then. To me, it was the ultimate betrayal. I couldn't believe that my mother, with whom I had this extraordinarily close relationship, could be doing such a thing to me.

My mother had doted on me. My mother had been obsessive about me, overly ambitious, overly protective. Ironically, the one childhood hobby I was allowed was probably the most dangerous of the lot, but fortunately for me, my mother never seemed to realise it. I had a passion for horses, and although I never owned a pony of my own, I spent every spare moment riding, and because I was quite good at it was given plenty of opportunity to help out at various local riding stables. Other than that she barely let me out of her sight.

Indeed, upon reflection our relationship had been almost unnaturally close. She even breast-fed me ages longer than I am sure was natural. Years later she would describe to me how my teeth had torn her breasts to pieces. I used to think, 'How old was I, for Christ's sake? Twelve?'

Then out of the blue my doting, obsessive, protective mother was sending me away to boarding school.

I felt that I was being abandoned, which I more or less was. The trust that I still had in my mother, despite her erratic behaviour, was totally destroyed.

And the whole experience turned out to be every bit as much of a nightmare as I anticipated.

I am dyslexic – only in those days nobody knew anything about dyslexia. I was just the thick kid who couldn't read or write. But until it came to sitting entrance exams for boarding school I had always got away with it pretty well.

I think I was quite a bright child, able to live on my wits. Certainly in primary school I managed to get by. I always had an answer for people and I was usually, somehow or other, in the top part of the class. I think a lot of small children aren't very good at writing and I concealed the worst of my deficiencies by copying. To me that was a kind of drawing – although I could only do it up to a point. When it came to reading, in the early stages there were usually illustrations and I would get by with a kind of educated guesswork. I was a natural busker.

My fall from grace began when I started to have to do my own reading and studying. The entrance exams finished me off. I failed almost all of them including, to my mother's abiding disappointment, one for a school in Blackpool which she had chosen because of its nice scarlet uniform. The only one I managed to pass was for St Anne's College in St Anne's-on-Sea, the genteel near-neighbour of Blackpool.

Maybe I should have ensured that I failed that one too. When my parents took me for the interview it seemed totally unreal. I still didn't believe it was happening. We met the headmistress – a dear little old lady with a bun, or so she seemed to me then, but I, of course, was at an age when everybody over twenty-five was geriatric – and I was accepted, much to my parents' astonishment, I think.

When my mother delivered me there some weeks later the reality hit me like a punch in the gut. I begged, I pleaded, I howled and I sobbed. But she still left me there. I felt utterly betrayed and I don't think I have ever asked people for favours since.

To make matters worse the dear little old lady was no longer headmistress. Instead we were greeted by two spinsters who were joint heads, Miss Foden and Miss Thompson. One was quite upper-class Irish, and one was quite upper-class English. They were very much a pair and the school they ran was a funny sort of place, to say the least.

The building, in Clifton Drive, St Anne's, looked like a dolls' house.

It was a private school full of supposedly nice middle-class girls whose parents all wanted them to have that sort of education. In fact, I got practically no education at all. My parents completely wasted their money.

I have no idea why people have children and then send them to boarding school. I was miserable. Utterly miserable. I think there is a perceived wisdom that all those initiation ceremonies and stuff that you hear about just happen in boys' schools. Not true. Girls' schools are just as bad. At least, St Anne's College certainly was. Girls always seemed to be having their heads stuck down lavatories.

The night I arrived I was ordered by some of the older girls to open my tuck box. They wanted the contents for themselves and intended to get them. It was just at the end of the war, so food was of even greater importance than it usually would be to schoolkids. I didn't care. I didn't ever want to eat again, so I just tugged at the lid of the tin, and in so doing took the end off one of my fingers. You can still see that it's a bit deformed. All I did care about were my beloved rabbits, Loppy and Lena. I was terrified that someone might take them or harm them in some way, so I was always looking for new hiding places for them.

My day-to-day life was thoroughly miserable. I was continually in a mess. I was self-conscious. I couldn't properly recognise the words I was supposed to be able to read and write and so I was confused and frustrated by my inability to do what everyone else seemed to do with consummate ease.

I have always had quite an imagination though, and looking back I think I was rather good at coming up with ideas for essays. We were once asked to write an essay about firework night, something that was not a feature of life in the Broadbent household, we already had enough fireworks going on on a daily basis without any extra sparklers and twinklers. So I came up with the story of a worm that got chopped in half by a firework and then formed a relationship with its other half, because they were obviously very compatible, and they hid from the war in an air-raid shelter with some ants.

Another essay subject we were given was food. Well, honestly! You eat the stuff, don't you? The best I could do was to invent a pig and its friend discussing the delights of pig swill.

The silliest subject, it seemed to me, was milk. What can you say about milk, for God's sake? I turned Milk into a Grand National horse, a grey of course, and I thought that was quite clever. The teachers, predictably enough, did not. Possibly my best effort was when we had to write an essay about trees. I invented a story about all the leaves being secrets that people had told trees. Every autumn trees drop their leaves and that's how secrets are kept. Yet again, nobody was impressed. Nowadays you would at least get brownie points for originality I think. Then they were only really interested in grammar and spelling, both of which, in my case, of course, were abysmal.

My dyslexia led to me frequently getting into trouble when I really didn't deserve it. Once in religious education class I was sent out of the room because I quite innocently asked what fornication meant. The teacher thought I was being cheeky. Actually I had just seen *Bambi*, about the adventures of a young deer, and I was trying to work out the connection between it and a passage in the Bible because I didn't realise *fawn* and *forn* were spelt differently. As it happens I didn't know that until very recently when it was pointed out to me during the writing of this book.

In order to cover up my deficiencies I became the school clown. Every time class was stopped because I couldn't read – as it often was, that was how the teachers so summarily dealt with my problem – I would put on my clown's hat and try to make everybody laugh.

When that failed I resorted to violence. I had always had a tendency to be aggressive when I, anyone, or anything I cared about, came under threat. Before even reaching school age I virtually beat to a pulp a far bigger boy who had thrown stones at our family dog. At boarding school my aggression ran out of control, and invariably manifested itself in the same way. I would launch myself at people, knock them over, grab their hair and bang their heads on the floor. And I wouldn't stop until someone came and pulled me off.

Now I look back, I realise I was actually deeply distressed, not only by my learning difficulties and the insensitive, thoughtless way I was treated by the teachers, but also by all that was happening at home. I didn't understand that then. I simply descended into a state of pure latent fury.

There was something else about St Anne's College, which was part day school and part boarding school. It had a particular heady kind of atmosphere. I felt then that there was something different about a lot of the teachers. I later realised that the school had more than its fair share of gay teachers, a situation that could well have been manipulated from the top. There was also quite a lot of bonding going on among the girls.

As far as I know, it wasn't a question of real sexual relationships, just heavy crushes which I think probably remain pretty much the norm in all-female schools. And in my first term I think I behaved much the same as everybody else.

But then something happened to me that, because I was so young at the time, is difficult to explain and possibly even more difficult to understand. I fell in love. It certainly wasn't a physical thing in the adult sense. Neither was it anything like the schoolgirl infatuations going on all around us. There was something so good and pure between us, in stark contrast to all the mayhem that was going on at home with my parents. I even remember wishing that they were out of the way so that I could give my entire love and affection to this person.

The girl I fell in love with, Bernie, was about five years older than me and went on to become joint head girl – along with Thelma Holt, another pupil at St Anne's then, who was to become such a successful actress and producer. Bernie was very, very beautiful and quite brilliant, everything I was convinced that I was not. I remember when I first saw her that I couldn't keep my eyes off her, which, as I had already learned to blush, was a problem from the start. Bernie was quite tall, about five feet nine inches, very slim, and had the colour of skin that I have always wanted, with a half-tanned sort of Asian look to it. She had mad, dark hair and very dark eyes. I used to look at her and think, 'I *must* remember those eyes.' I would do that over and over again. There was something about her that was androgynous, and I don't mean in any way butch. There are people who have a sort of charismatic dual sexuality and I think Bernie was one of them. She was extremely special, and I think everybody, including the two headmistresses, realised that. I loved her to bits. Indeed, for most of my life I have been unable to feel that much for anyone again.

Although it wasn't a crush I suppose it started like that. At boarding schools you do have prefects coming around and kissing people goodnight, and I suppose that was how it began. Eventually girls would say to me, 'I'm not going to have a crush on Bernie again, because obviously yours is different,' – which was pretty extraordinary coming from kids.

It *was* different, though. Bernie was different. I realise now that she was partially a mother substitute to me, at a time when I felt abandoned by my mother, but that wasn't the way I thought about it then.

Meanwhile, I was getting into more and more trouble at school. I continued to appear to be very bright when I was talking to people, then seeming to be very stupid as soon as it came to putting anything in an exercise book. It looked as if I was just refusing to work, I suppose.

There was no bridge between the two sides of me. I didn't work because I couldn't work. I was treated like an idiot so I behaved like an idiot. Not only did nobody else understand what it was all about, I didn't myself. I didn't realise that I had these difficulties because I was physically and mentally *unable* to learn to read properly. So at first I would cheat and then I would give up.

There was a plus side. The prefects and staff lived in a different house across the road. I behaved so appallingly badly that I was ultimately banished there so that they could all keep an eye on me. That meant I was living in the same house as Bernie – who had her own room. Now this was supposed to be punishment?

I think a lot of the teachers were jealous of my relationship with Bernie. There was one teacher who used to make me knock on her door when all the girls were asleep and then go and fetch Bernie, who would go down to her room. I then spent half the night sitting at the top of the stairs in this rather nice house watching through the banisters for Bernie to return, at which point I would go along to her room and curl up with her. I had no idea what actually happened between her and the teacher, but certainly nothing wildly sexual used to happen between us. There wasn't any writhing around in bed or anything like that, just a tremendous amount of kissing, and an even greater amount of talking. It was a kind of exploration of life, really. Bernie talked to me about everything. She tried her best to keep me out of trouble, but I was already a lost cause. However, I think she was the one, even more than my mother, who planted in me the idea that I could go on stage professionally. Until then it hadn't ever seeped into my consciousness that that was what I wanted to do with my life permanently. It was just what my mother wanted me to do. Bernie turned it into something real for me, made it feel like my future.

We also talked about death a lot. We both believed that she was going to die young. It might seem strange for two such young people, but we were both quite sure of it, and quite matter of fact about it. We used to talk about how it would be when she wasn't there any more. That was when I became quite obsessed with remembering her. Not just her eyes but her hands too. I have always been a very emotional person. Bernie had remarkably long, graceful hands. I used to look at them and think that I couldn't bear for her to be buried in the ground, for those hands to be allowed to rot. I know that might all seem hard to believe of a ten- or eleven-year-old, but it's the truth.

I believe the way I felt about Bernie was the way most of us want to feel about people all our lives, and hardly ever do. She was all that mattered, and the only thing that kept me going. She was my support and my refuge.

My home life was falling apart, I couldn't do my schoolwork and didn't understand why, so my school life, such as it was, fell apart too. I became more and more aggressive. It was my defence mechanism, I think.

If anybody made a crack about Bernie, and some did dare occasionally, I would first blush and then go ballistic. I had the most terrible fights. I was always a bit of a bruiser. I might have been small, but I've always been physically tougher than I look, and, oh, could I fight – which, as it happens, I still can if pushed into a corner.

At school I would happily knock someone down an entire flight of stairs, jump down onto them and bang their head on the floor. I didn't give it a thought. I was constantly involved in fights that ended that way. It didn't matter if it was a tarmac playground or a marbled hallway. I didn't give a damn.

I was continually being sent to Coventry by the other girls, which didn't worry me too much as long as Bernie was still speaking to me. And the teachers were always banning me from things, special outings like going to the dance at a local boys' school, as a punishment. Big deal. I really didn't care. At least, that was what I told myself. I was actually deeply distressed, of course, but I knew of no other way of dealing with my feelings than to turn them into anger.

The only time the staff wanted to know about me was when they were putting on a Shakespeare play or indeed any other kind of show. Then I'd be dragged out of my cupboard and told to behave. I never could, of course.

The fact that I looked different to the others didn't help either. That was down to my mother. She connived with my grandfather, who, being a man who had even customised his army uniform, thought it was quite normal to make a few alterations to my school clothes. Connie didn't like the cut or the shade of blue of the school coat, so my grandfather made me a different one. It was a lovely air-force blue and made of top-quality gaberdine, but all I wanted was to be the same as everyone else, something I never seemed to manage. Neither did Mother like the shoes, so my shoes were different too. My skirt was cut several inches shorter than the other girls' because she reckoned I had good legs and should show them off. Consequently, walking around St Anne's at that age, I must have been serious jailbait. And in school I was teased mercilessly. But it stopped short of actual bullying, because I knew how to handle bullies. I beat them up.

Actually, I was lucky I didn't kill anybody. There was a girl called Anne in my dormitory who nearly had it on more than one occasion. I considered her a very irritating person. She took to running a steel comb down the side of her bed, which was also metal. The noise went on for hours. I asked Anne nicely not to do it. Several times. But she wouldn't stop. 'If you keep doing that I am going to come and get you,' I warned her. But Anne was foolhardy as well as irritating. Brrrm, brrrm. She didn't pause. So I jumped out of bed and attacked. I got hold of the comb and chucked it out of the window. The silly creature promptly found another object to run up and down the side of the bed. Then I really went mad.

This time she knew she was really in for it, so as I got close to her bed she leapt out and ran into the corner of the room where there was a range of cupboards on top of which were some suitcases. She started to argue with me. I just couldn't be bothered with any more of it. I reached up for one of the suitcases and bashed her over the head. However, this was just after the war. The case was made of cardboard, Anne's head went straight through it and she couldn't get it out. Her head was stuck. Absolutely. She proceeded to run around the dormitory with the suitcase over her head like a headless chicken. We all thought it was rather funny, until she started screaming. I tried to open the case, but it was locked so she kept on running, making so much noise that inevitably Matron came in. She found the key, and released my victim who emerged like some terrible jack-in-the-box, weeping and wailing.

I was in my usual awful trouble, but while Matron was still thinking up a punishment dreadful enough, something else happened. And Anne was the one to suffer again. The next day was fire drill. It was a bit primitive at St Anne's, but I adored it. One by one, we were put in a kind of sling four storeys up and had to crawl down the wall while being lowered to safety. Being a dancer and a bit nimble in those days I was rather good at it and always went first. But on this occasion, as part of my punishment and as a reward for poor Anne, she was sent first.

Unfortunately, because Matron was so busy telling me off for my disgusting behaviour, telling me that I shouldn't be allowed to live and should probably have been put down at birth and so on, and I was responding with my usual dumb insolence – fully chronicled in all my school reports – she was somewhat diverted. She harnessed Anne the wrong way so that the poor girl was attached to the free end of the fire-drill contraption, and instead of going bumpety bump down the wall, she just dropped. From four storeys. Well, Matron grabbed the rope and we all realised what had happened when we saw that her hands were burning up and her skin was coming off in shreds. Most of the girls rushed to help. I'm afraid I didn't move. I thought it served them both right. I didn't really consider that a girl was being hurtled to her probable death. I just thought it was all a kind of justice, that proved there was a God in the world after all. I had no intention whatsoever of grabbing hold of that rope – it was steel, I knew how much it would hurt – but Anne did arrive more or less in one piece at the bottom with all those people grimly hanging on. A further result was that Matron, who was having trouble finding her hands and was busily occupied with trying to stick them together again, was no longer in a state to tell me off any more.

Another of my misdemeanours was to lead a hunger strike. During the war a ghastly glutinous butter substitute was produced, from engine oil, I think. We lowly junior pupils had our butter rations taken away from us to be given to the staff and prefects while we were left with this awful stuff. I thought that was totally unfair – which it bloody well was. So, following in the footsteps of my Grandfather Broadbent, who in his early days as a trade-union leader had been quite a one for organising worker protests, I organised a hunger strike. I said that I didn't mind somebody else having my butter ration if I could allocate who it went to – I would happily have given my butter, even my beloved bacon or anything else to Bernie, of course – but I was not handing it over to people who made me sit at a table and eat lumpy porridge. That was another of my grievances. Eating this horrible porridge with great indigestible lumps actually made me physically sick, but they still made me do so. For once the rest of the girls stuck with me on the butter strike. We refused to eat anything until butter rations were distributed fairly. And we won the day.

The Girl Guide troop was another area of school life into which I did not settle well. I hated the bloody Girl Guides and I particularly hated their bloody badges. I never got any badges for anything. The only thing I liked were paper chases. I used to contrive to be the one leaving the trail, then I would tell the other girls I'd meet them at the riding stables nearby – which was one of the few places where I did fit in.

In fact, I was so good at riding that I was once spotted at a show by people involved with international show-jumping who offered to fund me at the famous Porlock Vale Riding Academy in Somerset. And, as in addition to dreaming of being a ballerina I also dreamed of being National Velvet, I was furious when my father refused to let me be launched into a riding career on the grounds that I'd be on the scrap heap and miserable by the time I was forty.

I was, therefore, always welcome around horses. So instead of laying some silly trail I would get a horse and go for a gallop on the beach. This arrangement suited the other girls too, because nobody in their right mind wanted to go chasing around after bits of paper anyway. It was such a waste of time. But, inevitably, in the end I was found out. And, perhaps equally inevitably, in the end I was expelled.

The final nail in my coffin came when the headmistresses claimed that I had been spotted walking through St Anne's in my boater with chunks out of it – I had virtually destroyed the thing hurling it at people from five floors up – screaming repeatedly at the top of my voice: 'St Anne's is a lousy bloody school, St Anne's is a lousy bloody school.'

As it happens, I don't remember actually doing that. But I did used to put on a limp when we were walking along in a crocodile while hissing at people we passed by, 'Don't send your daughter to our school, it's horrible.'

I felt my end there was dealt with in an overly dramatic fashion. First of all my parents were summoned to the school. I was called to the headmistresses' office and made to kneel in the middle of the room. My parents, I knew, hadn't seen each other for some time and had their own problems. Also, I don't think either of them knew the other would be there. The shock of seeing each other under those circumstances must have been pretty overwhelming. Nonetheless, looking back, I am a bit astounded that they allowed me to be left kneeling in the middle of the room like that. At the time, though, I just took it for granted. I did, however, think it a little unkind in view of services rendered for certain teachers in the past – particularly the one for whom I had stood watchdog while she had been visiting Bernie in the middle of the night. For the best part of an hour staff and pupils were wheeled in one by one to complain about me. They all had something derogatory to say, including the drama teacher and the art teacher, in whose classes I had always done rather well. Every person who came in described this monstrous child who was rebellious, insolent, avoided work, hit people, and generally behaved atrociously. Matron was among the most vitriolic. But then, she didn't have a lot to thank me for – although it had been a considerable time since the 'girl dangled from end of rope' incident, to my intense satisfaction the skin on her hands had yet to heal.

As ever, I didn't allow myself to care. I just shut myself off from it all. I had only one fear. There was a low window near to where I was kneeling, and I thought, 'If Bernie comes in and speaks out against me, I shall throw myself through that window.' I don't remember how many storeys up the headmistresses' office was. I have no idea if jumping out of that window would have killed me, but it wouldn't have done me much good, that was for certain. I didn't care either way. If Bernie had joined in the demolition of that evil Shirley Broadbent, an eleven-year-old girl accused of bringing the entire idiot school to a standstill, there would have been nothing left for me, at home or at school, nobody I trusted any more. I did think about my beloved rabbits and what would happen to them if I jumped. But even Loppy and Lena couldn't have stopped me.

Bernie, however, did not take part in this ritual humiliation, bless her. She should have done, because by then she was head girl. But I learned later that she had refused.

When it finally ended, and I was presumably considered to have been ripped to shreds satisfactorily, my parents took me for tea at an elegant little tea shop nearby. I was really terribly upset of course, but I had already learned how not to let that show. Nobody could make me cry. I felt strongly that some strange injustice had been done and I was full of defiance. So we sat in this tea shop and my parents never even mentioned what had happened. Indeed, I hardly remember them talking to me at all. I think I was already a great disappointment to my father, while my mother would never admit that I ever did anything wrong, never tell me off about anything. They were poles apart about me.

And they were in this dreadful state with each other because my mother was having this big on-off affair and I suspect my father was involved in something too. I never really knew because they wouldn't discuss it with me. But in that tea shop, to my astonishment after what I had just gone through, I was pretty much ignored while they went at each other hammer and tongs.

I was then sent back to school as if nothing had happened. Apparently I had been to all intents and purposes expelled, but for some reason I've never understood it was agreed that I would stay on until the end of term. Perhaps it was because St Anne's College had not finished humiliating me. They had another go at the annual prize-giving.

They made me stand up in the middle of the assembly, in front of all the parents and the entire school, who were told that among the academic triumphs of girls who were going on to university and great things, the only prize they could give Shirley Broadbent was for her expertise in making excuses about why she never did any work. Somebody made a speech about how I was attracted by the crack of the whip – which I found rather disturbing even then and have never quite understood unless it was a reference to my horse-riding ability – and the smell of greasepaint, and was destined for some sort of devil's life.

It seems I was lucky, or unlucky depending on how you look at it, to survive long enough to experience the joys of that prize-giving.

Years later, looking through some of my father's papers after he died, I found the letter one of the headmistresses had written to him halfway through that final summer term at St Anne's. It was a letter I did not know existed. Curiously, but somehow typically in view of the fact that Broadbent family life had ceased to exist, neither of my parents ever discussed it with me. I'm not sure whether I'm proud of the letter or ashamed of it, but it was such an extraordinary thing to be written about a child of that age that I cannot resist printing it in its entirety.

It was true that I changed during that period of my life from being a funny but fairly conventional and reasonably behaved, happy little girl, into a bit of a monster who felt she had to take on the world. However, nobody but nobody, except possibly Bernie, ever attempted to try to find out why.

And I think the letter probably illustrates more clearly even than my own memories the devastating effect that the break-up of my family, combined with my dyslexia and misery at being sent away to school, had on me as a child. I never fully appreciated the extent of this until well

41

into adulthood, when I spent years going to see psychiatrists to deal with problems that I am sure dated back to those days.

Dear Mr Broadbent,

I am extremely sorry to have to write you this letter. As you were kind enough to say in your letter to me at the beginning of term, the relation [sic] between Miss Thompson and myself and you and Mrs Broadbent has always been very cordial, and I should like to think it would remain so until Shirley left. But Shirley herself seems determined to ensure that there shall be no regret on either side when she leaves. Since it was settled that she should leave here at the end of this term, her attitude has been that that day cannot come soon enough, and in the meantime she will do as little work as possible and defy all school rules. The entire staff complains of her gratuitous rudeness, which at times borders on insolence. She makes no secret of the fact that she is glad to be leaving, and appears to hold this entire school in contempt. This is having a most disastrous effect among certain girls younger than Shirley. I have tried appealing to her sense of fair play, with no effect at all. This week-end we seem to have reached a climax. On Friday she deliberately cut a special elocution lesson, which Miss Knight had remained at school after her usual time to give to Shirley. As a result Miss Knight has, very properly, refused to allow Shirley to take the elocution exam to-day [sic], as she had not even learned the test piece by the end of last week. In addition, over the week-end Shirley was extremely insolent to the staff on duty, so much so that I have recieved [sic] an official complaint about her from the staff. I have therefore refused to give permission for Shirley to dance at a Masonic Party on Saturday, and have further warned her that if this continues it is doubtful whether Miss Thompson and I will feel able to permit her to remain here until the end of term.

I cannot imagine what has come over her. Until last term Shirley was a straightforward and very pleasant child, who, though not over fond of work, was at least honest and pleasant to deal with. During the last term and a half a most disastrous change has taken place in her, which is apparent to all of us. I feel quite powerless, as I can, apparently, make no appeal to her. I have to consider the good of a great number of girls, and if Shirley persists in using her influence to undermine authority, that influence must be removed.

It is with the greatest reluctance that I write to you thus, and I feel sure that you will add your authority to mine in attempting to persuade Shirley that we should all prefer her last weeks here to be pleasant ones, rather than to part abruptly in such a way that her connection with this school will be broken permanently. Believe me it is sheer desparation [sic] which causes me to write this letter to you.

Yours sincerely,

Joyce M. Foden

So there it was, my condemnation in writing from my headmistress, complete with spelling and grammatical errors which, of course, I as a dyslexic would remain unaware of had they not, to my considerable amusement, been pointed out to me. Who knows, maybe the staff of St Anne's College were ill equipped to teach anybody to read and write properly, not just dyslexics like me!

Anyway, the letter seems to suggest that I knew I had been asked to leave at the end of that term. I have no memory of that, although threats of expulsion were a constant feature of my life at the school. I certainly left ultimately with no regrets except that I would be moving away from Bernie, the very thought of which shattered me.

The day my mother came to collect me she refused to let me wear my school uniform for some reason, probably just her usual insistence on being different, and demanded I leave the school dressed in a completely inappropriate and very adult outfit she had bought me. I felt even more self-conscious than usual, and everything seemed to be so muddled and rushed that I didn't even get chance to say a proper goodbye to Bernie. She was standing in the hallway with the two headmistresses when I was hurried past, clad in a grown-up pale-grey suit and teetering on high-heeled shoes. All we did was look at each other. And I just knew somehow that this would be the last time I would see Bernie, which was a terrible feeling.

Otherwise I didn't give a damn about being expelled. I was an awkward, blushing, self-conscious eleven-year-old, with no home life left worth mentioning, unable to read or do anything else much except dance. I thought that I couldn't be more miserable.

CHAPTER THREE

J ust a few months later my worst premonition came true. Bernie died. I was aware of it before I was told. I heard her voice in the night. And I knew something terrible had happened.

She said, 'Beloved child.' I have never told anyone this before writing this book because I didn't think I would be believed, and it was just too important, too precious, to allow anyone ever to mock me.

It is, however, the absolute truth that I heard her voice as clearly as anything in my life, and I just knew she was dead.

I was staying with my Grandparents Pike in the bungalow they had on Hobson's Moor just outside Mottram in Lancashire. I was always being sent there during school holidays supposedly because I had a bad chest and was prone to bronchitis and, for some crazy reason, at that time people believed the damp moorland air was good for chest complaints. It also left my parents free to carry on with their various adventures.

The cottage had few home comforts, and it certainly didn't have a telephone. In the morning I trudged down to the nearest village and from a telephone box there I called my old headmistress Miss Thompson. She confirmed what I already knew in my heart. Bernie was dead. By then she was at university in Dublin. She had been wrongly diagnosed with meningitis when in fact she had polio, and by the time this was discovered it was too late.

I felt numb. I didn't think life was worth living without Bernie. I didn't see the point in going on. I hadn't seen her since leaving St Anne's. She had written to me and I had scribbled notes back, but that had been the sum of our contact. Now suddenly she had gone. The only person in the world who even began to understand the immensity of my loss was my mother. I don't remember ever discussing with her the details of my relationship with Bernie, but she seemed to know instinctively that there was something special between us, and, being Connie, she just accepted it and did her absolute best to comfort me. Nonetheless, Bernie's death was a loss that influenced everything that I was and did for many years to come. Certainly, I think my behaviour became even worse because of it, and eventually led to my being expelled from a second boarding school, a school which should have been a dream place for me, but turned out to be anything but.

My mother was always determined that nothing would get the better of her or of me. And thank God she was like that, or I think we would have all gone under.

Somehow or other my mother got an audition for me for The Arts Educational School at Tring and, even more remarkably given my propensity for misbehaviour and my inability to read or write properly, I was accepted.

It was supposed to be a very special place and it was certainly housed in a very special building, an incredibly beautiful magnificent mansion built by Sir Christopher Wren. But I didn't want to be there any more than I wanted to be at any other boarding school. All I wanted was a proper home, something I felt everyone else except me had.

Then there was my north-country accent. Everyone else at Tring spoke in well-modulated southern tones. Except me. I was deeply embarrassed by my accent. One word I really couldn't say was 'envelope'. I remember asking, 'Has anybody got one of those things you put letters in?' They must have thought I was totally mad. I used to walk around looking at what other people did and listening to the way they spoke, but I still couldn't work out how to do it right. I was convinced that my way was wrong. I just felt inferior in every way there was, including, as always, the way I looked. I felt so ugly I would apologise to flowers. I used to think I'd horrify them if I went near them, and the same with children. I used to think that if flowers could see me they would be disgusted, and that little children would just run away from me. I was only all right with horses because they were all right with me.

I even had a problem with the dancing because my face would go red whenever people looked at me – and people do tend to look at you when you are dancing. So I would be standing at the barre doing what I was doing and being perfectly all right until the teacher approached and started poking at me and saying things like, 'Long neck. Chin up. Pull your shoulders back.' I would just change colour. Only people who have suffered serious blushing as a child will know the agony of it. I used to write misspelt letters to God saying, 'If you will do something about my blushing I will give all my blood away. I obviously have too much. How can I be a ballerina with a red face?'

As usual I got into trouble even when it wasn't really my fault as well as when it was. There were ponies at the bottom of the huge lawn at the front of the college, and, still being horse-mad, I would get up early in the mornings and nip down to talk to them. Once I was on my way back into the house when I saw the principal, Mrs Rickman, doing physical jerks in front of a big window. She was stark naked with her tits down to her knees. I had never seen anything like it. I just fell to the ground laughing. I think I may have been in shock actually, but she spotted me and was absolutely furious. I was promptly banned from her classes, and she was a very important person in the ballet world, so I was deeply in disgrace. Although, as it happened, I reckoned the musical comedy dance classes she ran were not so hot, and that I wasn't missing much.

Shortly afterwards, I was accused of having lesbian tendencies, something which, despite Bernie, I really had no conception of. I have no idea if the accusation was linked with the episode with Mrs Rickman, but even the possibility that it might have been still worries me deeply.

It all stemmed from half the dorm being found one Saturday night huddled together under my bedclothes. Actually we were listening to *Saturday Night Theatre* on the Home Service, a seriously big event for me and one which everyone else seemed to enjoy as well. I had been brought up on the Home Service during the war and was an avid radio listener, then as now. However, the teacher who found us was convinced that amazing sexual things were happening beneath my bedclothes. Actually all that was happening, apart from radio listening, was that we were scoffing Marmite sandwiches which I had sneaked down into the kitchen and stolen the ingredients for. I was, and still am, very partial to a nice sandwich in bed at night – although my preference, of course, is my all-time favourite sandwich filling: crispy well-done bacon. But there I was in trouble again.

I still wanted desperately to be a dancer, and knew that I could dance, but as far as The Arts Educational School was concerned I was apparently just a little red-faced misfit. I was also a total failure academically. The school prided itself on having a high academic standard, so I was considered a disaster. In every class I attended I was sent down to a lower and lower level until I finished up, in my worst subjects, French, maths and English, in the juniors along with the little kids, I was angry. Anger was my only defence and the emotion I remember experiencing most of all. It was the same old problem. I couldn't spell. I couldn't read. I just didn't see words. I was dyslexic, only I had no way of knowing that, and at the time neither did anyone else. I just gave up. There seemed no alternative.

At home, or what passed for it, the madness continued. My family was going up the spout, and all I could do was watch. Don't ever tell me that children don't realise what is going on when their parents' marriage is falling apart, because they damn well do.

My mother and father both did the classic trick of each trying to turn me against the other. I have to admit my mother was worse than my father at that. She really did pull out the emotional stops and worked very hard at successfully turning me against my father. She went to considerable lengths. She was an avid visitor of fortune-tellers, although she did become rather unpopular because she had a habit of claiming other people's spirits. If the medium had said she was seeing a one-legged Chinese man hopping around waving a budgie in his right hand, my mother would have said, 'Yes, yes, I can place him. He's here for me.' She would take me along to séances with her. Then afterwards she would say, 'They have told me never to trust your father.' It was pretty wicked of her really.

She also had a habit of being overly generous with other people's money. She did this both to my father and the other men in her life, all of whom were completely under her spell. In some way my father turned his frustration and fury on me. I've always thought that part of the problem he had with me was that, unlike Chris, I was old enough to understand what was going on between him and my mother. I had even seen him break down and cry, and I think that made him very uneasy. By nature he was a gentle man, not somebody who would ever hit another person. Yet once when I was home from ballet school he just lost control and turned on me so violently that I ended up falling down a flight of stairs. It happened over something very minor – Chris and I bickering again, something we did constantly at that age. It was then that I learned not to make a sound when I was being hurt. You could have cut my head off and I wouldn't have made a squeak. It was an extension of the dumb insolence I displayed at school really. It stayed with me. I had this stubborn attitude to anyone in authority – do what you like to me, it doesn't affect me in any way. Inside I would be completely broken, but I behaved as if I was untouchable. I even took that attitude into the theatre with me later. I had to re-programme myself, to learn that directors were there to help me, and that they weren't plotting my downfall. But back then I felt the whole world was against me, and that I was completely alone.

The man my mother eventually left home for was a former army colonel called William Barratt, rather upper class and well spoken, whom she considered a very romantic figure. Bill didn't like me because I reminded him of my father – as I would, being my father's daughter. He developed a penchant for making me stand outside the house at night if he considered that I had misbehaved in any way, which I found very frightening, particularly in view of the location involved.

My father had remained in our family home in Ashton with my brother, while my mother had contrived to move into my grandparents' remote moorland bungalow – their main home was above their tailor's shop, of course – yet again displaying that avid romantic streak of hers. I think she saw herself as Cathy in *Wuthering Heights*, continuing to be attracted to isolated places even though she was the most gregarious person I ever met.

I didn't find it romantic. I hated the place. And standing alone outside in the darkness was a dreadful punishment to me. I have no idea why my mother let Bill do this, but in his defence I will say that she had already managed to reduce him to an emotional wreck, as she did so many of those around her.

Divorce, of course, was a very big deal in those days. I was either twelve or thirteen when my parents eventually divorced, but Bill took longer to leave his wife. He ran a chain of dry-cleaning shops that belonged to his wife and, like so many men, he kept getting cold feet about abandoning this very safe, rather rich world. So for a time he was just a frequent visitor to my mother's bleak and isolated bungalow.

Meanwhile, my brother and I were shuffled between our parents. We seemed to be constantly on buses between their two homes. Then to get to the moorland bungalow, we had to walk about two miles up a lane with nothing except stone walls and sheep around us and, in the winter, it would be pitch black because there was no lighting.

We both found it scary, particularly because Bill's wife, Gladys, knew all about her husband's liaison with my mother and their moorland love nest, and would turn up outside yelling and brandishing a horsewhip. She would also lie on the ground in front of the garage so on countless occasions Bill nearly ran her over in his car. As Chris and I walked back to the bungalow, I was always convinced that she would leap out of the darkness and attack us with her whip.

Once when my mother had taken me shopping in Manchester, Gladys did physically attack her in Kendal's department store. True to form, I flew at Gladys and absolutely flattened her. I did the usual.

51

Knocked her down and kept bashing her head on the floor. I continued to do so, too, until I was finally picked up by the manager by the scruff of my neck and my backside and chucked out of the store onto the pavement outside.

It's a vivid memory and one I never failed to think of when, during my *Coronation Street* years, I would walk through Kendal's, usually with people calling 'Hello Alma' and wonder what those *Corrie* fans would make of it if they knew that I had nearly killed my mother's lover's wife in that very store, and indeed, bashed her head on the same marble floor that is still there.

I don't think my father ever knew about that incident. Certainly, on my mother's instructions, I never told him. I learned not to relate to either parent anything of what happened while I was with the other. The worst thing about the whole situation was that I never felt right wherever I was. If I left my father to go to my mother that was wrong, and if I left my mother to go to my father that was wrong too. My mother made me feel it more than my father. And I feel very sorry now that the relationship I had with my father disintegrated in the way that it did. I didn't understand that he had become a totally beaten wrecked man. I didn't understand that at all.

I don't know where I was most miserable, caught between my warring parents in their disparate homes and relationships, or back at school.

Salvation, albeit temporary, came in what might have seemed like an unlikely package in view of my chronic insecurity. At Christmas everybody at The Arts Educational School auditioned for a pantomime or some kind of show and I was sent up to the London Palladium to do an audition for a panto at the Finsbury Park Empire.

By this time I was in such a mess that I had lost all desire to go on the stage, but I did have an idea that if I got into a pantomime at least I wouldn't have to spend Christmas with either of my parents. Not only did I no longer have a home worthy of the name, but I didn't seem to have any of my things left, either, except my rabbits which I never let out of my sight. My mother would probably be spending the festive season in a hotel with Bill, so the choice was either to sleep on a hotel-room floor listening to whatever was going on between them or to spend it with my father, who was in a terrible state because he'd been left with my little brother. But he didn't seem to like me at all any more.

Nonetheless, I didn't hold out much hope of being picked at the audition even though I knew I was good at tap and you always had tap dancing in panto then. Apart from anything else who would want a dancer with a red face? However, a quite extraordinary thing happened.

To my total astonishment once I walked onto that stage in the London Palladium, in a wonderful theatre with an amazing history, for this major audition, I instantly changed into a person who didn't blush, a person who was, I suppose, a performer. Instead of being the one who couldn't do it, as I had expected, I was the one who could. You would have thought that with all my complexes and insecurities I would have been completely over-awed and gone to pieces. The opposite happened. I did it. I got hired for the chorus of *Babes in the Wood*.

At that moment my life was transformed. I know it sounds like the most terrible cliché, but I felt quite simply as if I'd come home, as if I'd found a kind of family that would always be mine. Just looking up and around at the back of the scenery was the most unbelievably comforting sight. I felt absolutely at peace. That has never altered. Only anyone who has been lucky enough to find the one thing they can really do in life will understand what I mean. In all that I have done wrong over the years, going into the theatre, becoming a performer, remains the one thing that I know I got right.

I never yearned to be famous, to be a star. That wasn't it at all. I merely wanted to be taken into the world of theatre and to become a part of it. Joining the company at Finsbury Park, just knowing there was this routine, that everybody was there, that there were going to be a lot of laughs, and that I really was a part of it all, was a source of absolute joy to me.

However, I didn't totally change character. My propensity for getting into trouble did not abandon me. In fact, I nearly got thrown out in the first week.

I was gazing at the principal boy and I fell straight into the brass section. I was completely mesmerised. Only a pretty heavy fall could have jerked me out of my trance-like state, actually. The trombonist booted me out with one foot. I shot through the pass door, was back in line pretty fast, and more or less got away with it.

Then I got into terrible trouble with the ponies, which I used to look after, catching them when they came off stage. It seems extraordinary now that we had real ponies, galloping around a theatre, unattached to anything except a bearing rein, but we did. They were pretty high spirited too, and would come belting off towards a stagehand who was scared of them. Nobody else wanted to try to catch them, but with my love of horses I was up for it. The routine went like this: pony into the wings, bang, straight into your tummy, bearing rein off, rug over, round the back, down the ramp, into the horsebox, make sure it was tied up, back for the next. One night I couldn't find one of the rugs. The producer found me, wearing my finale costume, lying face down under a piece of scenery trying to pull this blessed rug out.

Now, messing up your costume, particularly your finale costume, was a cardinal sin. 'You're out,' he bellowed.

I was mortified. However, he did not carry out the threat, although he may have wished he had when I was responsible for the magician going up in flames.

The magician did a guillotine trick. He had a bucket on stage with a pretend head, covered in red goo for blood, concealed in it. You know the kind of thing – the magician puts his own head through the guillotine, there's a chop, it's actually a cabbage that drops off, but he does a swap and the cabbage turns into the blood-smeared head, which was hidden in the bucket.

Well, not in this show it wasn't. Earlier in the magician's act I had to dance around a maypole with him. So there I was skipping around the stage with him when the bucket attached itself to my costume. I clanked around the maypole trying to get rid of it until the head fell out and rolled across the stage. Of course, the magician was furious with me.

The next thing he had to do was a fire routine in which he came on, clicked his fingers and made flames appear. Unfortunately he was in such a rage with me that he must have overloaded his fingers. He just went 'ta pumpf' and was engulfed in flames. But his anger was still directed at me. He leapt about the stage trying to beat the flames out while at the same time trying to strangle this small chorus girl.

Miraculously we both survived. He suffered no lasting damage and I was allowed to finish the run. I was even given my first words to speak on stage – I had danced and sung before but never spoken – in a routine with a then very famous ventriloquist's act, Daisy May and Saveen. I had to ask, 'Is Daisy May going to Nottingham Fair too?' Pretty profound stuff, that.

I loved it, though. I really loved it. Going back to school at Tring after Christmas was a terrible let-down, and things just went from bad to worse. The academic side totally disintegrated. I more or less stopped going to lessons. If at the age of twelve I was going to be sent to join the five-year-olds, then quite frankly I didn't see the point.

On one occasion I decided to have a bath instead. The house had once belonged to the Rothschilds and had unbelievable bathrooms off the dormitories, with huge baths, some of which even had bubbling jacuzzi-type fittings. I settled myself in with my radio, planning to have a nice hour's listening. Then I heard footsteps and voices. To my horror the headmistress, a formidable Margaret Rutherford lookalike, was showing some parents and a child around the school. They had to walk through two rooms to get to the bathroom, and the bathroom didn't lead anywhere. I was trapped. At first I thought I'd have to jump through the window, then my panicking eyes were drawn to a big cupboard in the corner. I leapt out of the bath, pulled the plug, picked up the radio, grabbed the towel, and shot into the cupboard.

I heard them come in and eventually, after what seemed an inordinately long time, I heard them leave. When I emerged there was steam everywhere, the bath water was still going glug glug glug, and there were wet footprints on the floor leading directly to my cupboard. The headmistress hadn't opened the door, presumably because she hadn't wanted to make things even worse. But she knew damned well what had been going on and it didn't take her awfully long to find out who the culprit was. It was usually me, I'd been missing from lessons again, and in any case, for some reason I always owned up.

On another occasion I'd gone wandering around in the middle of the night and was caught in this wonderful glass-lined quiet room which none of us were supposed to go into. I think I'd been to the kitchen scavenging for food again. Suddenly I heard Matron coming, so I just dived into a big tea chest that happened to be there. However, it turned out that light bulbs were kept in it, and the reason that Matron was on the prowl at three o'clock in the morning was that she had woken up to find that the light in her room wasn't working and had gone in search of a new bulb. She opened the lid of the tea chest and there I was inside. Now this was the kind of house you could easily believe was haunted. Matron went into shock. I reckon I nearly killed her. She just screamed and screamed. She thought I was a ghost. I made soothing noises and when she eventually realised that it was me she just said, 'What on earth are you doing here?'

'Tidying up,' I replied.

No wonder I already had a prize for excuses under my belt. Though why I told her that I have no idea. It was quite good though really, because there wasn't much that Matron could say in response.

Nonetheless I ended up in detention. Predictably, I spent a great deal of time in detention. That was a joke too. We had to make notes all the time which we were supposed to copy out later. I couldn't do that of course. Again nobody realised why, or indeed cared. You should have seen my notes, all doodles and scribbles, mostly drawings of horses' heads. I used to pretend to write, to mime writing if the teacher said write this down. I would just scribble something. Anything.

Food figured quite a lot in my misdemeanours, largely because I never seemed to be given enough of it. One of my tricks, when we were taken out on any kind of outing, was to dress myself up the way I thought a French schoolgirl would dress, under these big cloaks we all used to have to wear. Then I'd run off from the main group, take off my cloak, knock on the doors of unsuspecting local householders and ask for food in my terrible French. I was quite successful at that.

I also used to sneak off at night down to the village for fish and chips. Another thing those cloaks were very good for was concealing a fish supper. There was a ridiculous school rule that you had to curtsey whenever you passed a teacher, and one night, when I tried to do just that despite reeking of vinegar and with my arms wrapped around my illicit parcel, I dropped the lot at the feet of one of the senior dancing teachers. Yet again I'd broken all the rules, not least having left the school alone at night and without permission.

Even my dancing caused problems. My wonderful time in *Babes in the Wood* made no difference at all to the blushing and terrible embarrassment I experienced when I was back in class. My paranoia about blushing became so extreme that I would smother my face with toothpaste to lighten it. And the school made matters worse by doing terrible things to me.

On one occasion I had to dance before an extremely distinguished panel, all patrons of the school: Alicia Markova, Anton Dolin and John Gilpin. It was a quite terrifying line-up, and in addition the whole school was sitting on the floor. I knew that as soon as I opened the door to the ballet room I would start to blush. I was sure that everybody would fall about laughing when they saw me, because that was what they usually did. Indeed, I spent my whole ballet life at that school looking down so that people couldn't see my face. I looked like a headless dancer because my head was so far down. No wonder I couldn't do pirouettes.

Anyway, I gritted my teeth to walk into that ballet room and then the principal, who had after all been trained by Pavlova and had extremely high standards, said, 'You've got holes in your hairnet. Return to your dormitory and make yourself tidy.' Well, actually there wasn't much hairnet left. I was always a mess. And my hair always had a mind of its own. It had decided to poke itself through.

Mortified, I duly set off to go back to my dorm to find another hairnet and tidy myself up. I was in a hurry. After all, the entire school were waiting for me. I had to run along endless corridors and up the wonderful main staircase. The school was enormous and my dorm was miles away. You needed a taxi actually. By the time I came puffing back to the ballet room I wasn't red in the face any more. I was purple. I just wanted the ground to open and swallow me up. I still don't understand the thinking of people who could do that to a child.

Ironically enough the main cause of my expulsion was something for which you might have expected to win praise at a stage school. But then initiative was not encouraged at either of the educational establishments that decided they could do without me.

The summer after appearing in *Babes in the Wood,* which had so delighted me, I heard that the older pupils at Tring, the sixteen- and seventeen-year-olds, were being auditioned for pantomime at the Theatre Royal Drury Lane. I could think of nothing better than being part of this. But I was allegedly too young. These auditions were for individual appearances in various pantomimes throughout the country, and although the selection process which had resulted in me going into *Babes in the Wood* had been similar, I had been sent as part of a school troupe.

Keen to escape from both my school and my parents, I was determined to get in on the act. I decided I would sneak off to London on the train, but I pestered the older girls so much for details about the audition and what was going to happen that a couple of the nicer ones smuggled me onto the bus with them.

A momentous thing occurred that day. The producer, Freddie Carpenter, took a shine to me and kept calling me back to do a bit more and then another bit. I remember that the others were getting quite cross about this while I just stood in the middle of the stage feeling completely at home again. I was so absolutely bewitched by it all that I didn't really take in what it meant when he suddenly said, 'OK. So where would you like to go? You can go to Newcastle, Glasgow, Bradford or Edinburgh.'

Somehow I managed to mumble that I'd like to go to Glasgow. I had a friend who lived there. In what was for me an unusual flash of practicality I thought that at least I might have somewhere to stay.

After that I settled down again to school life, or the nearest I could get to it until the contract arrived. Then all hell broke loose. I hadn't been supposed to be at the auditions and the school liked to be in control. I had broken the rules again. Nobody there was pleased that I'd got a job. Not one little bit.

The pantomime went on until the end of March which meant that I would miss virtually the entire spring term. I was issued with an ultimatum. If I did the pantomime, I was out.

My parents became involved at this point, of course, and the row reached epic proportions. My father had more or less washed his hands of me by then. My mother, naturally, was over the moon, particularly when she found out that I was the only one from the school who had been picked. She thought it was wonderful. Together she and I decided that of course I was going to take the job. The prospect of my being expelled for the second time did not faze either of us at all.

The school duly carried out its threat, and I was out on my ear once more. It was several months before I was due to start rehearsals and I had no home worth mentioning to go to – or none that I wanted to go to anyway.

And that was how I ended up living and working in Soho at the age of thirteen-and-a-half despite it being totally illegal, of course. Probably because my life was so chaotic at the time, my memory is a bit hazy about exactly how it happened.

I do remember being allowed back to the school briefly and after lengthy negotiations between my parents and the headteachers, in order to sit certain compulsory examinations. And I also remember the only ones I passed were for drama and dancing.

But Soho quickly became the nearest thing to home that I had experienced since my family's troubles had begun. It was through the pantomime producers that I moved in to the Theatre Girls' Club in Greek Street. The excuse was that I had to be in London for fittings and things. Whatever the reason, I grasped the opportunity with both hands.

The Theatre Girls' Club was a wonderful place run by Miss Bell, a woman to whom I owe a great deal. It was a hostel for women in theatre. Their ages varied a great deal and went up to people in their forties, I think, who were still struggling. I was by far the youngest and had to lie about my age to be allowed there at all.

They charged thirty bob a week all in. We slept several to a room and the place was run like a boarding school in that we took turns to wash in the morning, set the tables and generally help out. But there all resemblance to boarding schools, certainly the ones I had been to, ended. I fitted in for a start. Totally. I felt I really belonged somewhere at last.

Most of the girls were off auditioning all the time, but I had a job to go to. I was just filling in time until the pantomime rehearsals started. Then, when I eventually went to Glasgow I found that theatre life for me was just like the first time in *Babes in the Wood*. Total bloody bliss.

At first I did stay with my friend, and later I went into digs. The pantomime was *Cinderella*. It starred Stanley Baxter as Buttons and a six-foot-tall ex-*Ziegfeld's Follies* girl called Carol Eric was the principal boy. I was extremely taken with both of them. I was in the chorus but if anybody was chosen for a special spot, to give Stanley or Carol a flower or something, and it wasn't me I was absolutely furious.

Right from the beginning, one of the joys about the theatre for me was stage make-up. Once I had that on, as many layers of it and as many eyelashes as I could muster, I just became a different person. There was no question of blushing. From the start the theatre gave me a freedom I can't explain.

This was a top pantomime in a top venue – the Theatre Royal, Glasgow. I had no qualms about that whatsoever. I thought the whole experience was sheer magic. There were about twenty-four of us in the chorus but I got myself noticed because I kept trying to put little bits into my dance routines to make people laugh – just as I had in Grandfather Broadbent's theatre in Ashton-under-Lyne when I was four. The more I succeeded in getting laughs, the more I did it. To my delight, I got a little rave notice in *The Stage*. Of course it put my mother in ecstasy and she kept it for me, as she did nearly all my early notices and photographs.

I loved the life of the theatre so much that even an early experience of the worst kind of showbiz landlady didn't put me off. Several of us stayed in dreadful digs where the landlady had so many children she used to shuffle them around and put them in our beds while we were working. When we returned, worn out after two shows, the children would have wet the beds. I didn't care. I built up this little life for myself within the confines of the company. Everybody else was much older than me of course, and it was during those early pantomimes that I began to develop this absolute paranoia about getting pregnant, which kept me sweet and virginal for far longer than may otherwise have been the case. There always seemed to be girls going home with two bottles of gin to sit in a hot bath or off to see a back-street abortionist. I was already determined that wasn't going to happen to me. Apart from anything else, I wasn't prepared to risk anything that might interfere with the daily theatrical routine which meant so much to me.

In between shows I would go across the road to a little café and sit there eating Scottish meat pie and chips – which were about as good as you could get I reckon – with a copy of *Reveille* propped up against the sauce bottle. I thought it was the most magical thing in the entire world.

I may have been only thirteen, but I decided that I wasn't going back to school, and neither was I going back to my fragmented family.

I was quite determined that I was never going to leave this new world I had discovered.

CHAPTER FOUR

⁓

When *Cinderella* ended so my life in Soho really began. I persuaded Miss Bell to take me back into the Theatre Girls' Club in Greek Street. She shouldn't have agreed given my age. Despite my fibs I suspect she had a jolly good idea of how old I was. Neither of my parents objected – my father because he was past caring, and my mother because I was starting, however humbly, to live her dream. Mummy phoned me every day and visited occasionally, and that seemed enough for her at the time. I don't think either of them worried about me, really. They both had enough worries of their own. It has to be remembered that we had all just survived a war and once the bombs stopped falling you didn't worry about the safety of those close to you, even girls of my age, in the same way that people do now.

In Soho my life was transformed. I'd never fitted in in Ashton-under-Lyne. I hadn't fitted in at either of my boarding schools. Suddenly I found myself in step with everybody around me.

Howard and Wyndham's gave me a contract for pantomime and summer season which ran for several years. Between those, I lived in the Theatre Girls' Club and, along with all the other girls, hawked myself around looking for work. We were in the heart of the red-light district just before the fifties. It was a rumbustious time when London's Soho became a haven for gangsters, England's equivalent of Chicago in the twenties. I was caught up in the excitement of it all and completely oblivious to the dangers. I barely noticed the seedier side.

I was already, at the age of thirteen, earning my own living. As well as auditioning for all sorts of things that never materialised, I would do stints at the various Soho nightclubs that were doing big business at the time and always looking for new acts. Several times I was hired by Al Burnett, father of my present agent Barry Burnett, for spots in shows at the Stork Club and I also worked at The Ambassador, where Shirley Bassey starred for years. I had become a Soho showgirl, dancing half the night away in chorus lines, lying like mad about my age and resolutely dodging any attempts from anyone to send me back to school, certainly on any kind of permanent basis. It seems extraordinary now but back then I just took it all for granted.

We didn't start work in the clubs until well after midnight, and most of us used to walk through Soho and then home again in the early hours of the morning. We couldn't afford taxis. There were no tourists in those days, just the people whose way of life was in that part of London. I used to leave the Theatre Girls' Club about 11.30 p.m., and walk right through Soho past all the prostitutes, who seemed really ancient to me. They became my friends. I didn't regard them as being different to anyone else and I knew they would watch out for me. If any men went to approach me the girls would call, 'Leave 'er alone, luv. She's a professional dancer and she's just a kid. You leave 'er.' And then to each other, 'Keep your eye on 'er will you, darlin'?' Thanks to them I could walk the streets in total safety day and night. I never batted an eyelid at any of it and surprisingly I probably felt safer in Soho in those days than I have anywhere else in my life. There was no question of getting drawn into the prostitutes' way of life, largely because they were much older than me. In those days, you never heard of young girls being on the game. The women I knew would never have allowed the kids you see on the streets today to join them. They really were tarts with hearts of gold.

The only time I ever remember having problems in Soho was when the police decided to clean up the area and move the regular prostitutes on. This meant the punters, unable to find what they were looking for, took to following any young women around. One night I woke up to find a huge man just standing by my bedside looking down at me. I froze. Fortunately an equally large policeman burst in almost immediately and carted him off, telling me, 'You're all right now, love. You're all right now.' It transpired the man had followed me back to the Theatre Girls' Club and had been spotted sneaking into the building by the policeman.

Getting work was rarely a problem in those days for a keen and able young dancer, although its quality did vary. At the Theatre Girls' Club we would get calls from all sorts of people, usually men's organisations of one sort or another, asking for a troupe of dancers. Some of the gigs were pretty dreadful. I remember once we went to an American army base and did a routine for a party in the mess. I was invariably asked along because I was good at tap. But I was only taught the routine, which consisted of continuous time-steps to the music of 'The Sheikh of

Araby' while turning in different directions, on the bus on the way there. So unfortunately I hadn't quite got the hang of exactly which way I should be turning or when, and more or less wrecked the whole routine. But I realised, as I was being knocked off stage, that people were laughing and so milked the situation mercilessly for more.

Afterwards the GIs gave us stockings, make-up and all sorts of things that were still hard to get hold of at that time. Some of the girls started drifting off with the men, and I was terrified about what might happen to me. Fortunately we had a Polish trombonist with us, a real sweetheart, who befriended me and I ended up sitting on the bus with him eating cough sweets and waiting for everyone to finish whatever it was they were doing.

I was never precocious in that direction. Partly because of my fear of getting pregnant, I never had any sort of relationships with boys until I was much, much older. Even then I wasn't particularly enthusiastic. I don't remember having any sexual urges of any sort for years and years. I was too deeply in love with the theatre. I read somewhere that Dan Leno, the Victorian music-hall star who was one of my great heroes, used to go to the Theatre Royal Drury Lane when he first started working and say his prayers on the steps. So I did the same. I made a bargain with God on the steps of the Drury Lane theatre, 'I don't mind if everything else goes wrong. I don't mind if I never have a relationship with anybody. I don't mind if I haven't got a proper family and I don't have anything, but please, please, please can I just be in the theatre.'

I have to admit that to this day, much to everybody's embarrassment, I will occasionally hurl myself on my knees there. People often think I'm drunk, and on one occasion in the middle of the night I was told to go home by a policeman. I may have had a lucky escape. After all, I was sitting on the steps talking to the theatre at the time. You can get certified for things like that.

When it came to auditioning, I was full of enthusiasm. There was a group of about eight or nine of us who used to buy one copy of *The Stage* between us. Then we'd all go to the Silver Grill in Leicester Square and squash up around a table over a single cup of tea or coffee because it was all we could afford. Eventually, after five hours or so, the management would get fed up with us, so then we'd buy one order of Welsh rarebit or beans on toast and slice that up between the lot of us. We'd meticulously dissect *The Stage* and take it in turns to go rushing off for auditions. Later on there was television too, but at the beginning the auditions were for pantomimes, summer seasons, cabaret, revue, dancers abroad and so on. I found it exciting just imagining what the jobs would be like.

We used to share our make-up and all our rehearsal things, leotards, tights, the lot. People were always shouting out things like, 'Anyone got any tap shoes?'

The auditions would start at ten in the morning and go on until six at night, and somehow or other we used to keep that Silver Grill table going right through, with people running in and out letting the others know what was required for each job. 'Oh Christ, they want you to do back flips and splits.'

I even remember auditioning for a stand-in with Wilson, Keppel and Betty who did a famous sand-dance routine. They were always auditioning for another Betty. I don't know what they did with their Betties, actually. Our changing room was the loo in Leicester Square tube station. It was like a cattle market, with fifty million people trampling all over you as you struggled into a leotard that was supposed to show off your shape and make some theatrical producer hire you. Amazingly enough the mirror we used to use while we applied all this extraordinary make-up and pulled on whatever outfit was needed was still there in the Leicester Square ladies' until only last year. For me it was a real slice of theatrical history.

There were some jobs I had my own reasons for not even bothering with, particularly anything at the Windmill Club. By this time it was apparent that my prayers to God concerning my upper anatomy had paid off. I wasn't growing any tits at all. And tits, in the forties and fifties were very definitely in. It wasn't that I minded taking my clothes off, it was just that I thought if I went to the Windmill and they asked me to take them off they would laugh. So I didn't go.

The pantomime and summer seasons took me all over the country. I worked with all the great comics back then – Jimmy Logan, Chick Murray, Tommy Cooper. Nobody rushed home after a performance. Chick Murray, who I thought was one of the greatest comics ever, liked to work out his act with other people. We dancers would go round to Chick's place and he would stand up and start doing his thing.

'I went to the door and I turned the knob to get out of the room, because that's how you get out of a room.' Now, that may not sound so funny written down here – unless, of course, you ever saw Chick perform. It was all in the delivery, which was hilarious.

All the dancers would be sitting on the floor with various variety artists coming on to them. That was the downside. People used to come after you for necking sessions all the time. I was still very young, very disinterested, and very terrified.

Tommy Cooper also made a big impression on me. But then Tommy made a big impression on everyone. He was larger than life in every way and I adored him. He had the biggest feet I have ever seen. He looked as if he was wearing Little Tich boots. He was always doing extraordinary, wonderful things. We were in summer season in Southport when we were asked to attend a fireman's ball. They sent cars for everyone except the poor chorus who were forgotten as usual.

But Tommy wasn't having that. He dialled 999 and said, 'There's a fire at the Garrick Theatre. For God's sake send the fire brigade.'

Then when the fire engines arrived he went out and told the men, 'Right, now you lot can take the girls to the party.'

It was a memorable season, that one at Southport. Derek Roy was actually the lead comic, Tommy was yet to become a big star, and Eve Boswell, the singer who was known as 'The Forces' Sweetheart' along with Vera Lynn, topped the bill. I thought I'd died and gone to heaven just being there with those three. Nothing but nothing would have made me quit. Somebody once dropped me during a lift and I broke two ribs, but I was so determined not to be off that I never mentioned the damage. I was doing cartwheels in the air with broken ribs.

I adored Eve, whom I understudied. She took me under her wing and was lovely to me. But she did have problems elsewhere. There was some kind of tension between her and another woman in the show. When something went missing from Eve's dressing room, the other woman was accused of stealing it. She promptly threatened legal action against Eve, simultaneously claiming, for some unknown reason, that our 'Forces' Sweetheart' was a lesbian. Eve's husband initiated a counter action. He came into the theatre one day with a huge sheaf of papers, making various allegations. Everybody was asked to read all this stuff, but only one person did. Tommy spent about twenty minutes in his dressing room, in complete silence, studying the papers meticulously. At the end he looked up and said, 'It's no good. There's not a laugh in it.'

Everyone thought that was hilarious – apart from Eve and her husband. The following day a notice in laboured legalese appeared on the board at the stage door. It began along the lines, 'I, the understated, Eve Boswell, wish to make it known that at no time have I ever had a lesbian relationship.' The day after that another notice appeared beneath it, 'I, the understated, Tommy Cooper, wish to make it known that at no time have I ever peed in the dressing-room washbasin.' Now, how could you not love that man?

He did have a temper though. He and his wife Dove, a big woman who was almost as much of a character as Tommy, had the most tremendous fights. We all always seemed to end up in Tommy's dressing room after the show while he told stories. But more often than not Dove would interrupt and tell the tag. Then the bottles of booze would go flying and the dressing room would end up covered in broken glass. Gin, whisky, whatever, Tommy would send the lot flying. It must have cost him a fortune, and it was certainly quite a spectacle. But then, you wouldn't steal Tommy Cooper's tag line would you? Only Dove would ever have dared.

I did have my problems in Southport, however. There was a rather unpleasant series of incidents which, particularly as I was a sixteen-year-old virgin at the time, would nowadays probably be regarded as serious sexual harassment by the boss. Things were rather different in the fifties. I was locked in the dressing room by this man, a senior member of the management, who then tried to jump on me. When I wouldn't play, he took his revenge. First of all he made me stand on stage from ten in the morning until lunchtime because I had a hole in my fishnet tights. I just had to stand there – wearing only my leotard and tights and in high-heeled shoes – with all the stagehands around. They were divine to me, thankfully. But he was a right bastard, keeping this horrible punishment going for a week – all for that one crime of having a hole in my tights. He proceeded to get nastier and nastier and threatened to stop me getting into the West End because of my terrible behaviour. Even if I had behaved terribly, I had no idea whether he had that sort of power – with the benefit of hindsight, almost certainly not, but it seemed like a very big deal at the time.

Then one morning he called me into his office, which was on the top floor of the theatre. 'You'll never work for Bernard Delfont again,' he threatened, leering at me. I knew how I could have got on the right side of him but I had no intention of doing so. Suddenly I blew. I had a pair of brand new pointe shoes with me and I whacked his head, two direct blows right across the skull. As he was reeling from that I kicked him hard so that he fell and cracked his head on the washbasin. Without knowing what damage I'd done I rushed out, locking the door behind me, and ran out of the theatre.

Much later in the day I bumped into some of the George Mitchell Singers and confessed. They guessed that he had probably been trying to get out of his office on the top floor for several hours. They were right. He needed medical treatment too. Not surprisingly he decided that I had to go. I was out. Sacked.

But to my surprise everybody stood by me. The stagehands and all the cast, including Eve and Tommy, stuck their necks out for me, bless them. They said I'd been victimised and if I was out then so were they. It seemed to me then that for once in my life I had experienced some justice. I think I loved the theatre and theatre people even more as a result.

It was just after that, in, I think, my third panto in Scotland, that I started going out with my first real boyfriend, a journalist called John Law. There was no sex though. In spite of, or maybe because of, the world that I moved in I still didn't want to know about it. However, John was a really clever comedy writer who was responsible for me being rather better at auditions than some of my contemporaries. He used to write me audition numbers, and there is no doubt that he played a significant part in my eventual escape from the chorus line. I remember in particular a parody he wrote for me about some idiot doing an audition. It began something like this:

Though my make-up's sad, my hair's as bad,
And my voice is tragically wheezy,
I'd do anything to be in your show,
But I know it's not that easy . . .

And ended rather desperately:

Be an angel and answer my plea,
There's no business like show business for me,
I'm down on my uppers, I haven't had suppers,
I'm so much thinner, what happened to dinner?
Give me a job, in the name of humanity,
You've got to have something for me.

Auditions were an absolute cattle market. Both Johnny Briggs,
Coronation Street's Mike Baldwin, and I remember all too clearly the big
open film auditions that used to be staged regularly in Monmouth Street
by Ronnie Curtis, who cast many of the Elstree and Pinewood movies
at the time. Ronnie used to point at the people he wanted, but unfortunately, as one of his eyes was set at a jaunty angle, shall we say, Ronnie
appeared to be looking in one direction while pointing in another. No
one was ever sure whether they had been chosen or not. I am certain
quite a lot of people were picked by mistake.

With John's help I was able to make myself just that bit more
interesting. I figured that there were always dozens of dancers up for
everything, so, somewhat precociously for a chorus girl, I auditioned for
the lead in *Where's Charley*, a musical version of *Charley's Aunt*. I got
down to the final two for the part playing opposite Norman Wisdom,
which gave me considerable encouragement.

One of my favourite jobs during that period of my life was a revue called *Five Past Eight* which was put on in Scotland by Howard and Wyndham's. It was produced by Freddie Carpenter, who had taken a shine to me when he had hired me for *Cinderella*.

I was delighted to hear that he was looking for eight very different girls and that he was more interested in personality than physique.

I had always had some problems as a chorus-line dancer because my shape never seemed to quite fit in with other people's. Later, when I auditioned for the Television Toppers, a top troupe at the time, I was the same height as all the other girls but my neck was so long that my shoulders were about four inches below theirs. So I stumbled through the audition with my shoulders hunched up around my ears. It was, however, probably a good thing that they didn't hire me. It would have been difficult to sustain that position for three hours on stage.

So I was thrilled when Freddie took me on.

He then became responsible for a rather momentous decision in my life – I said goodbye to Shirley Broadbent forever.

He insisted that I change my name. 'You'll never be taken seriously in this business with a name like that,' he told me firmly. 'You just couldn't succeed.'

I did his bidding instantly, never dreaming for a moment that one day an actor called Jim Broadbent would win an Oscar. Almost everybody changed their names in those days. Particularly if they were called Shirley Broadbent.

However, finding a new name wasn't easy. I picked Barrie with a pin from the phone book, and was pleased with my chance choice because of its connection with J. M. Barrie, the writer of *Peter Pan*. Then I thought of Amanda because of my lifelong devotion to Gertrude Lawrence, who always wanted to be called Amanda, as indeed she was in *Private Lives,* which was written specially for her by Noël Coward. But I thought that would be too pretentious so picked Lynne instead.

Then Equity turned that down because there was already a Lynne Barrie listed, so I asked a friend to choose a book for me and open it at random. The book was *Rival Experiments,* by H. G. Wells and it opened at two pages that were blank except for a one-word chapter heading: 'Amanda'. I reckoned that was a message from Gertie, and Amanda Barrie I became.

My mother, I suspect reacting differently to the way most mothers would, loved my name change. 'How wonderful, darling,' she announced. 'Why didn't I think of that?'

From that day on neither she nor any of my family called me anything but Amanda – except Mandy sometimes.

For myself, I had absolutely no regrets and changed my name without giving it a thought. But sometimes nowadays I do rather wish I'd stuck with the name I was born with.

Five Past Eight, which played all over Scotland, notably Glasgow and Edinburgh, opened up a whole new world for me. The world of revue was really big news at the time, and with my leaning towards comedy as well as being a dancer and able to sing a bit, I was particularly well suited to its mixture of different items.

We all stayed in some fairly downmarket Glasgow digs, and the young and barely known Des O'Connor, who was also playing Glasgow in a variety show, was booked into the same place. He would come bounding down to the breakfast room where the rest of us would be sitting like dead fish and say, 'Right, point to something, point to something.'

At first we thought he was barmy. Then we realised what he was trying to do. This was an exercise to make sure he had a gag ready about anything and everything. Someone would point to the pepper pot and Des would begin. 'Well, I met this man wearing a pepper pot . . .' Then it would be something else. Picture frame. 'There was this man walking down the street with a picture frame round his neck . . .' After a bit whenever he came in for breakfast we'd all shout at once, 'Salt cellar! Sugar bowl! Curtains!'

I can't remember how funny the jokes were, but it made clear how people like Des became so brilliant at what they do. It's sheer hard work as well as talent. Bob Monkhouse was another one who did the same kind of thing as a wit sharpener. But to do it at crack of dawn over a Glasgow showbiz landlady's idea of breakfast – that was real dedication.

During *Five Past Eight* I became good friends with a young woman called Jane Taylor who was also in the same digs. We had both worked in TV with Benny Hill and we got into a habit of having long telephone conversations with him late at night when we got back to our digs. The only telephone was a payphone in the hall to which we had restricted access. We weren't supposed to receive phone calls late at night and we certainly couldn't afford to make many. So we used to crouch under the hall table until Benny phoned us, then we'd grab the receiver, pull it back under the table with us and talk to Benny for hours.

After about eight years of panto, summer season and countless jobs in between I eventually became a regular dancer at one of the top London clubs, Winston's, early in 1956. I worked there for more than four years while continuing with pantomime and summer season and punctuated by lots of TV, including commercials. Winston's, where Danny La Rue made his name and Lionel Blair did the choreography, became a very important part of my life. It was where I first worked with Barbara Windsor, Judy Cornwell, Jill Gascoigne, and the West End musical star Maggie Fitzgibbon. We were all showgirls then, at the start of our various careers.

Like me, Barbara Windsor lived quite close to Winston's and she and I were always bumping into each other as we toddled down Oxford

Street in full make-up, mini skirts, false eyelashes, the lot, in the middle of the night.

I met some extraordinary people at the club including several of the gangsters who used to more or less run Soho back then. Those were the days of the Maltese Mafia when two legendary gang leaders, Jack 'Spot' Comer and Albert 'Big Alby' Dimes, once fought each other with knives up and down Frith Street for almost an hour in the middle of the day. A huge crowd gathered to watch, but when the pair were arrested the case was thrown out of court because of lack of witnesses. Even a vicar allegedly accepted £14 to swear that the fight never happened. Mostly these rather frightening men were extremely gentlemanly to us girls. But there were exceptions.

Our dressing room was not very salubrious. It actually doubled as the meat store, and to one side there were two huge refrigerators. There was barely room to move, which was about par for the course backstage at all of these clubs. The dressing room had been constructed out of a load of tiny cupboards underneath the stage. It was small and airless and there used to be between six and eight of us squashed in there. Every few minutes some commis-waiter would come blundering through, lean across us, and pull half a dozen bloody rump steaks out of a fridge. All too often we'd end up with blood dripped all over us, which was particularly unpleasant as we were usually in a state of undress or only wearing these silly little bikini type objects which passed for costumes.

As if all that wasn't bad enough, one night this big hefty man came into the dressing room and just wouldn't go away. He stood there alongside half a dead sheep staring at us for what seemed like forever. Now we didn't like that one little bit.

The stage manager tried to get him to go, but he wouldn't budge. He just carried on staring. Eventually I could stand it no longer. I had no idea who he was and I didn't care. I hit him over the head with a chair and he went reeling off, more than a little concussed, I think. Only later did I learn that he was Alby Dimes's minder, a fact that was mildly disconcerting even to me, and that he had just come out of jail. Apparently when he came round, he went quite mad, threatening to smash up the place and do me all sorts of damage.

Alby Dimes was a regular at Winston's and we'd all seen him around and passed the time of day with him. So after I came off stage I went over to where he was sitting and said that I was sorry I had hit his friend, explaining that he wouldn't leave our dressing room.

'He shouldn't have done it,' I said. 'It's not nice being stared at like that when you haven't got any clothes on.'

I was very naive. Everybody else was horrified when they realised what I was doing. But Mr Dimes pulled up a chair for me and sat me down and agreed with me. Like most of his kind he was always very polite with women, priding himself on treating them well and behaving properly in their presence. Indeed, if we had a bad audience who heckled a lot, it was usually Alby and his henchmen who would make them shut up and let us get on with the show. So it was quite in charac- ter for him to send me a huge bouquet of flowers the next day. It stunned a few people at Winston's when they arrived though.

I quite swiftly became part of the furniture at the club. It was a crash course in show business, no doubt about that.

I'd been there a couple of years when the choreographer walked out. Lionel Blair had already moved on to other things and his successor just threw a wobbly one day and left. Danny La Rue came in to the dancers looking for a volunteer to take over. Everyone looked at me for some reason and suddenly I was a choreographer and in charge of all the other dancers. Though I say it myself, I was quite well suited to the task and did rather a good job. I set all the numbers up.

I also had to choreograph the strippers, in as much as you could choreograph strippers in those days. Danny and I used to audition them together.

There was one hilarious audition where everything and everyone seemed to go from bad to worse. First of all a rather big girl came in and walked around the room bending down and studying the chairs. 'Can we help you?' we asked. 'Are you looking for anything?'

'I just want to look at the size of the chair legs.'

'Any particular reason?' asked Danny.

'Oh, it's just part of my act.'

Now that made Danny and me a bit nervous. There were some very nasty shaped chair legs at Winston's, and the thought of what she might be intending to do with them was something neither of us could face at that time of the morning, so we stopped her right there.

We had to audition about twenty girls, and an extraordinary number of them that day were trouble. There was one who came up to us early on and asked if we were ready for her. We told her that we weren't. She'd have to wait her turn on the list.

'Well, please can you tell me straight away when you're ready for me?' she asked. 'And please don't keep me waiting for too long.'

Naturally we just thought, 'Get her!' And we almost made a point of making her wait.

Meanwhile, there were other little treats in store. One girl, dressed in a royal-blue velvet outfit, proceeded to strip to 'Rhapsody in Blue'. Unfortunately her zip stuck fast and I had to go and rescue her. I had to unzip the whole top half of her costume, which set me off in helpless giggles. When she started again she was so nervous she removed everything on the first bar of her music.

Another came with a toothless mother who wouldn't leave her side. The girl was actually very beautiful but her act was a joke. It was supposed to be the Dance of the Seven Veils. Unfortunately it was more like The Mummy Returns to Unwrap Itself, or somebody climbing out of swaddling clothes. She was sort of draped in dirty bandages.

Next was this girl who did an act with plastic bananas. She stuck them in her G-string and as she ran around the stage she made them squeak. By then Danny and I were hysterical. Matters were made worse by the first girl coming up from downstairs, asking, 'Are you ready for me yet? Are you ready for me yet? You can't keep me waiting. You can't keep me waiting.'

We were beginning to find her really annoying. Out of spite, I'm afraid, we left her until last. When she eventually emerged she had a lot of props, including several mats, one of which had spikes sticking up all over it, and a box which made a chinking sound as she carried it onto the stage. First she took a paraffin lighter out of the box and dramatically set fire to her breath. This blaze of flame burst across the stage, while she stood there with paraffin and the protective gunge fire-eaters use dripping down her chin. We all ducked in a hurry.

'Oh my God, we can't let her breathe flames over the customers,' I whispered to Danny.

'Oh I don't know. If anyone wants their steak well done it could be useful,' he replied.

Then she lay down on her bed of spikes and asked for volunteers to stand on her stomach. When we all declined she moved on to her next routine.

'Now please, please could you all be very, very quiet,' she said. 'I am about to do my finale.' At which point she knelt down on the floor, reached into her box, brought out handfuls of broken glass, and began to smash them into herself. All over. Repeatedly. With disastrous results. She ended up covered in blood and bits of broken glass with her hands in ribbons. As she knelt there bleeding she wailed, 'I told you, I told you! You kept me waiting too long!'

It was then that we realised, to our horror, why she'd been in such a hurry. She had been put into a hypnotic trance which would allegedly stop the glass piercing her body, and by the time we let her perform she'd come out of the trance. She really was in a dreadful state. She was lacerated. As we didn't want to be sued I spent some hours downstairs in the dressing room with her, using a pair of eyebrow tweezers, borrowed from Barbara Windsor to pluck out the bits of glass and sticking tiny pieces of plaster all over her to keep her in one piece. She didn't get the job and neither did I follow her future career, but I suspect she may have gone on to be a window cleaner. Ironically enough, shortly afterwards I choreographed a strip routine about a window cleaner, which actually got a notice in *The Stage* describing it as the best and wittiest strip show outside Paris. The routine was written by Brian Blackburn, a brilliant writer who's now big in America, so it had very funny lyrics. But I was quite proud of that notice because it was almost impossible to get strippers who had any sense of music or timing in those days. Somehow or other though, I really got my strippers going.

Generally speaking the strippers and the dancers didn't mix. There was a kind of snobbery, I suppose. The strippers were the strippers. And the dancers were mostly middle-class girls who'd been to ballet school and failed.

The dancers did have vaguely risqué routines though. They changed the show every three or four weeks at Winston's, and when it was coming up to Wimbledon we'd do tennis numbers with racquets and balls as props. The dancers would always end up saying things to the audience like, 'Can I have my ball back? No, not that ball sir!'

It kept the audiences happy. We mostly got a pretty good bunch in Winston's, and the plusses of working there were enormous. The experience you got was invaluable. The worst sort of customers were the chinless wonders, the hooray Henrys and bits of fringe royalty who used to turn up. They were appalling. They used to think it was highly amusing to go downstairs to the gents' and come up with bits of old soap that they would break up and flick at us on stage. It was the fifties' equivalent of yuppies throwing bread rolls, I suppose. I think we did get the odd bread roll as well, which we probably ate.

We dancers were always hungry. We never seemed to get enough food. In between numbers we'd go on stage to pre-set the next routine, and we'd be gathered together behind a sort of Venetian blind while the waiters scuttled by serving the people out front. We would invariably grab a handful of chips off the nearest plate. They were usually tepid but quite nice, and it was often the nearest some of us got to a square meal all day. On one occasion Maggie Fitzgibbon, Barbara Windsor and I grabbed a handful of chips each, stuck them in our mouths, and realised too late that they were red hot. Naturally the curtain went up immediately and we had to spit the burning chips all over the audience before we could even begin to sing our next number.

Barbara Windsor was very much my contemporary in every way. She's about the same age as me, but even in those days she already seemed like a star. To me anyway. Her physical size never did anything to diminish her enormous presence. She always seemed to know what she was doing, and she always knew who everyone was. I never did. I've made so many mistakes in my career by not realising who was important and who wasn't.

Danny La Rue was in his heyday, of course. He was a big, big star in the West End. You could say he made the drag scene respectable, but it was more that that. I was a great admirer and saw how all kinds of audiences fell for him. He once advised me, 'Just learn your ad libs, dear.' Still one of the best lines I have ever heard in show business. Danny was great. He wouldn't take any nonsense either. No audience ever got out of hand with him. He would simply stop the show and say, 'Right, we'll wait then. I get paid for making a fool of myself. What's your excuse?'

Of course Danny went on to have his own club. It was that era when the clubs were seriously big business. People used to go to the theatre and then come on to the clubs to be entertained into the early hours. Winston's was one of the leading clubs, as was Churchill's just across the road. I was never aware of any particular rivalry between the clubs, but if you became a regular at one you were inclined to stick to it and not move around too much.

You never knew who was out front. Some very impressive people would turn up. Ava Gardner was a regular visitor, and one night Judy Garland came along, which caused me great embarrassment as I had the total humiliation of singing 'Swannee' with her about three feet away from me. Ultimately I was so mortified I muttered, 'Oh, sorry,' crossed myself and ran off.

Nonetheless her husband Sid Luft, whom I'd become quite friendly with when he'd visited the club alone on previous occasions through our mutual love of horses and racing, insisted that I meet her. It was an astonishing experience. There she was, this legend. You couldn't believe anyone could be so small. She didn't appear to have a neck. I remember thinking that she wasn't built like other people. She was tiny and yet she had a huge ribcage, which must have been why her voice was so extraordinary. She hardly spoke to me or indeed anyone else. She was appearing at the Dominion Theatre, and I think she was already in the kind of trouble with drink and drugs that led to her early death.

Early on during my time at Winston's I moved out of the Theatre Girls' Club permanently. I still didn't have any money, but I was working all the time. Television had started to become important, and I was doing quite a lot of it during the day as well as working at Winston's at night, so they wouldn't keep me at the Theatre Girls' Club any longer. It's a hazy period in my life I'm afraid. I am not always sure where I was living or in precisely what order I was appearing in each show or TV programme. It was inclined to all blend into one. I didn't have a permanent home to give my life any structure. Sometimes I used to stay with friends, and occasionally I'd visit my mother who by this time had produced my sister Caroline, who is sixteen years my junior. They were living with Bill, who had finally left his wife, in a fifteenth-century cottage in the village of Disley, just outside Manchester.

Although it was very exciting to have become immersed in so many varied aspects of showbusiness, it was also totally chaotic and there are considerable aspects of that period which remain something of a blur.

At first I stayed in Linden Gardens in Notting Hill with John Law, who had moved down to London from Scotland and had a flat there. We didn't go to bed together though. It was still only the mid-fifties, contraception was medieval and my absolute terror of pregnancy remained a great deterrent, and may or may not have been connected with my mother's gruesome descriptions of my birth. I just did not want a child in or out of wedlock. There was no way I could have had an abortion, as so many of my contemporaries did. It would have seemed like murder to me.

John was a lovely man. He used to say he didn't mind if I didn't love him as long as I stayed with him. He was just setting up as a professional comedy writer and he continued to write material for me. We used to sit up all night with these wonderful people who came to his flat and talk comedy. John wrote material for all of them. Marty Feldman, Barry Took and Michael Bentine were regulars, long before they became big names. Michael Bentine was always doing his act. He had a glove puppet he called Glovie which got itself into all sorts of trouble, culminating in it acquiring a gun and shooting itself. All this took place behind John's sofa.

Also, during this time I did a number of terrible gigs with Marty. I will never ever forget doing Tottenham Working Men's Club with him, before going on to Winston's. We were a disaster. Marty was a comic genius, but at Tottenham Working Men's Club nobody but nobody laughed at him. They didn't understand him at all. He just wasn't working men's club material. He was already quite off the wall. We did a cabaret act with little sketches and I remember having to sing a terrible number, 'The Railroad Runs Through the Middle of the Track'. Then Marty would pick me up – I was very light in those days – and rush off with me through the tables. The members of Tottenham Working Men's Club remained singularly unamused.

After a while I moved into my own flat in Romilly Street in Covent Garden. I'm not entirely sure quite how or why. Although John had said that he wanted to marry me, that was not what I wanted at all so it did not seem fair to stay with him any longer. It was also to do with the pressures of having to help my family.

My mother's life disintegrated yet again when Bill died suddenly and unexpectedly after a short illness. He had never divorced his wife nor left a will so my mother was left virtually penniless. I ended up with her, Chris and Caroline all sleeping on my floor. Suddenly I was the major breadwinner. This was the beginning of my providing for my mother to some degree or other until her death. Although she never failed to do her best to be independent, and was always willing to work, she was not always able to. Whatever income she achieved invariably seemed to need to be supplemented regularly by cheques from me.

At that time I did eventually manage to get my mother a job at Bermans, the theatrical costumiers, but she had never had to work in her life before and she was a disaster. Like her daughter at school, she was soon asked to kindly vacate the premises.

Nonetheless, Mummy still managed to contribute in her inimitable way. She never quite grasped the concept of not being able to have what you couldn't afford to pay for. As a consequence all sorts of things were inclined to walk out of shops with her. She would never have considered herself a shoplifter in a million years, and would have been absolutely horrified if it had been suggested to her that she was one. It was just that, if we needed something, and in particular, I have to admit, if I needed something, my mother would go out and get it.

She would say, 'I've got you a skirt for your audition.' Then, as I was going out through the door she would call after me, 'But don't wear it if you're going down the Strand.'

On one occasion we were together in Jaeger when I just happened to mention that I rather liked the waste-paper basket in the loo, because it had a horse on it. A few days later she returned from Jaeger clad in the big cloak she nearly always wore and this enormous waste-paper basket suddenly arrived in my flat. How she walked out of Jaeger with it, I will never know.

Her amateur status in the area of unofficial acquisition of necessary unaffordable items, was frequently in danger of becoming professional. I have absolutely no idea how she never got caught. Groucho Marx had an act where knives and forks would come flying out of his arms in all directions, and that was exactly what used to happen with my mother. Things would fall from her sleeves and pockets and from the depths of that cloak, sometimes even when she was going past the cashiers on the way out. But she was never even stopped.

A favourite victim of her tendency to take whatever she needed, as and when – including the many colouring books I was presented with as a child – was WHSmith. It was all a bit of a game to her, really. I could always tell when she was going to strike because she would acquire an air of extreme nonchalance and sing a little song to herself.

Food was, as ever, of major importance and perhaps I had inherited some of these unfortunate tendencies from my mother. I was the number one food scavenger. I used to go to Lyon's Corner House with all the other dancers. It was self-service and considered very avant-garde, but how the place ever kept going with the behaviour of the hordes of hungry dancers who went in there, I'll never know. You could take as much salad and bread and butter as you could pile on your plate. And we did. By God, we did.

I've never been very partial to salad, but there were all sorts of other tempting bits and pieces. I'd eat as much as possible and take the rest of it home for the others. Just like my mother I never thought of it as stealing. I used to justify it to myself by thinking that if Mr Lyon could meet me he would be sure to take me out to dinner, and as he'd been denied the pleasure I'd not spurn his kindness. 'I'll just take another three bread rolls, thank you very much.'

Somewhere, in the middle of all of this, soon after I split up with John, I finally surrendered my virginity at the age of twenty-one. The first man I slept with was a choreographer. I can't explain why I chose him instead of poor John except that he was extremely good-looking and had a phenomenal physique, something I have always rather liked. He was also married.

I hadn't waited because I wasn't interested. I was as interested as everybody else. It was just that I hadn't got around to it somehow, and I did have this almost pathological fear of becoming pregnant.

Ultimately it was something of a relief to get it over with. But, partly perhaps because I was still worrying about pregnancy even while it was happening, I don't remember being particularly impressed with the experience. However, he was a nice, clever man whom I found very attractive and I was beginning to have this thing, which stayed with me for quite a while, about it being impolite to say no. Also if somebody goes, 'I love you. I worship you. I adore you. I really want to go with you,' and all that, you do find it rather charming, don't you? You don't want to say, 'Well, I don't fancy you a bit.' Actually, I would do now, but not when I was young. I thought, 'Gosh, someone feels like that about me. Aren't I lucky?'

I think that may have had something to do with my background. But I did know, because of Bernie, that I didn't feel the same way. I don't actually think that was anything to do with her being female. I think it was simply because she was the person she was, and because, although we were both so young, there was this very special feeling between us which I have kept on looking for through most of my life.

◀ What do you mean, 'Don't phone us, we'll phone you?' I was a baby with attitude.

▼ Ashton-under-Lyne's wedding of the decade. My mother and father did it in grand style.

▸ Butter wouldn't melt. Me, aged four, with my prize – a box of chocolates – after winning a talent contest while supposedly 'on holiday' in Llandudno. Note the children who had lost the competition in the background.

▾ My first major stage appearance, aged four again, in *A Christmas Carol* at my grandfather's theatre in Ashton-under-Lyne. I'm sitting on Santa's knee.

▲ Aged eight, with my baby brother Chris. My body language gives me away – I was still thinking up ways of getting rid of him...

▼ In chemistry class at St Anne's, I'm seated far left. From the expression on my face, I think I was planning to blow the place up.

▶ Jailbait time. Back again 'on holiday' in Llandudno, aged thirteen. I had been dressed by my mother in one of my stage costumes, which really was far too old for me.

◀ With my mother in Babbacombe, Devon in 1959. I'm the one with the double-A cup.

▶ Barbara Windsor and I share the billing at Winston's Club, which played an important part in both our early careers.

◀ An unlikely pair of bookends. With Una Stubbs in the revue *On the Bright Side*.

▶ Still in fishnets. *The Merry Widow* in 1959.

▼ As a clown in the revue *See You Inside* at the Duchess Theatre, with John Dane. It didn't last long, but I did get spotted.

(VANE ▶)

(▶ DEREK BALMER)

(AQUARIUS LIBRARY ►)

▲ Me, Sid James and that famous asp. After all this time I still receive as much fan mail for *Carry on Cleo* as I do for *Corrie*.

◄ My name in lights in the West End for the first time in 1963. It was my proud mother, naturally, who took this photograph outside the Lyric Theatre.

▶ 'Kinky Boots'. I sang the song, dressed like this, in an early Jimmy Tarbuck television show. I was his original Tatty Head

▼ With Billy Fury and his dog Dibby on the set of *I've Gotta Horse*.

▲ With Elspeth March in *Public Mischief* – my West End debut as the lead in a straight play.

▶ A picture of serenity. This was taken while I was in *Public Mischief*. Proof that the camera can lie.

CHAPTER FIVE

Meanwhile, my mother was trying to rebuild her life and keep a home together for Caroline, and for Chris too, when he wasn't with my father. Naturally, being Connie Broadbent, she went about things in extremely bizarre ways.

She needed to work because Bill had contrived to leave her virtually penniless. Her car had been removed by his wife immediately after his death, along with almost everything else of value. For a long time it even looked as if she might lose the cottage they had shared. Unfortunately my mother was not qualified for anything. However, this did not daunt her at all. She behaved as if she was qualified to be President of the USA. There was no point in suggesting she apply for social security benefits because she wouldn't listen. It didn't occur to her, even under those circumstances, that she was a person who needed that sort of help. She was never one to shirk her responsibilities. If there was a problem she would face up to it, and by God, if anybody would beat it she would. That was one of the many reasons why I adored her. And I hope I have inherited a little of that side of her, because you need it in this world.

Her first project was to take on running a bar in Babbacombe, on the outskirts of Torquay in Devon, where she had honeymooned with my father. Typically, it worked like a dream for about ten seconds and then all hell broke loose. Some cigarettes went missing, and as my mother did have this propensity for making things disappear, I was not entirely astonished to hear this. Eventually, she had to be rescued and was more or less banished from Babbacombe for life.

Next she embarked on what seemed to be a rather more sensible and straightforward course of action, far less likely to cause problems. But naturally with Connie, this did not turn out to be the case.

She got herself a job in the millinery department of the Manchester department store Marshall and Snellgrove. All seemed to go well until she picked up her first payslip. The store operated a staff-discount service on everything they sold, and my mother had taken full advantage of this. So much so, it turned out, that she had spent almost twice as much as she had earned. Thus, she left shortly afterwards.

After that, she applied to manage a public house and restaurant in Manchester – spun a likely story no doubt and got the job. Accommodation came with it, so she moved in with both my brother and my little sister, taking with her all that remained of the Tudor furniture she had acquired during her time with Bill in Disley. Naturally this venture ended in tears too. I was appearing at the Manchester Palace at the time. I was telephoned after the show and summoned to rescue her from the car park of the pub. I found her, with Chris alongside and Caroline tucked under one arm, surrounded by all her furniture. Then my father turned up at around 1.00 a.m. to collect Chris, leaving Mummy, me, Caroline and the furniture to our own devices.

Ultimately my mother thumbed down a passing coal truck. 'I am in desperate trouble,' she called dramatically as the coal truck pulled to a halt.

A large, good-looking driver clambered out and in no time at all had loaded the furniture, which any antiques dealer would have killed for, into the back of his open truck. My mother climbed up beside him and we were duly taken back to her Disley cottage, fourteen miles or so away, which had been shut up for several months. I found myself sitting on the back of the truck, and thinking, 'One minute on the stage at the Palace, the next I'm in the back of an open coal truck covered from head to foot in coal dust, with my lunatic mother in a totally lunatic situation.'

There was no food at the cottage when we arrived so the coalman carried all the furniture in, then gave us his sandwiches. He ended up staying the night. It was all perfectly innocent, but my mother was so grateful and so wonderful to him, he seemed to think he had struck up a relationship with her. We couldn't get rid of him. I was willing my mother not to be too nice to him. She never knew when to stop. She didn't have that instinct to put the brakes on what she was doing. You really couldn't help adoring her though, and I do often think that if she had ever met the right person the sky would have been the limit.

She believed she could have run the biggest company in the world or anything else come to that.

There were other curious sides to her too. She was terrified of ever appearing prejudiced towards another human being. Actually I am a bit the same, but my mother, as usual, went to extremes. When they first had black porters on railway stations she wouldn't let them carry her luggage. Instead she would insist on carrying her own suitcase and would still tip them.

There was never a day with Connie Broadbent when something unbelievable didn't happen. One of my oldest and dearest friends, Beryl McLaren, a neighbour from Covent Garden, once described my mother as 'a cross between an angel and a demon'. I do understand what she means. Connie was a paradox. My sister Caroline was later to put it another way. 'Our mother is the only person I know who could have an asthma attack and eat a chocolate biscuit at the same time.'

One thing is certain. My mother's determination could never be questioned. Connie Broadbent did not know when she was beaten, and indeed virtually never was.

Once properly reinstated at Foxhole Cottage, Disley she suddenly decided that her financial salvation lay in turning the place into a hairdressing salon. She had never done any hairdressing in her life, but that didn't deter her for a moment. She went to a hairdressing school in Manchester, claiming to be a trained hairdresser whose husband had died so she wanted to go back to her old job. 'I only need to brush up on modern techniques,' she told them.

Within forty-eight hours she had persuaded them to give her a certificate. Then she went out and bought hairdryers which she arranged in a row in front of the big old log fire amid all her beautiful pieces of antique furniture in her picturesque cottage.

I turned up one day to find all these ladies sitting in a line under dryers. Within minutes my mother had somehow acquired a full diary of clients, all blissfully unaware that Connie Broadbent didn't know whether it was Christmas or Clacton as far as hairdressing was concerned. She was doing it all from a book. I couldn't believe it. She was handling about seven people on her own, doing Mrs So-and-So's cut and Mrs So-and-So's colour and perm, the lot. And making them all tea.

It was a summer's evening, and in between all these varied tasks she was outside in the back garden on her knees to God with a hairdressing book open before her desperately reading tips on bleached ends while praying at the same time.

'Please God help me, please God help me do Mrs So-and-So's ends. Please God do not let me fail at this, because I will let my family down.'

She didn't fail. She did it. She bloody did it! Somehow or other she made a success of being a hairdresser. Eventually she employed staff, who all stayed with her for years. She even taught my brother the trade she had taught herself and he became a very good hairdresser, at one point running his own salon.

My work remained the nearest thing in my life to stability. I was beginning to build up quite a pedigree of work in TV, alongside people such as Peter Sellers and Spike Milligan who went on to be such big stars. Throughout the fifties there were countless TV shows, many of which I have forgotten all about and of which there is little record any more, because it was all live in those days.

I do remember clearly appearing in the very first *Morecambe and Wise Show* with Alma Cogan. It seems hard to believe now, but it was a total flop. I think it was because Morecambe and Wise were modelled on another famous double act of the time, Jewel and Warris, and they had yet to formulate their own style. They were already very funny though and were great to work with. However, I managed to disgrace myself when my skirt fell off doing some gypsy dance. And this was live TV remember, so the entire television-watching public got a grandstand view of my knickers.

I was also chosen to do a TV show called *On the Bright Side* with Stanley Baxter, Betty Marsden, Pip Hinton and Ronnie Barker. The other dancers were Judy Carne, Una Stubbs and Greta Hanby, a Royal Ballet dancer. The dancing was choreographed by a brilliant man called Alfred Rodriguez. The standard all round was pretty high, and the show won a number of awards.

Other TV work included a show called *Cool For Cats,* which featured all the hit numbers of the week. It was like a forerunner of *Top of the Pops*. Then there was the legendary *Sunday Night at the London Palladium*, *The Harry Secombe Show*, *The Dave King Show*, *Saturday Spectacular*, and *Seven Faces For Jim*, which was written by Frank Muir and Denis Norden for June Whitfield and Jimmy Edwards. I worked on a host of other less well-remembered shows too, as well as TV commercials.

And every night I was still appearing at Winston's Club. The most important qualification for anyone living that sort of life was not so much great talent as great endurance. I never got enough sleep, so my big problem was keeping awake. I'd be working on some TV show all day from about nine in the morning until about seven in the evening, then I would go home, sleep for an hour or two, grab something to eat, then set off for Winston's Club where I would work until about four the following morning. The money was lousy. I had to have two jobs, particularly as I was helping support my mother and Caroline.

I used to have a telephone alarm call booked for 7.00 a.m. in order to get the bus out to the BBC rehearsal rooms at Shepherds Bush, which meant I would have been in bed an absolute maximum of three hours. I remember once being woken by the phone and falling asleep again kneeling by the side of the bed answering it. I used to fall asleep on the bus and regularly miss my stop. I got in the habit, as I climbed aboard, of asking people to give me a shout at Goldhawk Road. Once I was doing *The Jubilee Show* which was an Edwardian music-hall production with Hugh Paddick, and I actually dropped off right in the middle of it with rather dramatic results. I was sitting on a lovers' seat at the time and when everybody else got up, it toppled over and I fell off it flat on my face. It had been a particularly long day but I was told off by the director who, reasonably enough, pointed out, 'I just can't use you if you can't keep awake.'

At least when we were rehearsing we got a short evening break. I used to rush back to my flat where there was a bath in the bedroom cupboard. Maggie Fitzgibbon, who had become a good friend, had given me my first TV set, which I thought was wonderful. I just used to jump into the bath and sit there in a complete daze watching TV. Then I would try to get an hour or so's sleep, but no more. I had to set the alarm to give me time to do my hair and make-up and eat something before going off to the night job.

Frozen food had just been invented, and I lived on fish fingers, as well, of course, as my favourite bacon sandwiches and anything I could steal from Lyon's Corner House if I had time to go there.

Being a chorus girl was not as glamorous as it might sound. We were like the army in eyelashes. Totally regimented, totally anonymous, and there to be abused by anyone passing – from lead comic to stagehand – who fancied a grope. Certainly how we looked was a total illusion.

On stage, and on screen, in things like *Saturday Spectacular*, we appeared to be wearing all these wonderful costumes. Anyone watching would imagine that a great deal of time and trouble was taken in dressing us. Not a bit of it. Bermans, the famous theatrical costumiers where my mother had been so briefly and unsuccessfully employed, used to dress us in about two and a half minutes and the costumes had always been worn and worn. They may have looked all right on stage or camera, with the right lighting, but they were ancient, tatty things, and all too often the sort of outfit suited to an old drag queen. I would invariably have problems because my boobs were never big enough for anything to fit. I always ended up with padding in my top. Indeed, so much padding, and all pulled together so tightly, that I sometimes ended up with cleavage at the back. There was certainly no cleavage at the front. In fact there was nothing to hold my tops up at all, however tightly they were tied. The consequence was that they were always falling down. I'd do some energetic dancing step, and whoops. Lost it again!

The shoes were another nightmare. They were kept in a big theatrical skip at Bermans, a huge wicker basket, which we had to rummage through in a desperate attempt just to find two shoes we could stand up in, never mind dance or run down flights of stairs. They were smelly and worn right down. There was never a proper pair to be had. One shoe was invariably a good size and a half different to the other. Usually they were what we used to call Silver Surgicals, because they were just like surgical boots only silver. They really were awful things.

Also, if you are a dancer and you wear fishnet tights all day, come the evening you have fishnet feet, and your Silver Surgicals are full of sweat and the odd bit of skin that has been dislodged. It was not, by any means, comfortable being a walloper. Limping off home at the end of the day with these throbbing feet was the most painful thing. And having extricated one pair of fishnets which had worn their way into my feet, I'd be off to Winston's where I would put another pair of fishnets on top of the indentations left by the first pair, thus creating the double agony of cross-angled fishnet scars. Then I'd have to stuff my poor feet either into yet another pair of Silver Surgicals, or these three-inch heeled 'naff batts' as we always used to call them.

Naff batts is *Polari* for awful shoes. *Polari* is a wonderful language which was used a lot in London showbiz circles back then and has since been adopted by certain sectors of the gay community. I believe it stemmed from travelling circus folk who, being of varied nationality, invented this common language.

All members of the royal family – with the exception of the late Princess Diana, of course – wear naff batts. But not as naff as these terrible winkle-picker things with three inch stilettos in which we were expected to dance the can can or similar. Doing the splits didn't hurt a bit. In fact, it was a relief to sink into them because standing upright was such agony. We were more than dancers in those days. We were endurance experts. I've seen dancers absolutely unable to walk.

The make-up for TV was the worst thing of all. In the beginning of television they had all sorts of funny ideas. We weren't allowed to wear our ordinary make-up but were made to wear a gooey khaki stuff which they believed – quite mistakenly in my opinion – looked better on screen. We actually looked as if we were in camouflage and had just been pulled out of the Korean jungle wearing khaki masks. Most of the time we were so small in the background nobody would have noticed if we'd come on with somebody else's head on. But every so often we had to do these terrible close-ups. There we'd be in our Silver Surgicals, laddered tights, costume with somebody else's tits sewn in, and a lot of sweat under the armpits. The whole ensemble would be topped off with the greatest indignity of all, a feathered headdress taller than the Eiffel Tower. There was nothing to attach it to because they made us scrape our hair straight back, so these great wobbly headdresses were just balanced on top. Then, barely able to move, we were supposed to go and do the routine that we'd learned during the week. We danced like stiff-backed string puppets as we tried to keep them on. And guess whose was always falling off? There we were with these feathers the size of a small palm tree coming out of the tops of our heads, which were supposed to make us look like really glamorous showgirls. Nobody looked less glamorous than me tottering around in my surgical boots.

Once we were dressed it was almost impossible to go to the loo, because the performance of getting into a very tight leotard, fishnets and tight everything else was such that it took so long to dress and undress that you'd be sure to end up being off when you should be on. It was the worst at the BBC where the loos were always miles away. I remember once confessing to Lionel Blair when we were in the middle of a routine on live TV, that I was bursting to go. 'If you do, darling, be sure to breaststroke off in tempo to the music,' he replied.

That was how it was with early live TV. You just kept blundering on whatever happened. It was nearly all live. There was no choice but to plough on somehow through the disasters.

Costume calamities were routine. Once on *Cool For Cats* we were dressed up as Red Indians, performing 'Tequila Sunrise', a huge hit that was top of the pops for weeks. All the boys were wearing rubber wigs and, on camera and under the powerful studio lights, their heads got too hot and the wigs started to bounce off. Ping! There went the first. Ping! There went another. By the end, they had all gone. Imagine the spectacle, all going out live.

There were a lot of sudden camera cuts in TV back then. The dancers would be spotted doing something wrong in shot so the director would just cut to another scene regardless of any kind of continuity. I remember in a variety show doing a spectacular version of 'Let's Face the Music and Dance' where we all had to dance on top of giant musical instruments which had been built into the set. Quite ambitious stuff. The camera went wrong so they cut to another one which was focused on the George Mitchell Singers who were there for some completely different reason, and certainly weren't supposed to be in shot. They were all sitting huddled up in their overcoats because it was freezing in their part of the studio. After a bit the first camera started working again. So it was back to us. Then it packed up again. Back to the George Mitchell Singers. And so on. It must have been very confusing for the viewers, but I guess they were pretty used to it. Part of the fun of watching TV in those early days was trying to guess what was actually supposed to be happening on screen.

Another number that I remember very clearly indeed was 'Tuxedo Junction', which we did for a show called *Chelsea at Nine*. It turned out to be sheer agony. The choreographer was very athletic, and he thought that if he could do something everybody else could too. We had to do some very intricate stuff on ropes, which involved running flat out across the stage, then swinging up into the air on the ropes, finally landing in the splits on the floor. We learned to do it in a gymnasium where we managed just about to get through it although by the second day we were so sore we couldn't move and we had no skin on our hands. I remember us all going to the pub at lunchtime and the only thing on the menu was chops, but nobody could cut them up because we could barely move our arms and our hands were raw. There were the five of us, three boys and two girls, just sitting there, aching from head to toe, groaning, and trying to feed each other. I even began to feel a certain very limited sympathy for Matron's condition following the steel-rope-with-girl-hanging-from-it incident back at St Anne's.

But little did we know, the best was yet to come. In the studio the ropes were attached to an iron scaffold above us. It transpired, however, that the scaffold was not properly attached to anything. We took off, gamely swinging on the ropes, and the whole lot moved. We went straight through Vic Lewis's band. We scattered them. There were trombones flying, music stands flying, and we were swinging wildly out of control. There were dancers hanging on for their lives while being hurled up in the air. Eventually we swung down, rather stupidly still trying to make an act of it by doing the splits, but the whole scaffolding came down with us and we were dragged for yards along the floor. Now that was pain. People ask, 'Is it nice being a dancer?' Most dancers would probably reply, 'Only when it stops.' Half the time dancers don't want to move, and the other half they are virtually unable to move. You will never see a dancer walking if they can stand still, standing if they can sit, or sitting if they can lie down. I remember watching films in those days and seeing dancers like Vera Ellen rushing around doing amazing things and there was never a mark of sweat on them. I was incredulous as I was always red faced and bathed in sweat. In my innocence I didn't realise until much later when I started doing films myself that they all had minions in constant attendance wiping them down every few seconds.

I get told off nowadays because I am not very interested in taking exercise. As far as I'm concerned I had enough exercise in my dancing days to last a lifetime. I make Sherpa Tensing look like a beginner in terms of the number of things I've climbed up and down and over.

The worst thing was having to trust some half-awake camp boy dancer to catch you at early-morning rehearsals. Some of them scared the wits out of you, they really did. You just knew they were going to let you go straight over their heads. There was one who did just that when I was supposed to land round his neck. He missed me and ducked, so I went straight over his head and hit the wall. Splat. I was spread-eagled like a starfish, and scraped myself down six feet of wall. I lost two teeth in that escapade too. But the choreographer just called, 'OK. From the top . . .'

'I think I've broken my back teeth.'

There wasn't even a pause.

'. . . and a five, six, seven, eight!'

So you just got on with it. Indeed, I suspect I would probably rise from my grave if somebody called, '. . . and a five, six, seven, eight!'

You were thrown about. Hurled. Dropped. As a chorus-line dancer you never had a name. We were 'them', or 'the kids', regardless of age – and some chorus dancers could be quite an age.

It was, 'When are *they* coming in?' 'Well, *they* can start first.'

We were totally anonymous and supposed to obey orders instantly and without question. We got through it thanks to a mixture of herd instinct and terror. We were always either struggling to keep awake or battling the pain because something had been pulled or bruised or broken while some unfeeling bastard of a director or a choreographer was shouting, 'Come on kids! Come on!'

By the time I was about fifteen I felt like a very old horse.

Something you do not experience in a chorus is any sense of ego. In fact, I defy anyone who spent as long in choruses as I did to ever develop one. There is a saying, 'You can get a girl out of the chorus, but you can't get the chorus out of the girl.' I know that's true of me. I'm still inclined to take food parcels with me wherever I go just in case nobody feeds me. I'm surprised if I'm treated well by people I'm working with. And I never ever walk when I can stand, stand when I can sit, or sit when I can lie down.

In 1959 my career changed direction briefly when I was asked to be a hostess on *Double Your Money* with Hughie Green. Apparently, Hughie had picked me out of the chorus in one of my many TV dancing appearances because he reckoned I was funny. Whether or not I was supposed to have been being funny at the time, I have no idea.

I was delighted because people got recognised on those shows and I thought *Double Your Money* might prove to be a route out of the chorus line before I became so bruised, battered and worn out that I wouldn't be capable of moving on to anything else.

This did not turn out to be the case. To start with I just wasn't the hostess 'type'. Hughie's hostesses were supposed to have either immense tits or endearing cockney personalities, like little Monica Rose who got it so right she turned the whole thing into an art form. I was supposed to provide my own clothes and I just didn't possess anything like the right sort of stuff. I didn't go to cocktail parties. If I had had time for partying, I doubt I would have been going to the sort of dos which called for the kind of clothes I was expected to wear on *Double Your Money*. 'Bring three or four gowns,' they would say. Gowns? I owned absolutely nothing that could have been remotely described as a gown, except perhaps a candlewick dressing gown with Bovril stains down the front. I ended up buying all these rotten little frocks.

I was dreadful. There I was on stage looking extremely peculiar and I realised that I had absolutely no idea what to do. It was a complete mystery to me. I was supposed to deal with the money, hand it out to the contestants and keep track of where they were up to. I was, of course, hopeless at that. The more I tried to concentrate and get it right the more of a muddle I would get into. I was invariably passing out the wrong amounts while desperately trying to catch the contestant's eye, mouthing, 'They'll sort it out later.'

It was an immensely popular show of course, and very professional. Hughie Green was almost certainly the most professional TV presenter of his kind at the time. He came to the UK having had similar experience in Canada and he was very different from anyone we had seen before on British TV. By God, he was slick. He had the whole thing worked out down to the last eyelash flick. He knew absolutely how to handle his audience, and, boy, could he turn on the charm. 'Sincerely folks' was his catchphrase and anything less sincere than Hughie Green at work on an audience is hard to imagine. It was just his act. He was mechanical. The total professional.

Hughie had everything so under control that all the contestants seemed to say the same thing when they went off. Whether they had won or not they would say, 'We've had a lovely day, Hughie,' and Hughie would grasp their hands in his and sink into sincerity mode. But even *Double Your Money* had its unexpected moments. One night we had a taxi driver who was doing really well answering questions on horse-racing. Then, for his £1,000 question he was asked something that was more or less impossible, a bit like, 'Which horse came thirteenth in the Grand National, and what colour were the jockey's underpants?'

On camera the taxi driver took it brilliantly. He was totally pleasant and amiable. 'It's fine, Hughie. It's fine. Don't worry. Good luck, everybody. God bless you all,' he said, followed by the obligatory, 'I've had a lovely day, a really lovely day.'

However, when taxi drivers are crossed they are, in my experience, inclined to let you have it. For all the loveable charm there is likely to be an explosion if you don't give them the right tip. Once the show was over, this taxi driver went absolutely bananas. He started to shout and smash the studio up and his mates came down from the audience and joined in. It was mayhem. They were after Hughie in a big way. We all had to flee out of the back door. I remember following Hughie and thinking that I'd never have believed he was capable of moving so fast.

CHAPTER SIX

❧

Later on in 1959 I had my West End début at the Phoenix Theatre in the stage revue *On the Brighter Side* which had grown out of the TV show *On The Bright Side*. I was working with much the same cast as the TV show, with Stanley Baxter and Betty Marsden starring, and with Ronnie Barker again. This was early in Ronnie's career, when he was Stanley's understudy. Off stage, he was nothing like a comic genius. He looked more like someone who worked in a bank. But he was brilliant, even then. You gradually became aware of this wonderful dry wit spilling out of Ronnie all the time. He was also the man everyone turned to when there was a problem.

These were the days when the Lord Chamberlain was in full flight and you couldn't do anything without being censored. It was the era when lines like, 'We have fairies at the bottom of our garden,' were banned. The whole thing was ridiculous. We were in revue, for Christ's sake, the whole point of revue was to be near the knuckle.

I remember that we did a number called 'Little Nell' in which the Old Curiosity Shop was a brothel. There was one line in it – 'All this knocking and banging must stop in our old curiosity shop' – which the Lord Chamberlain promptly banned. It was Ronnie, with his quick comedy brain, who came to the rescue with something about bringing a donkey in and the line, 'I will not have that noisy clip clop through my old curiosity shop.' We got that one past the Lord Chamberlain even though it was actually much ruder in the way it was done, with that rather risqué mention of a donkey which the audience picked up on soon enough but fortunately His Lordship missed.

Ronnie always had an amazing head. When we were touring we used to sit up at night for hours writing 'quickies'. Those were the items in revue when somebody walks on stage from one side, says something quickly, then walks straight off the other side. They were just one liners, but terribly important. Silly stuff like, 'Ooh! Doesn't the boss dress nicely.'

'Yes, and so quickly!'

The secret was often in the speed of the delivery. 'Quickies' fascinated Ronnie and me, and we used to spend forever trying to make them up. In between desperately trying to think up more and more funny ideas, something I have always been obsessed by, we used to play cards and drink wine, which was very avant garde at the time.

Ronnie and I became very special friends during that show, and it was he who introduced me to antiques, which have remained a great passion of mine. We used to go snooping around antiques and junk shops together, and he taught me all about Victorian postcards. Of course, Ronnie has more or less retired from show business now and has his own antiques business – a way of life that I have always thought would suit me down to the ground, and in which I have dabbled at various stages in my life.

Judy Carne, Una Stubbs and Greta Hanby were also in the show again. Una was this cute, doll-like person who was always immaculate and in control, in stark contrast to me. My bit of the dressing room was always in a terrible state. That hasn't changed. You can ask anyone who has ever worked with me.

So imagine my humiliation when we were on tour and I went into the dressing room one night to find Una had not only cleared up my corner but had also turned out my entire suitcase and tidied it up too.

Some people are just born drip-dry. Whatever they have been through they come out looking all right. Not me. Not ever.

My entire personal life around that time was chaotic. All too often in a show I would find myself wildly attracted to the leading lady but, of course, go into total denial, refusing to admit it to myself or anyone else, and balance it by going to bed with the leading man.

That was what happened when, in 1960, I was in a tour of *The Merry Widow*, starring Vanessa Lee. I ended up having an affair with the actor Richard Curnock who was playing opposite me. I had a huge crush on Vanessa Lee, which she had no idea about, of course. I did confess to her years later, and she roared with laughter and apologised for all the trouble she had unwittingly caused me, not to mention poor Richard.

At the time though it was no laughing matter. At one point Vanessa had to sing to me on stage, and I didn't so much turn red as purple. What I should have done, if I'd known what I was about, was to have hurled myself at Vanessa Lee's feet instead of those of a married man like poor old Richard.

We were soon discovered in rather unfortunate circumstances by his wife, the cookery writer Margaret Costa, who at the time was something important in the Marriage Guidance Council, which added to her embarrassment. She stormed into a room while Richard and I were in bed. After this I meekly succumbed and agreed not to see Richard for a year. However, shortly afterwards he and I bumped into each other by chance in London and continued more or less where we had left off. One thing led to another and Richard ended up having to put up with me for God knows how many years.

Mind you, I did my best. I threw myself into his life, as I have always been inclined to do with my partners. This even involved trying out recipes for Margaret Costa when she was taken ill, so that her newspaper cookery columns could continue. On one occasion 200 oysters were delivered to be test-cooked in a variety of different ways. I think I am still getting over that.

Richard was also a wildly enthusiastic fisherman so, when I was in London, I ended up coming off stage in whatever show I was in and spending the rest of the night going fishing with him, sometimes in the River Thames and sometimes further afield.

After a while he left his wife, acquired a flat in Endell Street and we both moved in. I used to make bread paste, steam the hemp for his bait, untangle his fishing lines, and do all those things for a fisherman that show how much you care. But unfortunately the flat didn't have a proper bathroom, just something called a 'Bink' in the very small kitchen which, as its name suggests, was a kind of cross between a bath and a sink. It was not remotely suited to the cause of personal hygiene, particularly if you were having rather a lot to do with dead fish at the time and what you really needed was a power shower and a steaming tub at regular intervals in order to fumigate yourself. So, at a stage in my career when I should have been perfectly groomed, beautifully dressed and looking like Una Stubbs, I was wandering around the West End looking like a fisherman – more often than not carrying a bag of live maggots and, thanks to that Bink, smelling like a fisherman too.

The relationship between Richard and me came under strain when I began to be quite sought after in the West End. I never stopped working, and that put pressure on us. I think Richard wanted all the things from a relationship which were regarded as normal. But I wasn't doing what other people were doing, like planning a home, planning a future. I was just swimming like mad in order to keep afloat.

When one day Richard and I were walking down Regent Street, and he suddenly turned to me and said, 'I want you to have my child,' I nearly threw myself under a double-decker bus. The disruption of my early life had had a very severe effect on me, so much more than I realised at the time. I never thought that I would like to get married and have children. The thought of getting pregnant or having a child still terrified the living daylights out of me. Indeed, I have never felt old enough to have children, and I still feel that to this day. I'll go to my grave thinking that I am not old enough to have a child, that I'm just not capable. On the other hand I think that's probably true of most people but it doesn't seem to stop the rest of the world having children.

It was early 1962 and my nineteen-year-old brother Chris came to stay for a while. The two of us had become great friends by then and we got on like a bomb. I took him shopping for his first pair of winkle-picker shoes, and, completely by accident, he met the Beatles who were shopping in the same store. They had just begun to take off and a wildly excited Chris got to say a quick hello. He then insisted on wearing the winkle-pickers straight away and kept falling over them all down Oxford Street. I also bought him a very expensive designer coat, which he's still got. It cost me a fortune. Every penny I didn't have. But I didn't regret it.

Chris and I had a ball. We used to go to the pictures endlessly. We'd see one film, have a hamburger, still a novelty food in those days, then go and see another one. We adored each other's company. Richard got more than a bit fed up with us. I actually think he might have been a little jealous.

One night I was cooking lamb chops on a gas stove alongside the Bink when Richard suddenly started to hurl the chops around the place. Now a lamb chop, when it's hot with the fat attached and really shifting, can play havoc. 'All is not well in our relationship,' I thought. 'Something is amiss.'

I really should have stuck at it with Vanessa Lee.

Following *On the Brighter Side* and *The Merry Widow* I switched from theatre to film with a small role in *Doctor in Distress*, which had a large and impressive cast including Dirk Bogarde, James Robertson Justice, Mylene Demongeot, Samantha Eggar, Barbara Murray, Donald Houston, Leo McKern and Dennis Price.

This led to an extraordinary proposition from James Robertson Justice who was known to have royal connections. Over a drink in a bar one evening James asked me how I would feel about giving the then fifteen-year-old Prince Charles a lesson in sex. I was so shocked I nearly fell off my bar stool.

James was obviously quite embarrassed about putting this to me, and went round and round in circles before finally finding the words. Eventually he said, using what I thought was a rather splendid euphemism, 'I am one of eight people who have been selected by the royal family to launch the young royal males into their future lives. We have had a lot of discussion about who might be suitable for Prince Charles, and we are all inclined to agree that you might be very suitable. We don't really want people who are experienced, but on the other hand, they obviously have to know the ropes. Frankly, the main requirement is a sense of humour, and I know you have that.'

I think I suffered a sense-of-humour failure at that moment. When I could speak again I politely declined. I had a terrible image of having to face the Queen over breakfast the morning afterwards and her asking, 'So, Amanda, how was it?'

I have no idea whether or not James Robertson Justice had really been asked to arrange the deflowering of our future king. I also have no idea whether Prince Charles, whom I have since met several times, ever learned of what had been so presumptuously suggested, nor how he would have reacted – quite possibly with supreme relief that it never happened, I should imagine.

Shortly after that incident, in the autumn of 1962, I returned to theatre with the revue *See You Inside*, with Jon Pertwee, Moira Lister and Harold Lang. The show toured the country for ages before it eventually came into the West End. Although written by the very clever Barry Cryer, it was not as well received as it may have been by the critics, but I was fortunate enough to score quite a big personal success in it and a notice in *The Times* that did me no harm at all:

> The one good reason for seeing the show is the presence of Amanda Barrie, a doll-like figure with huge fluttering eye-lashes, a slack jaw, and clockwork movements, who is that rare creature a female clown, a role which she dances in one of the best routines of the evening.

Indeed, I think the impression I seemed to make in *See You Inside* was a major factor in my becoming established in West End theatre. Certainly

I was swiftly hired for the revue *Six of One* at the Adelphi Theatre, which was based on the life of Dora Bryan, already something of a legend. We became great friends and have remained so. Dora, whose real name, coincidentally, is also Broadbent (although as far as we know we are not related) led the show, of course. It also starred that very distinguished leading man of the time, Richard Wattis, who we all knew as Dickie.

While on tour before moving into the West End, Dora, Dickie and I started to get along extremely well, in fact rather too well. There had been some sort of muddle about rehearsal rooms and, on a wet day in Leeds, the three of us had finished up rehearsing outside a church hall because we couldn't get into it. There we were trying not to walk on too many graves going over a rather twee little number called 'A Versatile Trio' in the pouring rain. Understandably enough, we got the giggles. That was just the start. By the time we reached the West End, where we were directed by that famous old director of revue Billy Chapel, our giggling had reached epic proportions. I know that stories of actors corpsing each other can be extremely tedious, but it is the sheer idiotic scale of this particular episode which makes it impossible for me to overlook it. It was, however, nothing to be proud of. It really wasn't. We were supposed to be professionals, for goodness' sake.

During rehearsal I'd told Dickie a story about Sir Cedric Hardwicke, another very distinguished British actor, who'd been asked to do this prestigious play live on American TV. Understandably, Sir Cedric, quite a nervous man in spite of his talent and reputation, turned it down because of a bad heart condition. He used to hold his chest and tap it periodically, which was somewhat disconcerting for anyone working with him. But the American producers persisted. 'The thing is, Sir Cedric, we will get you the most experienced and able cast they told him. Everybody will be rock solid. There'll be double rehearsal time.

All you will have to do is just walk on and off and do your scenes. Everything will work like clockwork all around you.'

Eventually they persuaded him. Everyone on the set had such strict orders to look after Sir Cedric, make sure that no problems arose that by show time all the other actors were far more nervous than him. But for one poor actor it was just too much. The play opened with Hardwicke entering a room to announce, 'The papers have arrived.' The other man, sitting behind a desk, was supposed to respond with, 'Oh, my God!' Instead he sang, 'Wagon wheels.'

The stress of working with Cedric Hardwicke had overwhelmed him. He'd cracked. Hardwicke just stared at him in horror. He stared back. Then he started again.

'Wagon wheels. Wagon wheels.'

In the middle of a live TV transmission, the poor actor was having a complete breakdown. Suddenly, stagehands were everywhere. They grabbed Cedric Hardwicke and catapulted him into the next scene which was supposed to be in a plane travelling at 20,000 feet. A whole scene had been cut. There was chaos. Hardwicke was going blue in the mouth, and while he was allegedly in this plane at 20,000 feet, the other actor was being dragged past on the way out of the studio still singing, 'Wagon wheels. Wagon wheels.'

Now Dickie, although much respected and well known for his film roles and lots of very serious acting, had never sung on stage before. When it came to the West End first night he was very nervous. So in one of our early harmony numbers I quietly sang 'Wagon Wheels' into his ear to cheer him up. It did the job. In spades. Dickie just went. I joined in. Dora joined in. And after that we could never get through a performance without falling apart with the giggles.

All hope was lost a few performances into the run, during a number for which I was dressed as a daffodil, Dickie was a bluebell, and Dora was a primrose, and our hands were supposed to have been made to look like leaves, but actually just looked like long prongs. I had to do the first part of the routine alone, but then I was waiting to be joined by Dickie and Dora when I suddenly realised that Dickie was behind a mound on the stage in absolute uncontrollable giggles, heaving and sobbing. There was no chance that he was even going to be able to stand up, let alone be able to do the number. Dora was beside him, poking him, trying to get him to pull himself together. Then she started to go as well.

I was left alone in the middle of the stage doing the whole number dressed as a daffodil, not only singing, 'I'm a daffodil,' but also, 'I'm a bluebell. I'm a primrose,' with all this snorting and guffawing going on behind me. When eventually the curtain fell on a rather bemused West End audience we all went to Dickie and asked what had happened.

'Well,' he said, 'I was just sitting here with my prongs on the end of my arms, dressed as a bluebell, ready to do my bit, and I realised that I hadn't taken my glasses off, and I couldn't do anything about it because of these bloody silly prongs. Then I remembered that my mother had wanted me to go into the clergy. So I started to wonder how on earth I'd ended up as a bluebell.'

The two images had sort of merged for Dickie, and rendered him quite unable to function. And it meant pretty much the end of any chance of doing that number properly for Dora and me as well. From then on, whenever we tried to do it, all we could think of was Dickie Wattis, the potential clergyman who'd become a bluebell. The problem was that this went on throughout the run. Every day we'd get a telling off. It would be, 'Miss Bryan, Mr Wattis, Miss Barrie, please come down to prompt corner at five.'

We'd walk out of our dressing rooms, determined to behave, set eyes on each other and be unable to speak. We were taken down to prompt corner by the company manager, and told to pull ourselves together. We were told it was unprofessional, which it most certainly was. They tried everything. One night the poor man said to us, 'Would you all have a good look at each other and tell me what it is you see that is so funny.'

We'd been doing quite well until he said that, but then we just went to pieces again.

'Would you please realise you are in a West End show. You have an audience to entertain, people who have paid a lot of money to see you. Will you please go back to your dressing rooms and pull yourselves together,' he begged.

We tried, we really did.

This was the era of purple hearts. We were all into them. At that time in my life I thought they were wonderful things. They made you love the world and you could keep going for hours after you would otherwise be exhausted. They were a kind of tranquilliser and an amphetamine together. All you had to do was take half a purple heart and you could learn an entire play at a sitting. I'm afraid I really did think they were brilliant. But of course most people took about sixteen rather than a half of one, and they were very addictive which is why they ended up being banned.

But it was no big deal in 1962. This was the beginning of the decade when almost all young people experimented wildly with all the mind-changing substances available, and a lot of older people too. For my sins, I was even a pusher for a while. I knew a lovely man who had a chemist's shop in the Charing Cross Road. He was a mad keen theatre-goer with a daughter he desperately wanted to get on the stage, and he just used to give me the things by the box-load.

Of course, it quickly became known in the business that I had a regular supply and dressers were always arriving at the stage door from other theatres asking me for them. I didn't charge anybody. I just used to hand the pills out and say, 'Have a good show.' There were occasions though, I must admit to my shame, that if people whom I did not regard as my greatest friends asked, it was not unknown for me to give them a laxative instead.

The point was that Dora and I hoped purple hearts might be our salvation. We thought if we took a half or so before we went on every night it might help us gain control. It didn't. Meanwhile, in the true spirit of the era, Dickie thought he'd try Librium. That didn't help either. He was by far the worst of us. He was completely uncontrollable. We used to do everything we could on stage to stop him laughing. We even hit him. Nothing did any good. He would rush into my dressing room before a performance and say: 'I'm all right, I'm all right, I've taken another Librium.'

But Dora and I both knew that the chances of him being able to do anything without crying with hysterical laughter were absolutely nil. And the hysteria gradually spread into every number, into every part of the show.

At the end of the show there was a big glamour bit where Dora emerged as the star that she was and Dickie had to go on stage in top hat and tails and sing: 'She's the nicest thing that ever happened to me. She's the nicest one I know.' Dora and I would be doing our changes and she'd say, 'Oooh listen, Mandy, he's gone again.' And there at the top of a flight of glitter stairs on stage at the Adelphi Theatre in front of a packed house would be this shaking blancmange-like figure, otherwise known as the distinguished actor Dickie Wattis, making a squeaky bleating noise. Dora and I would run into the wings with Dora pleading, 'Come on Dickie, for goodness' sake. Dickie, pull yourself together. Come on, Dickie.'

Of course, it was just so contagious. The sight of this major pro dissolving was just too much for Dora and me. Night after night after night we collapsed alongside him. It was actually very serious, and I was well aware of that. It was also the only time in my life I have been terrified of laughter. The management threatened us with all sorts of dire consequences. One night they even brought the curtain down on us. Nothing did any good. We would, without doubt, have all been sacked were it not for the fact that amazingly enough, the show was a great success. When Dickie started corpsing Dora, in her inimitable fashion, would address the audience directly and include them in the joke.

'Ooooh dear, we just can't control Dickie,' she would say. 'He's not himself tonight.'

Almost invariably the audience loved it, and even gave the impression that they preferred things to go slightly wrong – it was pretty much the same culture as pantomime really. Involving the audience was one of the things great revue artists thrived on. And Dora was always the best, and still is.

The show ran for a year, and we never got through a performance without collapsing in hysterics.

CHAPTER SEVEN

A s *Six of One* stumbled to its close in the summer of 1963
something happened which was to change my life. At the
time I didn't really know whether it made me happy or not.
It certainly thrilled me. It also frightened me. It was to influence my
whole existence from that moment on.

I was to have a gap of three weeks before going into the already
acclaimed musical *She Loves Me,* at the Lyric Theatre, taking over from
Rita Moreno. I had also been hired to play Cleo in the film *Carry On
Cleo*, which, of course, was to turn out to be a real landmark for me. I
had already played a much smaller role in *Carry On Cabby*, and had
apparently caught the eyes of the producers. But my agent had made a
ghastly mistake. It transpired that the filming of Cleo actually started on
the same day that I was to go into *She Loves Me* at the Lyric. By the time

we found out it was already too late to drop out of one of them decently, even if I had wanted to. So lucky old me, not just eight shows a week, but two productions at the same time.

Faced with that, and having worked non-stop forever, everybody in my life urged me to have a holiday – something I had never had since those early and thoroughly uncomfortable experiences at Llandudno. Richard had been in America for almost a year. He had taken the opportunity to go there for a season of plays, including *Oh, What a Lovely War!*, which were being produced by Joan Littlewood. I had been on my own in the Endell Street flat with him returning briefly only once or twice. I really didn't have anyone to go on holiday with and I wasn't entirely sure that I wanted one, whether or not it would be good for me. Most of the people I knew were dancers, who were all like me and didn't really take holidays. My mother would probably have wanted to go to Torquay, her honeymoon venue and the place she had returned to like a homing pigeon after Bill had died, and I didn't fancy that either.

Then, during the last week of *Six of One*, I was told there were two people waiting at the stage door after the show and they wanted to give me a drawing.

It turned out that one of them was Kay Ambrose, a ballet artist who had also written books on various famous dancers and a well-known ballet manual called *Ballet for Beginners*, and the other was a wonderful wild Canadian called Ian Robertson who had once been a dancer with the Kirov Ballet and was Rudolf Nureyev's boyfriend. Kay handed me a drawing of me which she had completed during the show.

'I hope you don't mind,' she said.

It was actually very good and I was thrilled. Kay and Ian were very talkative and great fun. After a bit Ian invited me to join them for something to eat. I heard myself say, 'I'd love to.' It was completely out of character, quite unlike me.

We went to Rules, the famous old restaurant in Covent Garden's Maiden Lane, and we struck up this ridiculous instant friendship on the spot. So much so that when Kay and Ian told me that they were going on holiday at the weekend to Paris and asked me if I would like to go with them, it seemed the most natural thing in the world to say yes. I had never done anything like it in my life. And it turned out to be much more than a holiday, leading to one of the most momentous experiences of my life.

The very day after we finished *Six of One*, Kay, Ian and I set off for Paris – at the last moment travelling by train instead of plane because there was an air strike. Originally I had said I would go for a week, but they had already persuaded me to make it two, so I was armed with both my *Carry On Cleo* and *She Loves Me* scripts.

'There'll be plenty of time to work on those,' they had promised. Of course, somewhat predictably, that did not turn out to be quite the case.

Kay spoke fluent French and knew Paris inside out, including every club and bar it seemed. We all shared a room with huge shuttered windows reaching from the floor to the ceiling in a wonderful hotel in Montmartre, the artists' quarter. It was an old theatre place where pros had stayed for hundreds of years. The three of us fitted in there as if it were a pair of old shoes. We laughed non-stop from morning until night. Ian was outrageous and ridiculous and I suppose I was that way inclined too. We were about the same age, late twenties, but behaved and looked far younger. Kay was a bit like an old-fashioned ballet teacher and was much older. She treated us like a pair of children she'd adopted and taken off on a spree.

Kay was quite famous in the Royal Opera House and elsewhere for taking people over and looking after them. They became her protégés really. It was usually male dancers who she drew and fed and gave all the help she could in getting started, including making them the most incredible frilled shirts. There was never anything sexual about it, whether they were straight or not. In fact I always thought that Kay was completely asexual, and had quite possibly neither had nor desired any sexual experience at all. She never took on females though. I was the exception perhaps because I was a bit androgynous. I had no tits of course, and was very thin and boyishly shaped back then.

I adored them both from the start. I'd never got on with two people like I did with them, and for the first time I felt really at home with people. I usually felt like the odd one out, which I was in a way, because even in the show-business world most people of my age were getting married and settling down, starting families, doing all those sort of things that I was still actively avoiding.

After just a few days in Paris, Kay suddenly suggested we went to Cannes. We were on a roll by then. The next day we just clambered aboard *le train bleu* and set off for the south of France. I still had my scripts in my basket – a very fashionable thing to carry in those days – which also contained the remnants of a considerable number of purple hearts. The journey was wonderful. *Le train bleu* was an experience in itself. They brought us beautifully embossed playing cards to help pass the time, while elegant waiters fed us raspberries and strawberries, and served us drinks in crystal glasses.

But the greatest experience of all was waking up as we arrived in Cannes and seeing the south of France for the first time. The streets of Cannes were bright and bustling, the buildings looked like something in a picture book, the sea really was blue and everything was bathed in sunshine. It seemed so amazingly colourful to me, and I loved the warmth. You have to remember that my only experience of the seaside involved freezing to death on British beaches. I'd never been abroad in my life before, which was not at all unusual then, and suddenly I was being introduced to this extraordinary world of Cannes in the sixties.

Kay, naturally, knew where to stay and where to go. She found us another great big room to share in a little hotel in the Rue d'Antibes, just a stone's throw back from the seafront, the famous *Croisette*. I think she told the hôtelier that Ian and I were her son and daughter, so that they would let us have a family room, with four little iron beds in it that was just like the room you see in every Matisse painting.

We instantly became immersed in a nightlife that I hadn't known existed anywhere. It was all wonderfully adventurous and daring to me. That, coupled with being with Kay and Ian and feeling so relaxed and at ease with myself, a feeling I was not at all used to, led to the cracking open of a shell I did not even know I had.

The nightlife was a bit like a sort of underwater sea life, with people floating around in an apparently aimless fashion, never making any formal arrangements to meet, yet all turning up at the same club, as if by instinct, because that seemed like the place to be that night, and then floating off somewhere else.

There were the most extraordinary cabaret acts around, many of them dating back to the thirties, and still being performed by old men who'd once been quite famous and celebrated. There was one man who was terribly thin and looked like Charles Hawtrey. He used to have a disgraceful act where he did a ballet dance and halfway through would spin around and spray the audience with milk from this false top he wore. It was very French humour. We thought it was pretty funny too, but we were drinking a fair amount of wine every night.

A lot of the clubs were gay haunts, and Ian was in his element because there was plenty of opportunity for trolling – something else I had never encountered before. One of the places we started to frequent was a gay club called the Can Can. It had a very smoky, hazy, intimate atmosphere. People danced with partners of either sex – something else I had never seen – even though there was still a law in France that people of the same sex couldn't. The club just put somebody on the door who would raise the alarm if there were any police about and everyone would quickly switch partners and start dancing with the nearest person of the opposite sex.

On the very first night we were there, after sitting and observing over a drink for a bit, Ian and I decided to dance together. We knew all the music – it was just when the Beatles were starting to emerge and most of the songs being played were English, a lot of them the kind of stuff we now associate with Dusty Springfield, Cilla Black and the other big names of that era.

Ian was from the Kirov and not at all averse to some serious showing off, and I was a very good dancer. Almost before we knew what we were doing Ian was doing lifts and throwing me over his head. We completely stopped the entire club. We made quite a couple in those surroundings. Ian was extremely good looking with hair that had gone white in the sun, while I was so thin and brown that I think some of them weren't even sure what sex I was.

As we eventually sat down, having danced until about three in the morning, a very attractive dark lady with two enormous wolfhounds, came prowling round the place looking at people. She smiled at me and ambled off. It turned out this was Ginette, the owner of the club.

Kay said, 'You've made quite an impression, Amanda, so I want you to realise that if any of the women ask you to dance it would be very rude to say no.'

Now that was a pretty amazing thing for me to be told. You have to remember that neither Kay nor Ian had any idea that I had ever had any feelings that had been other than strictly heterosexual. Since Bernie died, I'd never allowed anyone in my life to know that there was even a tweak of anything else inside me. I had completely shut down on my leanings in that direction. I knew that I was attracted to women but in a more emotional way than sexual. Sexually I went to bed with men, but emotionally I was always attracted to older women. It never occurred to me to even consider sleeping with them though. There was a block inside me between a particular lurking sexuality that I had yet to recognise and my strange, almost other-worldly, relationship with Bernie. I never let any of it come to the front of my head.

So, when a few minutes later Ginette came over and asked me to dance I had never been so scared in my life. I thought my heart was going to come pumping down my nose. I was quite terrified of having that sort of physical contact with a woman. Indeed, if Kay hadn't given me my instructions I think I would have turned Ginette down. But I didn't. I got to my feet, and we danced together for the rest of the night.

Almost at once something clicked inside me. I was still scared, really scared, but my poor little heart was banging away and I realised I was feeling things I hadn't felt since Bernie. It was like opening Pandora's box.

It made sense of so much in my life. I understood at that moment why I suffered from this constant feeling of discomfort and not fitting in, why I blushed so easily. It was as if I'd always been trying to hide something that was so much a part of me, as if I had lived constantly in fear of being found out. Yet I hadn't even known what I was afraid of being found out about.

However, when I danced with Ginette I knew that I was never going to be quite the same again. And I was very aware that she was attracted to me. When we finally finished dancing I realised that people had been staring at us. There was a whisper going round the club in various languages. '. . . never seen Ginette dance with anyone all night like that.'

I was in a state of almost nervous collapse, and I was very grateful to be going back with Kay and Ian to the communal safety of our shared room. On the way, as we walked along the Rue d'Antibes with dawn approaching, Kay turned to me and said, 'That was very kind of you.'

She hadn't a clue about the turmoil I was in. I didn't reply. I had no words.

The next day I tried to dismiss it all. To tell myself that nothing momentous had happened. I idled the day away on the beach, and tried not to think about Ginette, tried again to deny the feelings that were rising up inside me. Nonetheless, I couldn't wait to get back to the Can Can that night. My heart was bumping. I was still terrified. But I couldn't have stayed away.

When we arrived, Ginette came straight up to me and asked me to dance. She spoke very little English and I spoke virtually no French. We danced all night again, and then after the Can Can closed, she took me to a funny all-night café. It was there, in a secluded corner, that she asked me if she could kiss me.

I said 'oui', which was one of the half dozen or so French words that I did know.

So she did. And I melted. We didn't take things any further than that. She didn't suggest that we went to bed, for which I was grateful because I wouldn't have known what to do and would have been quite incapable of coping. Instead she just went home and I went off with Kay and Ian.

But there is little doubt that in that instant I fell headlong in love with Ginette. It was the first crack in me really. I'd never let myself go before. I'd kept all my emotions reined in. I'd made myself believe that I didn't care what happened with my parents, didn't care about being on my own, didn't care about unsuccessful relationships, didn't care about hitting fish over the head. I'd convinced myself that I didn't care about anything much really – except my work. That moment when Ginette kissed me changed everything.

I cracked open and I dissolved. As soon as I got back to our hotel room I started to cry and I couldn't stop. I must have cried for twenty-four hours.

Kay and Ian were not only very concerned, they were bewildered. Eventually I told them what had happened between me and Ginette and what it meant to me. I told them about the feelings that had surfaced, feelings that had lurked inside me and that I had denied virtually throughout my life. They reacted very differently. Ian was delighted. Over the moon. 'You're my sister!' he cried exultantly. 'My blood sister!'

Kay on the other hand was terribly upset. I think she had taken me under her wing thinking of me just as a little dancer who was as asexual a creature as herself. I still believe that she thought of Ian and me as her children and it disturbed her to discover that I had this other side to me. However, as I was finding it so difficult to come to terms with, it was unsurprising that other people were too.

Ian was a great support. He talked to me for hours about it all. And somehow through the tears we carried on with this extraordinary holiday, all mixed up with me sobbing and realising I didn't know what I was, or what to do about it, and being wildly excited at the same time.

I am well aware that the majority of younger people nowadays just accept their own sexuality and that of others, but it wasn't like that in 1963. It really wasn't.

You have to remember that it was to be another four years before male homosexuality was legalised. And the only reason female homo-sexuality was not illegal was that when Queen Victoria had passed the law on sexual practices she had not imagined it possible for anything of that nature to occur between two women. Silly Queen!

I was confused, frightened, and yet ecstatic. For a while anyway. In the south of France, for the first time in my life, I seemed to fit in wherever I went, whether it was in the clubs or on the transvestite beaches. People were lovely with me and I was all right with them, whether we spoke the same language or not. It was all right to be bonkers and barmy.

We fell into a routine. In the evenings we went to the Can Can and I danced all night with Ginette. We were accepted as a kind of item, only leaving each other's arms when there was a police scare, which was happening quite a lot at the time because it was policy to periodically close down a club, and the Can Can appeared to be about to have its turn. So when whoever was on the door blew the whistle you had to change partners smartish. It was very funny. You'd suddenly find yourself dancing with the ancient ex-prince of some principality you'd never heard of. And as the only language I could speak anything of other than English was *Polari* I didn't have much chance of getting any sort of conversation going.

I remember once Ginette had to go away somewhere for twenty-four hours so she gave me the keys to the club. It was extraordinary to put so much trust in a near stranger, but at the time, in the middle of all this magical madness, it seemed perfectly logical. There I was with the keys to the safe, the bar and the door, which I was responsible for locking at closing time in the early hours. I'd only been in the south of France for a week or so and suddenly I was in charge of this camp club in the heart of Cannes. It was crazy.

Ian and I quickly got into the habit of staying up all night, chewing purple hearts out of the bottom of my basket so we could keep going. Then at about six o'clock in the morning we'd go to the beach and fall asleep on the sand all day. You've never seen anyone browner than us two. People would turn us over as they arrived there later and pour fruit juice down these two terribly hungover creatures.

I came to life at night, and during the day I was tired, exhausted and completely out of it. I didn't bother with the sea, I couldn't swim. But Ian was a very good swimmer and one day when he disappeared underwater, I was so worried that I put my head into the ocean and called for him. I almost succeeded in drowning myself while standing up, which shows how befuddled I was. I'd virtually lost my sense of reason. Ian talked and talked to me. Kay was very quiet. But Ian and I continued to talk and to get brown to the point of almost becoming black, and we got thinner and thinner because we never seemed to eat. I was supposed to be on holiday, resting before making a film and appearing in the West End at the same time. In fact I was a walking wreck, emotionally and physically.

We went, as had become our habit, to this very stylish beach alongside the Carlton Hotel. The south of France in the sixties boasted a quite remarkable mix of people and still smacked a bit of the decadence left over from the twenties so there was plenty of cabaret to watch through half-closed eyes as we lay baking ourselves in the sun, trying to build up the energy for another night of excesses.

There were all these be-cobwebbed bits of ex-royalty that had been deposed from various places and ancient queens of another kind, in their white pyjama trousers with gold dripping off them, looking a bit like Dirk Bogarde in *Death in Venice*, sitting around in corners waiting for their toyboys. They all had boats bobbing about out in the bay somewhere and they'd be endlessly speaking into walkie-talkies to their young boyfriends. 'It's time you came back now. You've been there too long. Where are you? Who are you with?'

It was obvious that the toyboy concerned had teamed up with somebody else's toyboy and that they were out on a boat doing whatever gay toyboys do together when they can't be seen. Every so often one would dive into the sea and swim back to shore and there would be great ructions on the beach in front of all of us.

The beach also seemed to be full of French men who'd run away from farming communities to have a sex change operation. They'd usually managed to get just half of it done, and would be prancing around with huge tits but having not yet had everything chopped off, and would invariably be quite happy to show you what stage they were up to. One of the most beautiful of the lot was a transsexual known as The Duchess. She looked like the most incredible film star. She would sing in the clubs sometimes and spend her days sitting on the beach with her extraordinary long legs stretched out before her with about half a dozen camp queens all around her. She'd been a man two years earlier, yet she really was a beautiful creature. She was so grand too. She put your ordinary film star to shame.

They found me quite intriguing of course because of having no tits and being so thin. I was very readily accepted in a way I just wasn't used to. Being a chorus girl at heart I was always ready to take my clothes off with alacrity, and I found it very amusing because I knew they weren't always sure whether or not I too was having an operation, or whether I was a girl or a rather pretty boy.

It was mad and it was magic. People used to come up and ask, 'Do you prefer women or men?' They could have been asking whether you would like tea or coffee. It was totally matter of fact. Nobody bothered about what anybody else was doing. Nobody judged you. It was extremely sophisticated in a strange way. Nothing was pushed at you, and yet everything was available. We were also aware of the tragedies. We could see all the beautiful people who weren't beautiful any more but were still trying so hard. I realised that in this community, desperately living out its swansong to the craziest limits, looks and appearance counted for absolutely everything.

Then there was a culture of men who spent all day having facials and getting their nails manicured who would then stagger out to the clubs and join the ranks of these ex-famous people doing hysterical cabaret acts. One awfully butch lady who did Edith Piaf impersonations was advertised as '*les yeux sinceres* – sincere eyes – because she would try to sing with this extremely sincere expression in her eyes. She was hilarious. It didn't matter what you could do, you had to look right.

At the end of the night, instead of going back to our hotel, we would be off somewhere with Ginette and all the other club owners until the early hours. We would often leave some drag club with the performers as well. They all accepted us, perhaps because Ian and I were performers too and Kay was a writer. We'd finish up eating with the chefs and the cooks at five o'clock in the morning somewhere. Then we'd take everything outside and watch the dawn come up over Cannes.

What an eye-opener for a girl from Ashton-under-Lyne straight out of the chorus.

We seemed to get invited everywhere. One morning we were drinking coffee in an old French café and somebody asked us upstairs for a drink. So we went up to a cavernous, white-arched room where a man dressed as a sailor wanted to show us his incredible art collection, one of the greatest I have ever seen. There were Monets and Matisses, everything. It was unbelievable.

On another occasion we got into somebody's car and were taken at dawn to this villa where a dethroned prince of some sort lived. Half-stoned we walked into his grey world. Everything was pale grey. The floor was pale grey marble and the walls were painted pale grey. He let his animals in and a grey whippet ambled by followed by a beautiful grey wolfhound and a grey cat with the most enormous yellow eyes. Even the dethroned prince himself was grey, except for his clothes, which were white. He must have been in his seventies and he had a wonderful elegance about him that dated back to the twenties.

Once again, everywhere you looked were these works of art. I remember just staring at a Picasso for ages. It was unreal.

That day we didn't sleep on the beach. We stayed in this amazing villa. The ex-prince took me into a bedroom where again everything was pale grey with the most beautiful eighteenth-century painted furniture like something out of a fairy tale.

'Would you like to sleep here?' he asked casually. 'We don't get up until lunchtime.'

Then he opened the window which reached from ceiling to floor. The sun was just coming up. And through the window I could see an orange and lemon grove that ran right down to the sea. It was just stunning. I remember taking a big gulp of the morning air. I wanted to clear my brain. To me it was like a dream. It still feels like that now.

People just didn't fly off around the world then seeing how the other half lived. I felt immensely privileged to be in Cannes and to have the opportunity to experience the way of life there, albeit briefly. It was sheer bliss.

And then there was Ginette, whom I had come to adore. I was completely under her spell. I refused to go to bed with her, though. I really didn't know what to do or how to go about it. Understandably enough, things did become a little frustrating and strange between Ginette and me. I couldn't explain properly because of the language barrier. I did try to get Ian to interpret, but God knows what he said to her.

Eventually I had to leave. The two-week holiday had stretched to three, and I was right on my deadline for returning to London. I had work to go back to. Eight shows a week plus a film. And for once, I wasn't all that keen. I had begun to discover myself, I suppose. I had certainly discovered that it was possible even for me to be myself. I would have liked a little more time to explore the possibilities. But as ever in my life that was not possible. I just had to get on with it and go back to work.

CHAPTER EIGHT

～

My return to London and my impending workload brought me down to earth with a big bump. Suddenly I was back in the real world and not entirely popular. I had managed to change shape and appearance quite dramatically in less than three weeks away. My skin was burned black. I was thinner than ever, weighing less than seven stone, and I looked even more androgynous than I had before. The producers of *Carry On Cleo* were not impressed. At one point there was even a chance that they might drop me, and I think they probably would have done had they thought they could find somebody else in time. Not only did I look a bit odd, but I suspect I was also behaving differently. I had undergone a life-changing experience after all.

The producers of *She Loves Me* weren't best pleased with me either.

I very nearly went from having two productions to do at the same time to having none at all.

'We know you're taking over from a Puerto Rican, but we're still going to have to whiten you up unless you fade – and fast,' they said. They also told me, albeit apologetically, that I couldn't have my name in green neon as Rita Moreno's had been. I didn't mind that. I said I'd never even had my name up in matchsticks before.

I had to go for the fittings for my Cleo costume. I will never forget the embarrassment of it for as long as I live. The costumier, Mr Schneider, was a man of Hungarian descent who was very respected in the business. He considered himself to be an artist and had a temperament to match.

At the time almost everybody wore padded bras, and I was no exception. As I stood before him fully clothed, he probably assumed that I was the shape of all other *Carry On* actresses. Showing me the designs for the costumes, he explained, 'Now, we want the bra to expose the breast. Only the nipple will be covered. And the breast will be pushed up, so . . .'

I kept saying, 'But Mr Schneider, I don't think I can push anything up. I don't have anything to push up.'

'No, no, no. Everybody has a little to push up. The straps will be there, the nipples will be covered and the breast will be exposed.'

He went on and on. He wouldn't listen. He was an artist. He knew best. In the end I unzipped my dress, took my padded bra off, and just stood there topless.

Mr Schneider stopped in mid-sentence and was silent for fully thirty seconds. I think he was in shock.

'Oh my God!' he yelled, before running to the phone.

I was left standing there – naked to the waist, weighing under seven stone, black from head to foot with no tits.

I could hear him talking to the *Cleo* producers at Pinewood Studios. Well, not so much talking, more screaming. 'What are we going to do? She has no breasts! I cannot make costumes for this! I am not the miracle maker! She has to have an operation!'

I very nearly burst into tears. It might sound funny now, but you have to remember that I was preoccupied with not being like other people, and already thought of myself as a monster and a freak. Suddenly this had been proved. I had taken my clothes off in front of someone and he had been totally horrified by the sight of me.

Eventually Mr Schneider returned. 'You will have to see a doctor,' he ordered.

'What for?' I asked nervously. I had heard him talking about operations. I knew about those kind of operations from the south of France where people had seemed to be perpetually in a state of change with bits being chopped off and sewn on.

'We're going to get you some injections,' he said. I knew about those from the south of France too. That was how the transsexuals grew boobs.

It was my turn to go into shock. There was no way I was going to have those injections. Cleo and I seemed destined to part company before we started. I was despatched to Pinewood so that the entire production team could discuss what could be done with my poor body. In the end they agreed that there was nothing that could be done and left it alone, relying on nothing more than clever camera angles to enhance my shape. The crazy thing is, just a few years later, after Twiggy had arrived on the scene, I might have been considered quite fashionable, but at that time anyone playing a role like Cleo in a *Carry On* film was definitely supposed to have big boobs. In my case any boobs at all would have been a result.

My shape was just one of the anxieties facing me as I prepared to launch myself into *Carry on Cleo* and *She Loves Me*. Although I was already a very experienced performer in many ways and always at home on stage, I had done little acting. I had performed mostly as a dancer or in short sketches in revues where I had been given a piece of paper with three lines on it and a few bits and pieces of instruction. It had never really occurred to me that I would do anything other than dance and be funny. I would have loved to have been a mime artist actually. This was the first time that I had had to learn scripts properly. At that stage in my life that was one hell of a task. My dyslexia kicked in of course. I just couldn't get my head around it. Over the years I have developed various techniques for dealing with what for me is the thoroughly daunting task of reading, understanding, and then learning a new script. But then it was an absolute nightmare and a little later was to be a major factor in my having a breakdown. I was in fact just starting to become rather ill, and the stay in the south of France chewing all those purple hearts, drinking everything in sight, and eating virtually nothing, not to mention the emotional turmoil I underwent, had certainly not helped.

I didn't realise it, but I had already developed an eating disorder. Some years earlier I'd developed a trick of making myself sick when I was nervous. It seemed to help me conquer the nerves and be able to function again. In order to get on stage I used to make myself sick. This is not at all unknown in the theatre, of course. Indeed, one of the more glamorous aspects of acting is listening to the sound of nervous performers being sick prior to their entrance. I became more and more nervous during rehearsals for *Carry On Cleo* and *She Loves Me*. Something physical happened to me around that time. It didn't show, but it was like a sort of internal shake. By the time we came to the start of filming, and my West End first night on the same day, I was in quite a state.

I had to be up at four for filming, and arrived on set to find myself surrounded by all these beautiful girls with thick billowing hair and beauty-queen shapes, with me in the middle, the tit-less wonder with its little red face, putting its make-up on and poking at itself. As usual I felt thoroughly inferior. When they took my wig off at the end of the day, I thought I looked like an earthworm.

I then had to rush to the Lyric Theatre for *She Loves Me*. It was crazy. I'd worked out what seemed to be the only possible way to do it. I had these two dear friends, a pair of lovely old queens called Naff and Na Na, and they agreed to pick me up at Pinewood and drive me to the theatre. So I hurled myself into the back of their car and scraped off all my Cleo make-up as we drove into the West End, where I ran into the theatre, put on my twenties wig, threw up, and galloped on stage to sing, for the first time in my life really, some serious music.

The next day I went through the same routine again. So it went on throughout the entire six weeks of the filming of *Carry On Cleo*. Under that kind of pressure my nervous condition naturally worsened, and I was physically sick more and more frequently. I think I had a mixture of bulimia and anorexia, only neither of them had been invented at the time, so I just carried on working. I was going to bed at midnight, if I was lucky, and getting up at four. It was sheer madness, but I was so used to having no sleep and working half the night that it never occurred to me that you couldn't do it forever without putting the most almighty strain on your entire well-being.

The really amazing thing, however, was that I got excellent notices for *She Loves Me* and for *Cleo*, which became, of course, a huge hit. *Variety*, the prestigious Hollywood weekly, said, 'Best discovery is Amanda Barrie as the poor man's Cleopatra. Her take-off of the Queen of the Nile gets nearer to the tongue-in-cheek sense of what the film-makers were aiming at than any of her more experienced colleagues.'

I was also sent a review from America which referred to my 'brilliant pastiche of Elizabeth Taylor'. Well, I didn't even know I'd been doing one, even though our film was supposed to be a kind of parody of the famous Hollywood blockbuster *Cleopatra,* starring Elizabeth Taylor and Richard Burton, which had just been released. Indeed, there was a terrific row when posters of me, which were a deliberate recreation of the Liz Taylor posters, were used to promote *Cleo*. Twentieth Century Fox successfully sued the *Carry On* producers and my posters were withdrawn. I felt a bit guilty about that because the pose had been entirely my idea, not some great advertising stunt at all. I simply suggested it, on the spur of the moment, at one of the photo calls. Beyond posing like her for the posters I really hadn't been at all aware of producing a pastiche of Elizabeth Taylor, brilliant or otherwise. If it came across as that then it was an accident. I played it the only way I could think of, a bit camp. The lisp just slipped out. One or two of the posher British critics were a little less effusive. The *Guardian*'s film reviewer Ian Wright wrote, 'In all senses, Amanda Barrie, a newcomer to the *Carry On* series, proves a rather less than ample Cleopatra.'

Poor Mr Schneider would certainly have agreed.

None of us realised at the time that the *Carry On* films were anything special. In fact, just the opposite. It wasn't just the posh critics who were dismissive. Really big-name actors didn't want to know about them. People looked down on the *Carry On*s, particularly agents, producers and casting directors.

Years later when I was up for a part in the TV play *Early Struggles* with Tom Conti, which was directed by Stephen Frears, he suddenly realised I'd done *Cleo* and said, 'Oh God, I'm going to have to think overnight. I've never employed a *Carry On* actor before.' He did employ me though, and I adored working with him. Actors would pay to work with Stephen Frears, and I do still consider *Early Struggles* one of the best things I have ever done.

There were definitely these prejudices, however, which were quite unfair because I don't think there has ever been a more professional bunch on a movie than the *Carry On* team. A roll call of just some of the regular stars of the thirty-one *Carry On* films – Sid James, Kenneth Williams, Barbara Windsor, Charles Hawtrey, Kenneth Connor, Hattie Jacques, Frankie Howerd, Leslie Phillips and Joan Sims – speaks for itself. They were all incredibly experienced leading artists and absolutely top notch at what they did.

They were also, with just one or two exceptions, most notably Kenneth Williams, lovely to work with. Charles Hawtrey was a real favourite of mine, on screen and off. Twice a week he would bring me a piece of Finnan haddock, because he thought I was too thin and wasn't eating enough – about which, of course, he was quite right although I didn't realise it at the time. 'I've got you a nice bit of fish for your supper, don't forget to eat it,' he'd say.

It was very sweet of him, but unfortunately I don't think the Finnan haddock ever quite survived the day's filming and the long trip home – via the small matter of a show at the Lyric – in an edible condition.

The *Carry On* scripts were superb too which is why, of course, the *Carry On* films have stood the test of time and are regarded nowadays as absolute classics of their kind. It wasn't like that then. We just got on with it. The pay was lousy, about £250 a picture. In view of their lasting popularity, it still rankles that we just got one-off fees without any deals for TV or video exposure, which didn't even exist then of course. The schedules were relentless too. It was about the fastest filming ever – seven minutes a day, a hell of a lot on a major film. As soon as we finished one scene we were straight into the next, because the next set would already be lit and ready to go. And, a bit like in *Coronation Street*, the highest standards were demanded of you. It was a hanging offence to be late or to arrive on set not knowing your lines. You just didn't. An entire *Carry On* was shot in six weeks, and the budget for *Cleo* was £160,000 – seriously tiny for any film, even in the sixties. *Cleopatra,* on the other hand, ran up a budget of millions and took almost two years to make. It is a joke to even attempt to compare the two films, but in terms of professionalism *Carry On Cleo* would not fall short. In order to keep to that kind of schedule and budget everything had to work like clockwork.

However, there were occasional hiccups and as ever, if anything was going to go wrong I was usually involved. Everybody, it seems, remembers the scenes of me in the film bathing in asses' milk. The milk was the genuine thing – not asses' milk, but certainly cows', 200 gallons of watered-down semi-skimmed. It used to go off from time to time, and they had to replace it. The bath had to be kept at a certain temperature, and on one occasion something went wrong with the thermostat and it got so hot it nearly killed me. My stand-in refused to go in because it was too hot, but like a fool in I went. 'I'll do it. No problem. It's not that hot.' As I climbed down the four steps into the bath, which was like a very small swimming pool really, the water seemed to press against me. The cameraman said, 'Just go in quickly, let me get one shot, then straight out.'

I did my best. But as the water passed my heart something went bang, and I passed out. Fortunately, one of the stagehands had stayed nearby, even though it was supposed to be a closed set, and he grabbed me by the wig so I didn't go right under. I think if I had done in that heat it could have been the end of me.

I remember reading at the time that when Elizabeth Taylor finished the bath scenes for *Cleopatra* she was given a week's holiday. I was given a cup of Pinewood Studios' coffee, then on to the next scene.

I really was naked in that bath – apart from bits of plaster over my nipples which looked pretty silly. Although tastefully shot from the back, this was very unusual in the early sixties. It seemed perfectly normal to me of course. I was an old chorus girl, more used to being undressed most of the time than dressed. But it was considered quite outrageous at the time. Because of it I was offered a *Playboy* centrefold, which I turned down. This was not out of modesty. It was simply because I was, as ever, paranoid about my body, particularly my breasts. Or lack of them. The Mr Schneider incident was still making me cringe. If I'd had an inch more tit I'd have said yes to *Playboy* straight away, jumped back into my bath of milk and done the backstroke for them.

I now regret turning *Playboy* down. As you get older you are inclined to realise that once upon a time your body may not have been quite as bad as you thought after all. I recently watched Cleo all the way through for the first time – I know actors always say this, but I really do have a horror of seeing myself on screen – and I watched myself climbing out of the bath and thought, 'Why on *earth* did I say no to *Playboy*?'

A couple of years later I made the first colour front cover of the extremely upmarket *Tatler* magazine, which both impressed and astonished me. But I would still rather have been in *Playboy*.

On another occasion while filming *Cleo,* I had to be rolled up in a carpet and a table was supposed to collapse on me. Again a stunt girl had been employed, but she was late, so, not having learned my lesson from the hot bath episode, I promptly offered to do the stunt myself.

But fortunately, for me if not for her, the stunt girl turned up at the last moment. They rolled her up in the carpet, but the table, which was a huge long trestle affair, collapsed far more dramatically than it was supposed to, breaking several of her teeth. If that had been me I would have been out of the film and out of *She Loves Me*.

By and large it was just a privilege to work with the *Carry On* cast. They were so good and there was never any nonsense with them. One exception to the latter, although certainly not the former, was Kenneth Williams. He was a genius of course, and so witty, but it was usually a cutting wit directed against somebody else. Like many people who worked with him I suspect, I was, quite frankly, terrified of him. You never knew what he was going to say or do and he had a dreadful sourness about him. He was also prone to bouts of quite fanatical professional jealousy and there was considerable unspoken rivalry between him and Sid James.

In fact there is little doubt, and Kenneth Williams certainly made his feelings clear enough in his diaries, that they thoroughly disliked each other. Now, I was too worried about doing a show at night and getting through a day's filming without falling over, to worry too much about who hated who, but I do remember one day when Kenny was at his trickiest and there was an incident in which I was involved. We had a caravan by the asses'-milk swimming pool, and in it hung about a dozen dressing gowns which were there for anybody who had to go into the milk. Because of my south of France escapade I was still too brown and so I had whiting on my body all the time, and somebody would chuck a dressing gown over me as soon as I got out of the water so that I would be kept warm and dry and hopefully not streak. On this particular day I was sitting in the caravan, desperately learning my lines because they'd just informed Sid and me that we were going to do an extra scene of about five pages, when I was suddenly called on set. I was required to be naked, apart from the sticking plaster over my nipples, so

I just grabbed the nearest dressing gown, which was hanging right by me and walked out. As I approached the set I suddenly felt something behind me ripping my dressing gown off. I ended up stark naked. Then the unmistakable nasal tones of Kenneth Williams hissed at me, 'My dressing gown, dear, I think.'

I half turned towards him. He was in a white rage, trembling, his lips pulled back in a kind of snarl, and there was real menace in his voice. Kenneth had this well-known thing about personal hygiene, of course. But there was no question of my having put on his dressing gown. The dressing gowns were there for all of us.

At the time I just thought he had it in for me. It wasn't the first time he'd been unpleasant to me – although this was by far the worst. It's quite vindictive to do what he did to a woman on a film set, with a full crew there, knowing she's got nothing on underneath because she's about to go into a nude scene. However, the truth was that the reviews had just come in from America for another *Carry On* film. Sid, who was much loved over there, had got wonderful notices. And Kenneth was not best pleased.

It didn't occur to me to think, 'This is a very twisted, sick man, and he's probably jealous because Sid's got all the notices, and people have been congratulating him all day.' I didn't know Kenneth then. I just thought that he didn't like me. It was only later that I learned that he had behaved that way towards everybody that day. It had not been anything personal at all. Kenny was simply beside himself with anger, because he didn't think anybody but himself should have good notices. Particularly not Sid.

Typically, it was Sid who came to my rescue. As soon as he realised what had happened he grabbed another of the dressing gowns and threw it over me. He was a lovely man and I adored him. I am saddened nowadays when I hear or read how miserable he was. I am sure he went through periods of his life, as perhaps most of us do, when he was depressed, but I find it hard to believe that Sid was like that most of the time. I worked with him a lot over the years and I always found him the easiest, most likeable and funniest of men. I defy any sad, tortured man to have the amount of humour in his eyes that Sid James had. I don't think he could have come across the way he did if he really was a depressive.

I became specially close to Sid. However, unlike Barbara Windsor, my relationship with him was confined to a shared love of horse-racing. It was very much Sid who was responsible for the growth of my abiding passion for the sport. I had always loved horses of course, although I never found time or opportunity to ride again after I left school and started to work for a living. I think my interest in racing began when Lester Piggott won the Derby with Never Say Die. But it was on the set of *Cleo* that I started to become quite fanatical. In the days before betting shops there were unofficial private bookies. At one point I became Sid's runner, placing bets and checking on our winners in between shots. If I wasn't on set with him I'd be tick-tacking him across the studio so that we could keep in touch with what was happening.

Like everybody involved with the *Carry On*s, Sid was a superb professional. However, there was the day when he just couldn't say 'Caesar'. As he was playing Mark Antony, he had to say Caesar quite a lot, which was something of a disaster. He was supposed to say to me, 'Right. What you've got to do is get Caesar back to your apartment . . .' And on the very first take for some unfathomable reason he said, 'Right. What you've got to do is get *Shakespeare* back to your apartment . . .'

I couldn't believe it. Sid didn't even realise what he had done. He just carried on, sometimes saying Caesar when he was supposed to, and then reverting to Shakespeare again. Eventually the director called, 'Cut.' But once it was pointed out to Sid what he had done, things went from bad to worse. Sid really didn't know whether he was saying Shakespeare or Caesar. He kept saying: 'Sorry, sorry!' Then, all over again, it would be, 'Right. What you've got to do is get Shakespeare back to your apartment . . .'

By this time he had started to laugh. We both had. However, when Sid really started to laugh he went into hysterics. Most people have seen Sid's laugh on camera. It was exactly the same off camera. My most vivid memory of Sid is of him shrieking with laughter to such an extent that his eyes ended up blood red.

Now this was the age when blue drugs were supposed to cure everything. That's the way it seemed to me. There were purple hearts to keep you going; turquoise-blue oblivon to calm you down,!and *couleur bleue*, which was a blue eye-drop that whitened your eyeballs, took away any trace of red and gave you a wonderful sort of blue-white eye whatever you might have been doing.

They must have used tablespoonfuls of *couleur bleu* in Sid's eyes that day, and they did manage to get one vital shot out of us – the one where I had to hold up the jelly asp. But finally they gave up. 'Go home, you two, just go home.' It's the only time I know of that happening on any *Carry On* film, which is a dubious accolade. But at least I got to the theatre early that night for once.

I remain extraordinarily grateful to the *Carry On*s. At the time they were just another job, but they had such visual impact that the images from them remain in people's minds. They were also, I think, very much part of an era. Somehow things like the *Carry On*s and *Coronation Street* have a special appeal and for some reason the public are kind enough to take them into their hearts.

It always surprises me that I receive just as many letters about *Cleo*, which was just one film made almost forty years ago, as I do about the Street. In spite of other people's kind opinions I have never thought I was any good in *Cleo*.

Meanwhile, in *She Loves Me*, a wonderful show with seriously good music, I was playing Ilona, a funny-sad character. It was a role that suited me quite well. I certainly like to think that I was better in it than I was in *Cleo*. I have never been very good at instant work. Some people make things grow and get them better and then hone it down to make them better still. Other people can just do it instantly. I've always been somebody who likes to work on something and let it develop. Which is why I have always felt better suited to theatre than film or TV. I invariably feel that I'm the worst in rehearsals, and I then work and work at it in an attempt to be not just better, but the best.

I enjoyed *She Loves Me*, in spite of the various pressures from outside, not just having to shoot *Cleo* at the same time, but also still being in a state of great confusion because of my unfulfilled south of France liaison with Ginette. I remember the first person I confided in about Ginette was my then agent, Alec Graham, a lovely man who was also a very clever lyricist and a famous writer of revue. I told him about her mainly because the title of the show had, of course, a particular poignancy for me at the time. Alec promptly rewrote some of the songs for me with different lyrics. One of them had lines in it like, 'Charming, romantic, the perfect café.' Alec came up with, 'Charming, romantic, the perfect gay bar; Everyone around me looks like Hedy Lamarr; Tables for two, Danny La Rue; But where are you, dear friend?'

I loved his version, and used to sing it to myself all the time.

In spite of being critically acclaimed *She Loves Me* did not last all that long after I went into it, largely, I have always thought, because people were inclined to get the show confused with the latest Beatles hit, 'She Loves You', and were half expecting to be entertained by the Fab Four. On the show's last night the lovely Ian, who I believe was having a particularly bad time in his relationship with Rudi, turned up in my dressing room. Kay was off writing a book in Russia or somewhere, and at some stage, fuelled by copious quantities of alcohol, Ian suddenly said, 'Oh God, wouldn't it be wonderful if we were back in Cannes?'

I was without a job and he was without Rudi, more or less. So we just went. Straight away.

The last-night party wasn't much, as the show had been brought off, so at about 10.30 p.m. we took off, shot around to Endell Street, where I grabbed my passport and a handful of nothing – you don't really need many clothes when you're thin – and got a taxi to Heathrow via Ian's flat where he too grabbed a small bag. We arrived at the airport at about 12.30 a.m., to discover that there was one night plane leaving for Nice two hours later. We took it, and, unsurprisingly perhaps at that hour, it was empty apart from the stewards. Then we got a taxi to Cannes from Nice and walked straight into the Can Can while everyone was having breakfast. I was back where I wanted to be. But I remained as reticent as ever about actually having a physical relationship with another woman.

There was still a kind of magic about Ginette and once more she made her feelings for me very clear. I just couldn't bring myself to take things any further, and, bless her, she didn't push me. It's probably one of the differences between men and women in love. Most men would just want to jump on you regardless of any doubts you might have and without taking into account the possible emotional effect. Women are more sensitive, I think, to someone being frightened and unsure. Also, Ginette always knew that I would be going back to England which probably made her think twice. The distance between Cannes and London seemed greater then than it does now.

I kept thinking of what Bernie said to me when we used to cuddle up together. 'This could change your entire life.'

I had it very much in the back of my mind that I really mustn't mess with my feelings concerning relationships with women. I adored Ginette and found her extremely attractive. But I could not bring myself to do anything about it.

Nonetheless, Ginette did change my life.

CHAPTER NINE

❧

Shortly after I returned from France, Richard came back from America and I decided to tell him about Ginette and the feelings she had awoken in me. This proved to be a mistake. He reacted as if I'd grown horns and was a sick animal.

There wasn't really much left between us by then. He'd been away for so long for a start, and our relationship had become very strained during the brief periods when we had been together. The night I told him I got very upset. I'd had a few drinks, but I was already in an extremely emotional state. After all, I had repeated my previous performance in Cannes – no sleep, too much sun, not enough food, too many purple hearts – and I was absolutely miserable at the loss of Ginette even though I was full of guilt and fear. It didn't take much to push me into a confession.

Everything that had happened in the south of France had been so important to me that I just felt that I couldn't have a relationship of any kind with someone I hadn't told about it. Also, I was trying to use Richard as a friend. He was quite a lot older than me and I thought that he'd be wiser. But he didn't show a lot of wisdom.

He just went absolutely mad. He was appalled. He was disgusted even though I hadn't actually done anything. I had just indicated to him that I had these certain feelings. His reaction devastated me. I already felt that I was peculiar, and although my feelings for Ginette seemed so absolutely right, I suppose I also half believed – probably still the view of the vast majority in the sixties – that my sexual leanings meant that there was something wrong with me, that I was unnatural.

Perhaps if there had been the type and range of television, films and books back then that there are now, I might at least have realised that I was not alone – that there were other people out there facing the same problems, learning to deal with the same discoveries about themselves. As it was I felt completely alone. The way Richard reacted merely confirmed what I already believed – that I was some kind of freak.

Richard returned yet again to America to continue his Joan Littlewood tour. In spite of the total breakdown of our relationship – my south of France revelations being the final straw – I continued to live in his flat, an arrangement that suited both of us.

However, as well as the turmoil I was in about my sexuality, I had other worries. The story I am about to tell may seem like light relief but I can assure you that it wasn't at the time.

I was left in charge of Richard's six canaries, which lived in an aviary built into an alcove in the living room of his flat. In the past a neighbour had looked after the birds, coming in frequently to feed them and check on their wellbeing while Richard was away, but the neighbour had moved and I was in sole control.

Richard was terribly fond of his canaries, and used to let them out of their cage to fly around the flat and from time to time dive-bomb visitors. I didn't intend to risk that. I didn't know much about birds so I just hoped that if I fed and watered them all would be well. This did not prove to be the case.

It began on only the second night after I had been left alone to look after them. I heard a strange sort of scratching and clawing noise and I noticed that one of the canaries was on the floor of the cage trying to stick its head under the water container. Now, although I was not all that up on bird behaviour, I had lived with these canaries for some time and I'd certainly never seen one of them doing this before. I realised it couldn't be because they were missing Richard, he'd been away too long, and it couldn't be because they were trying to tune into Radio 4. There was obviously something wrong with this creature. So I poked at it a bit, as best you can with a canary. I tried putting some water next to it, but it didn't seem very interested. There's not much you can do actually. I couldn't ask, 'How are you feeling?' or, 'Is everything all right, love?' I just had to leave it alone and hope for the best. Eventually time came for bed, and the next morning when I got up, it was still in this rather uncomfortable position. And it was stiff. 'This is a deceased canary,' I thought.

Knowing how fond Richard was of his birds, I reckoned I ought to try and do the decent thing for the poor creature. So I decided to take it out and bury it. We were close to St Giles-in-the-Field Church and I thought it might be nice for this canary to end its days in the church-yard. So I popped it in a carrier bag and took it along to the church, which was right near the Phoenix Theatre. I found a nice earthy spot in the churchyard where I proceeded to dig a little hole with a spoon that

I'd had the forethought to take with me. However, I was interrupted by a very angry verger.

'What are you doing desecrating the churchyard?' he shouted at me. 'How dare you!'

'I'm only trying to bury a canary,' I said.

'You can't,' he replied. 'Not 'ere, not in consecrated ground, you can't.'

'Why not?' I asked.

I then had an argument with him about even canaries being God's creatures. Eventually I found an easier way. I slipped him five bob. He let me bury the canary.

But the next night I heard the same scratching noise. Another canary had dropped to the floor and stuck its head under the water container. Well, by this time I knew that when they do this they are not happy birds. I thought, 'Either she's missing the other canary – or he is, because you don't know what sex they are, they could have been a pair of old queens for all I knew – or this is the same procedure happening again.' The next morning, there in the bottom of its cage was a second dead canary. Fortunately I had another Sainsbury's bag, so I toddled back to where I'd planted the first canary in the churchyard and proceeded to make another little hole. Yet again the verger arrived.

'You can't do that 'ere,' he said.

'But I did it two days ago and now this one's dead,' I told him. 'Please can I put it alongside the other one as they've always lived together?'

It cost me another five bob. Quite a lot of money was beginning to change hands. But I was relieved just to be able to bury canary number two and go home.

All was peaceful for about another week before I heard the noise again. Another bird was on the floor of the cage doing something funny with the water container. Not good news. I waited. Sure enough, boom, boom. Another one had gone.

So I got another Sainsbury's bag and toddled off to the churchyard once more.

This time the verger asked, 'Are you killing birds?'

'I am not,' I told him indignantly. 'These birds are of an age. And they're like light bulbs, when one of them goes, they all start going.'

Suffice to say another two birds died, leaving only one alive. I took them all down to the churchyard where they were buried safely together. At the cost of five bob per canary. I took solace back home with the solitary surviving canary and my hobby of drawing, which I did a lot of at the time.

Now another pride and joy of poor Richard's was a button-backed chair that had been his mother's and which he'd had re-covered, at great cost, with pale yellow velvet. True to my messy nature I managed to tip a bottle of Indian ink all over this chair. Indian ink is not easy to move on any surface, and as it sank in and spread over this pale yellow chair I thought, 'Five canaries down, one canary-yellow chair on the way. Oh my God!'

I panicked then and phoned my mother, which I always did when anything was wrong. 'What can I do?' I wailed.

'Try milk on it, dear,' she said. 'That brings stains out.'

Obediently I poured a bottle of the stuff over the chair. It spread nicely, sort of blended with the ink, curdled and went stiff. Within twenty-four hours the whole flat stank of stale milk. I didn't have a shower or a bath, just that blessed Bink in the kitchen, and there was no way I could get rid of the milk from that chair. It was the most disgusting mess you have ever seen. You know how velvet goes stiff and sticks up? Well, that's what happened to this chair. It looked like something out of Battersea Dogs' Home.

I had no idea what to do. I spent the entire day on the phone to my mother, who, having already made matters considerably worse, was no further help whatsoever. I was at my wits' end.

Salvation came in the form of a film called *I've Gotta Horse* with Billy Fury, in which I was to play Billy's girlfriend. The film was to be shot largely in Yarmouth, the biggest appeal of which was the healthy distance between it and the crime scene. I have never snapped up a job so fast. I have always said that I was keen to do that film, which featured Billy's Derby-placed racehorse Anselmo, because of my love of horses. The truth is that I think I would have taken almost anything which would have got me away from Endell Street. Fast.

However, even then my bird problems were not over. The last canary had one final trick in store for me. I had arranged for Miss Poulter downstairs, an elderly lady who had understandably not been prepared to look after six birds but was happy enough to take one, to look after the blessed thing in my absence. But while I was packing up, and just as the canary was due to be taken to its new home, it got out of its cage and, to my horror, flew straight through the window. Maybe it was looking for its friends.

So there I was in the middle of packing, which is never easy for me, with a stinking chair covered in milk-sodden, inky mess, five birds down in the graveyard and one wild in Covent Garden. Frantically I alerted everybody I knew in the neighbourhood and we all rushed into the streets to look for this canary. Miraculously we spotted it where it had alighted three storeys up on a warehouse building in a little alleyway off Shorts Gardens. It was sitting on a windowsill ducking every time a pigeon came past and swooped at it.

I thought, 'I haven't packed. I'm in big, big trouble in my private life, and that bloody bird is just sitting there.'

But in spite of my irritation I did feel sorry for it. There was no way

I could leave it there. So off I went to Bow Street Police Station, just around the corner, where they knew me, a mixed blessing under the circumstances, to ask them if they could lend me a long ladder. They did have one and obligingly carried it to where the bird was still cowering on its windowsill. But there was no way they were going up after a bloody canary, so they just left me to it. Even though I'm not good at heights, up I went. There was, however, no way I could reach to get hold of this bird. I even took its cage up there to try and tempt it home, by which time a group of people had gathered who were all killing themselves laughing.

I was quite frantic. 'Look, this is serious,' I shouted at them. 'There's an animal's life at stake here.'

It made no difference.

Eventually I came up with a device that solved the problem. I returned to the flat, got some wire coat-hangers, fastened them together, took a net curtain down, threaded the wire coat-hangers through to make an arch, weighed the bottom of the net curtain down with pennies and went up the ladder again with this enormous butterfly net which I hurled over the window. The canary fluttered into it, and I got the bloody thing down and back into its cage. I was duly rewarded with a round of applause from the watching crowd, which by then had grown quite considerably.

I wanted desperately to get hold of the bird and give it six blinding raps around the jaw. That would, however, have defeated the object of my day's adventure. I had rescued the darned thing. I had saved the last canary. Miss Poulter promised to buy it a friend in case it was lonely. But I'd become convinced by then that for months this canary had probably been telling the others 'I need my space' and may even have brought about their deaths in some devious way.

As far as Richard was concerned though, I would be held

responsible. And I suspected that even my possible switch to bisexuality would be far less upsetting for him than the death of five of his cherished birds and the ruination of his lavishly re-upholstered chair. So I didn't tell him.

I just took off quietly, and with a considerable sense of relief, for Yarmouth, Billy Fury, and what was to turn out to be a whole new episode in my life.

I'm not quite sure at what point I started to fall for Billy Fury, or him for me. I was still trying, albeit without much success, to convince myself that the thing with Ginette had been just a phase.

Billy and I started off becoming very friendly mainly because we were both such great animal lovers. In his dressing room and everywhere he went Billy was surrounded by big travel bags. In one there'd be eight Chihuahuas and in another there'd be some stray creature he'd rescued. He also had an Alsatian called Sheba and a Great Dane called Rusty. I thought it was rather wonderful that all his animals were strays or rescue jobs.

The film had been set up by Larry Parnes, Billy's manager, who for some reason asked me to look after Billy. It was no hardship to do so. Billy was an incredibly charismatic, incredibly good-looking boy – just a thoroughly beautiful creature. Men sometimes go through that stage in adolescence I think, when they are neither men nor boys but some kind of unique creature. Billy had that quality about him even though he was way past adolescence. It may have been something to do with the fact that he was already quite ill and knew it. I'm not sure. But he was an absolute sweetheart, and I adored him. During our three weeks or so on location in Yarmouth nothing actually happened between us, but I think a little flame was lit.

Working on the film started off pretty much like working on any other film. We had quite a nice little family set-up. I knew most of the other dancers quite well, particularly Sheila O'Neil who had been in *Six of One* and my friend Doreen Cran. Michael Medwin and Jon Pertwee also starred, and the director was Ken Hulme, Shirley Bassey's first husband and one of the funniest men ever born.

Ken had a great way of talking as if nothing ever went right for him. He'd say, 'Should it be I got up this morning? Should it be that I come here on set and find I have no actors?' Almost every remark he made started with, 'Should it be . . .' He was also one of those directors who would think rather dramatically on his feet. Somebody would point out that we were behind schedule and he would simply tear up a few pages of the script. This may be an apocryphal story in filmmaking, but Ken Hulme really did it.

'Should it be?' he'd say, followed by a ripping noise. Then, 'Well, we're not any more.'

So if anybody found the continuity hard to follow in *I've Gotta Horse*, that's why. There was another reason as well. About two and a half weeks into the location shoot Kenny discovered that he had been using the wrong film, which was also much more costly than that we were supposed to be using. Apparently the powers-that-be ordered that we re-shoot what we had already done on the correct cheaper film because even that would cost far less than carrying on with the expensive stuff. The two sorts couldn't be mixed because they wouldn't match. So we ended up literally re-shooting two and half weeks of filming in about two days.

Strangely enough I don't remember any tension. It was actually very funny. Kenny proceeded to shoot at speed. He'd tell us stuff like, 'Should it be that it rains in the middle of this, just mention it and keep going. Say something like, "Oh, it's raining. It was a much nicer day yesterday," then, whatever you do, just carry on . . .'

Of course all of this put the whole filming schedule out of kilter. We'd had permission to film at Epsom, which was to be cut in with newsreel footage of Anselmo actually coming fourth in the Derby, but we ended up going on the wrong day. It was the day of a big race and the stewards, quite rightly, just wouldn't let us through to the paddock.

'Take no notice,' ordered Kenny. 'Should it be that anyone tries to stop you, just walk. Walk! Push your way through. Take no notice.'

Michael Medwin, who was a racing man, tried to explain. 'You don't just push your way into a paddock with millions of pounds' worth of horse-flesh in it, Kenny,' he said. 'Not at Epsom. You just don't do it.'

Kenny wouldn't have it.

'Push your way through,' he continued. 'Stand by the nearest horse. Just let me get one shot.'

'No, no, no, this is a grey,' shouted Michael Medwin desperately at one point. 'Don't shoot me with a grey, for Christ's sake! Anselmo was a bay.'

This went on all afternoon. Owners and trainers were complaining about us. Kenny was running around after us with a hand-held camera. In fact it was very embarrassing for all of us who loved horse-racing. In the end the police were called but we contrived to escape without being arrested and, miraculously, with a few inches of film too.

People should watch *I've Gotta Horse* to spot the mistakes. The weather changed, the film itself changed, Anselmo was a riding-school hack, and the Epsom scenes were chaos. Never mind *Summer Holiday* and Cliff Richard, *I've Gotta Horse* was so terrible it should be the cult film of all time.

Somewhere along the line Billy and I laughed together. It always does something to my heart when I laugh with someone. And when Billy and I started laughing, my heart went thump. I just felt so relieved too because I had been so upset and desolate after Cannes. I was surprised and relieved at the same time to have those feelings for a man again. It was a bit confusing, true, but at least I knew what to do with a man, I did have a basic understanding of how it all worked.

We returned to the London area for more filming, mostly at Shepperton Studios and it seemed perfectly natural that when Billy sold his house in Richmond and had yet to acquire another property he should come and stay with me. I had moved back to Endell Street, while managing to keep the last canary in the care of Miss Poulter downstairs. Richard had been away in America for almost a year, apart from just a couple of brief visits home, and when Billy came to stay, I started by kidding myself that I was just providing him with a roof over his head for a bit.

Into this small central London pad, with two tiny rooms and a Bink, Billy brought with him his various animals, a quite hysterical suitcase with lots of socks in it, and a gun. Now Billy was the gentlest creature in the world, and what he was doing with a gun in his suitcase I have absolutely no idea. I just accepted it. I never asked him why he had a gun, and neither did I ever ask him if it was loaded. I did however handle it with great care when I was looking for his socks to wash.

People are sometimes surprised, but I have always happily done chores like that for those I have lived with. With Billy it was mostly me who got the surprises. Larry Parnes was the old-fashioned kind of pop star manager who looked after everything for his boy. He used to invest most of Billy's earnings for him, pay all his bills, and give him about £60 or so in cash every week, which was a lot of money in those days. Billy had a habit of crinkling up the bank notes and stuffing them in his socks.

I discovered this the first time I washed his socks in the Bink, which served as a washing machine as well as everything else. I realised the socks were full of paper and I thought it was probably tissue. I'm so messy myself that it would seem perfectly natural to me to find a stash of paper handkerchiefs in somebody's socks. But I discovered to my horror that Billy's socks contained those big crinkly five pound notes we used to have in those days, all scrunched up and sodden. So I ironed them and set them out to dry as best I could. When Billy came home all his money was hung up around the kitchen with clothes pegs. He didn't seem to mind. He was always easygoing, and I think he quite liked having someone washing his socks.

He also had a Saxone shoebox full of marijuana which lived under the bed, alongside the suitcase with the socks in it. Billy liked to smoke dope a lot. Once he forgot to take any with him when we were filming at Shepperton Studios. I ended up ringing my mother, who was staying with us at the time, to ask her if she could come out to Shepperton and bring the shoe box with her. Typically she took this request entirely in her stride.

'It looks like it's got the contents of a hoover in it, Mummy. Just wrap the whole box up in something and get a taxi.'

'All right, darling.'

'And don't go in the suitcase next to it because it's got a gun in it.'

'All right, darling. Is it loaded?'

'I don't know. Just don't touch it.'

'All right, darling. Do you want anything else?'

'No thank you.'

She duly arrived with fresh supplies of marijuana for Billy, and she never batted an eyelid.

Billy also liked to drink rum and Coke. We used to rush back to Covent Garden after filming, put on these identical denim caps we both had, and go on a pub crawl drinking rum and Coke.

Everybody around Covent Garden was really fond of Billy. My mother adored him, and he was absolutely divine with her. He was, without doubt, the sort of son anyone would have wanted.

I don't remember quite when Billy the lodger became Billy the lover, but I suspect it was pretty soon. I moved effortlessly from carrying maggots around and killing fish with Richard to rum and Coke and dope with Billy. I was, as ever, playing the chameleon trying to fit in with my partners. At first we kept our affair a secret. I knew vaguely that Billy had a girlfriend, although I think he must have stopped seeing her during the time that we were together. We just didn't talk about that. And I was still living in Richard's flat even though our relationship was dead. Eventually though it became public knowledge. At one stage my sister was staying with us as well as my mother, and we all piled into this tiny flat. My mother was, as usual, completely unfazed by anything that I did or was involved in – the dope incident being a very good example – and used to bring us tea and toast in bed in the mornings, get us up for filming, and feed us when we returned. In fact we struggled a bit when she returned to Manchester. Left to our own devices we never seemed to get around to eating much. Our principal sustenance was rum and Coke and as a result we were both like skeletons.

Quite early in our relationship there was an incident which I'm sure wasn't helped by this lifestyle. Billy collapsed in the studio during filming. He just went out cold. After just a couple of minutes he came around, very pale, but otherwise apparently OK. Nonetheless a doctor was called and, after examining Billy, he expressed a desire to speak to whoever Billy was with. Quite a lot of people knew that we were an item and so I was sent for.

'Do you know that Billy smokes marijuana?' the doctor asked.

I was a bit nervous because possession of dope was a serious offence in those days. Nobody got off with a caution in 1963. If Billy had ever been arrested on a drugs charge he would almost certainly have gone to prison, and I could just imagine the headlines. It would have been disastrous. So I avoided making a reply.

Then the doctor told me just how ill Billy was. He had TB, kidney problems and a serious heart condition – which, of course, was to ultimately cause him to die so young. I was shocked because I'd had no idea about any of this. And I was absolutely astonished by what the doctor said next.

'You make sure he keeps on the marijuana,' he instructed me. 'It's probably what's keeping him alive.'

Now, extraordinarily enough, I had never smoked dope with Billy at that stage. Indeed, I'd never smoked it at all. I was a bit nervous of it. However, mindful of the doctor's instructions, I proceeded to play my part in ensuring Billy had plenty of supplies.

Shortly after this incident Billy suddenly remembered that he'd left behind a number of marijuana plants in the garden of his Richmond house, which by then had new owners in residence. So one night after filming we borrowed a van and drove across London to repossess surreptitiously his precious plants. The house was surrounded by a huge security wall, and there are no prizes for guessing who had to climb over it. It wasn't a problem to me though. You can always knock an old dancer over a wall. There was one minor difficulty however. Innocent as I was, I didn't even know what a marijuana plant looked like. Billy had to describe them to me and then hiss directions over the wall as I stumbled around the garden in the dark. Eventually I located the blessed things and hurled them back to him to load into the van. We then drove miles to the country mansion that he had just bought where we replanted them. Billy seemed to spend very little time there, and this was my first visit, but from then on we used to go there occasionally for weekends. The place had a deserted feel to it and we'd sit around, surrounded by all his animals, drinking rum and Coke while Billy played music and sang some of his own material, much of which I don't think has ever been published.

I also used to go down to Brixton with Billy where we'd meet up with wonderful West Indians who were drug dealers, but I thought they were rather splendid. It was all very secretive. We would sit around a great big round table and they'd get all the stuff out and the deals would be struck over endless cans of Coke. Most of them were musicians of one sort or another and they adored Billy, who moved a bit like a black performer and was without doubt far better at what he did than he's ever really been given credit for. I didn't realise until later that he was never really able to sing to his full potential because of his health.

Ultimately, while we were actually staying in a hotel in Shepperton because the filming schedule had been stepped up to such a level that we seemed to be on set about twenty hours a day, I was persuaded to try dope myself. Ironically enough I was not persuaded by Billy but by some of the musicians who were working on the film with us. In fact, for some reason I can't recall, Billy wasn't there at all that day. The rest of us had been filming since dawn and it had been so freezing cold that towards the end of shooting they'd fed us all brandy to warm us up. You could not imagine that happening nowadays, but it was different in the sixties. Everybody else apart from me seemed to smoke dope, and the musicians were obviously living on it, which, in my experience, was fairly typical of musicians. I had once been in digs on tour and was in bed in the middle of the night trying to fight off an attack of bronchitis, when two musicians had rushed into my room, grabbed my Benzedrine inhaler and disappeared with it in order to remove the inside and eat it. I knew musicians did all sorts of things. Unfortunately what none of them did was to warn me to be careful of my first smoke. On top of a load of brandy and having been up since the crack of dawn, I must have smoked the equivalent of about three joints, and they were really heavy duty, although I didn't realise that at the time. I suddenly started to feel very peculiar. I dragged myself off to my bedroom where strange things started to happen to me. My arms seemed to get longer and I couldn't hold on to anything. The furniture kept changing size, and everything had a coloured haze around it. Then I had a massive panic attack. I thought I was dying, my heart was beating so loud and so hard. I remember finishing up face down on the carpet. I felt as if I was going into a kind of limbo, and as if something so difficult to describe I can only think of it as a black monster, was overwhelming me.

I understand it's pretty much unheard of to have such an awful attack of the horrors on perfectly ordinary joints, but, of course, I didn't weigh anything, I had drunk a lot of brandy, goodness knows when I'd last eaten, and I was, as usual, in a state of exhaustion. I know that I very nearly went under. All that held me together really was that I kept saying to myself over and over, 'What a fucking stupid way to die! Your mother is going to be absolutely furious with you!'

Eventually I managed to drag myself into the shower and I turned it to ice cold and sat slumped under it. Sheila O'Neil came to see if I was all right. She got me out of the shower and into bed and stayed with me. I know she was extremely worried about me, but calling a doctor would have meant us all ending up in jail. So I just had to sweat it out. I was too terrified to sleep and I had a curious time-slip experience too. I felt as if I had been in this state for days rather than hours.

In the morning I still felt absolutely awful, but I made my early morning call somehow, although I was shaking from head to foot. To make matters worse this was the day when I had a big song and dance number, 'You Get Dressed Up For a Man', to record. I watched *I've Gotta Horse* again recently and it was extremely weird to see that sequence and remember the condition I was in. But somehow I got through it and, amazingly, it doesn't look as if anything was amiss with me at all.

Billy took it quite lightly. He didn't realise how bad I had been. I don't think anybody did actually, not even Sheila. I felt such a twit. It was like getting drunk for the first time, only worse. It felt like the end of the world. Unfortunately the feeling didn't go away, for a very long time, particularly the time-slip experience. It was about then that I began to develop a kind of fear of being on my own that was to stay with me for many years. The time-slip feeling was quite extreme at first. Whenever Billy left me on my own while he popped out to get cigarettes or papers or something, I used to panic because I would think that he had been gone for hours when it was actually only a few minutes. It put me off smoking dope with a vengeance. I was afraid of the stuff for years. Fortunately Billy was quite happy smoking alone, and never put pressure on me to join him.

We were together for almost a year, and we became very close. So much so that, rather to my surprise, Billy proposed to me. He asked me if I would marry him as we were driving past the Star and Garter Home for Disabled Servicemen on Richmond Hill, right by the entrance to Richmond Park. I was stunned, and I remember that my first thought was, 'Oh my God, what a romantic place to propose!' But I don't remember what I actually said. I know I didn't give him a proper answer. Not ever. I just couldn't. Billy was really precious to me. I adored him, and I really did consider marrying him. But Ginette, and indeed the whole scene in the south of France, had changed everything for me. I wouldn't have dreamed of marrying Billy without telling him about that side of me, and Billy was one of those people I could just never tell. It wasn't that he would have been judgmental. It was just that he was so completely immersed in his own world of music and animals. In many ways he was like a child and I just couldn't have burdened him with my own worries and anxieties. He wouldn't have had a clue how to deal with someone else's troubles. So I just dodged the issue of marriage and for a while things went on much the same between us, with most of our time spent together in Richard's flat in Endell Street and occasional country-mansion weekends.

Then one night when we were actually going to eat together for a change and I was preparing a meal, Billy went out to buy some cigarettes and he never came back. Maybe it was my cooking. I never found out where he went that night or why. He just went.

Of course, at first I was worried. Had he had an accident? I called the police and the hospitals to no avail. Then the next day I called Larry Parnes, his manager. Larry wasn't there, or just didn't want to talk to me about Billy, which would have been perfectly understandable.

But somebody in his office said to me, 'Just leave it Amanda, he's had to go back.'

By which I gleaned that Billy had probably gone back to whoever he had been with when we had got together. I never knew for certain what happened. I had always thought, partly because of the gun although I make jokes about it, that there was this other side to Billy, and that he may have been involved in some kind of really heavy drug scene when he met me. But I knew nothing really. There was, however, something about the way in which that message was related to me that made me do exactly what I was told. I just left it. It was rather as if I had been warned off.

And I never saw, nor heard from, Billy Fury again.

CHAPTER TEN

ﹾﹾ

Work came to my rescue once more. Shortly after Billy left I was offered a season at the Bristol Old Vic, and I jumped at it. I had no desire to remain in Richard's Endell Street flat any longer. I knew it was time for me to move on, but the Bristol job meant that I didn't even have to make a decision. I was required to live in Bristol for several months. The decision was made for me.

At the same time I was asked to become a regular in the *Carry On* films. And that was another decision which was made for me. This time by Alec Graham, my agent, who thought it would be better for me to do some 'proper work' at the Old Vic. His reaction was indicative of the snobbery there was at the time towards the *Carry Ons*. However, aware of how well he knew his stuff I just went along with it. I don't regret not doing more *Carry Ons*, but again it was one of those moments when my whole life could have turned out differently had I taken a different route.

The first production at Bristol was the revue *See You Inside,* which I had already done in the West End. I had also been asked to do two other productions, *Hobson's Choice* and *The Beggar's Opera.* I liked the idea of doing a straight play such as *Hobson's Choice*, but the reality terrified me. It was a huge leap forward, and my nerves went into overdrive. I was nearly thirty years old and had been in the theatre since I was three, but I had never been on a stage in my life when the curtain went up without music. I shall never forget the horror of experiencing a curtain rising to silence for the first time. It was a huge shock. As Alice, I had quite a big role in *Hobson's Choice*, playing opposite Anna Cartaret, Rosemary Leach, the lovely Frank Middlemiss, and Thelma Barlow, who was to go on to become Mavis in *Coronation Street,* in a small part as one of the women who came into the shop. In spite of my terrible nerves I found that I loved doing it.

My mother, of course, loved it even more than me. She made the trek to Bristol to see me perform, as she did almost everywhere I appeared, regardless of her own circumstances. Years later when she presented me with a scrapbook which she had kept for me of high-spots of my career, I saw that she had pasted into it the *Hobson's Choice* programme from Bristol Old Vic, and written underneath it, 'Congratulations darling! Legit at last!' which was copied from the telegram Noël Coward sent to Gertrude Lawrence when she did her first play.

In *The Beggar's Opera* I played Lucy. It was hard for me, but I adored that too. I remember Dorothy Tutin, who had played Lucy straight, coming backstage and asking me, 'How did you get all those laughs?' Well, I don't very often miss an opportunity to get a laugh on stage. It always comes naturally to me.

I have always had two very great heroines in the theatre. One is Gertrude Lawrence and the other Kay Hammond, whom I believe was the best British light-comedy actress ever. Noël Coward wrote *Blithe Spirit* for Kay. I had seen her on stage in the West End, and there was one play called *Rape of the Belt,* which she did at the Piccadilly with Richard Briers in his first West End role. I must have seen it about twenty-seven times because I thought it was so wonderful. I had never seen anybody on stage who could be that funny while appearing to do absolutely nothing.

Kay was married to Sir John Clements, the very distinguished actor manager, who, after she had a chronic stroke in her early fifties that destroyed her as a performer, nursed her for the rest of her life. She was a friend of Dora Bryan's and, when we appeared in *Six of One,* Kay used to be brought to the Adelphi and be given a box there. Apparently she'd taken a shine to me but although I'd been aware of her being in the theatre at the Adelphi I had never met her.

At about the same time Alec, my agent, told me that Val May of the Bristol Old Vic wanted to talk to me about a new play he was putting on. We all had dinner together in Bristol, and it turned out that the play he was talking about was *The Killing of Sister George* with Beryl Reid. This could have been considered quite appropriate in view of my Cannes experiences, but *Sister George* was a brand new play then and neither Alec nor I had a clue what it was about until Val started to explain. Very hesitantly. He wanted me for the role of Charlie, Sister George's young female lover, but it took him some time to explain that Charlie was a lesbian. Indeed, it took him about five minutes alone to actually form the word. Under the circumstances I found this rather amusing. Alec, who was of course one of the few people who knew about my sexual confusion, kicked me very hard under the table and I just about managed to hold myself together

◀ *The Beggars Opera* at Bristol Old Vic in 1965. I played Lucy, Anna Cartaret was Polly and Richard Gale played Macheath.

▼ The play that was nearly the end of me. With Moira Lister, Dennis Price and John Fraser in *Any Wednesday*.

▶ Getting married.
Outside Caxton Hall on
19 June 1967.

(▲ ASSOCIATED PRESS)

▼ A favourite watering
hole. In the Nags
Head pub in the
early seventies.

(▲ TV TIMES/SCOPE FEATURES)

▶ Me and Katie Cupcake – joined at the hip.

▼ Among the veg doing my Eliza Dolittle bit in Covent Garden in the sixties.

▸ With Alfred Marks in *Twelfth Night* at the old Globe Theatre – otherwise known as *The Plastic Bucket*.

◂ Playing Hermia in the BBC's play of the month, *A Midsummer Night's Dream*.

◂ *The Country Wife*, also for the BBC.

▶ Following in Gertie's footsteps. In 1973 playing Lady Kay in the Gershwin musical *Oh Kay!*, written for my heroine Gertrude Lawrence.

▼ With my greatest fan — my mother Connie — at the first night party for *Oh Kay!*. I don't like the way she's looking at her glass. She probably took it home.

(◀ ASSOCIATED NEWSPAPERS LTD)

▲ Me and Humphrey Cushion – a creature with an unfortunate proboscis – my co-star in the children's TV series *Hickory House*.

▼ Just before the dinosaur got me. With screen husband Joss Ackland and that creature in the 1975 Disney film *One of Our Dinosaurs is Missing*.

(◀ AQUARIUS LIBRARY)

▶ With Paul Eddington in Alan Ayckbourn's *Absurd Person Singular*.

▼ With Robert Fleming in *Noises Off* at the Savoy

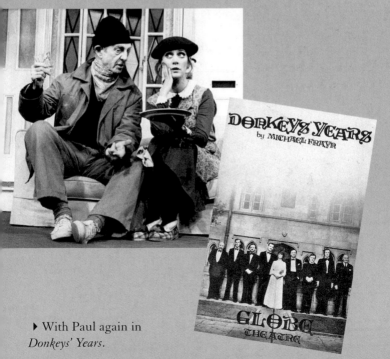

DONKEYS' YEARS
by MICHAEL FRAYN

GLOBE
THEATRE

▶ With Paul again in *Donkeys' Years*.

▲ Another heroine. My first appearance as Alma, with Pat Phoenix as Elsie, in Jim's Caff. Minutes later I had to sack her.

▶ Back in tights again. *Stepping Out* at the Duke of York's Theatre.

– even when Val remarked rather apologetically, 'Charlie is the sort of person who still has toys at home.' I could see my rabbits, Loppy and Lena, sitting up in bed going, 'Ha ha.' As you can imagine, I was quite intrigued by the prospect of playing Charlie. But my agent counselled heavily against it, on the grounds that he thought the role was too camp!

However, it was while *Sister George* was still under discussion that I got a telephone call just before curtain-up one evening which changed everything. The caller was Kay Hammond. Even though I had never spoken to her before I recognised her voice at once. It was very distinctive. Kay Hammond calling *me* at the Bristol Old Vic? It was unbelievable.

'Amanda, darling. They're putting on a play in the West End called *A Public Mischief*, and there's a part in it which I would once have played, and I think you should play it.'

This was like a summons from God. Nobody said 'no' to Kay Hammond. Her husband Sir John Clements was one of the play's backers, and the couple's influence was such that because they thought I should have the role, I was promptly offered it – without even an audition. I forgot all about *Sister George* and Charlie (the role was ultimately played by Eileen Atkins, to whom it certainly seemed to do no harm as she went on to have a wonderful career). Instead I buried myself in the script for *A Public Mischief*, a new comedy written by Kenneth Horne, and at the end of the season at the Old Vic went straight back to London to go into rehearsals.

It was then that my trouble really started. I was playing the lead in *A Public Mischief* opposite George Cole. I still had very little proper acting experience, and there was the small problem of my reading difficulties.

I had never had to deal with anything like as many words before. The prospect overwhelmed me. To make everything just perfect, I didn't even have anywhere to live either.

Richard was coming home from America and, quite understandably, had sent word to Bristol that he wanted me out of his flat. I didn't blame him. Any semblance of a relationship between us was long over. Besides, if I didn't return to Endell Street I realised I would probably be able to avoid forever the prospect of a confrontation with Richard over the death of his birds and the destruction of his precious chair – all of which still rather haunted me.

My mother came to the rescue. She usually managed to be around when I needed her, constantly flitting to and fro from Manchester to London or wherever I was working. She found me a flat in my beloved Covent Garden by following a group of building workers. She had to fight to acquire it, but that was something she was rather good at. She spotted a group of workmen going into a building in Bow Street, decided with her own particular logic that it meant they must be working on a flat, discovered that they were – two in the same property in fact – and found out the name of the letting agency. However, they didn't want me, or any other lone woman, as a tenant. This was during an era when landlords in the area around Soho were reluctant to rent to women because they feared that they might be working as prostitutes. But Mummy wore them down, as she was inclined to wear down almost everyone, with an avalanche of letters, phone calls and personal visits. 'My daughter is in *Carry On Cleo*, my daughter is in this, my daughter has done that.' She even took in to them every naked photograph she could find of me in *Cleo*, which probably proved their point actually. Ultimately the agency, Shaws, rang me up. 'We are so exhausted with your mother's persistence that we would really like you to have Bow Street,' I was told.

However, the flat was not yet ready and during rehearsals my mother booked us both into the Eros Hotel in Shaftesbury Avenue. So, there I was, homeless, confused about my sexuality, unable to read properly, and of course, the first thing I had to do was the read-through. I stumbled through making every mistake possible, and I don't think it looked as if I was any kind of actor. I just couldn't, couldn't, couldn't read it.

The director, Harold French, had naturally been anxious to hear the play come alive at the read-through at the St Martin's Theatre, and, adding another dimension to my terror, Sir John Clements and Kay Hammond were also there. Harold knew nothing about me, and, based on my performance at that read-through, I could not blame him for murmuring to Kay, 'Has she ever done anything, dear?' But I overheard him quite clearly and my despair was total. I just wanted to hide away somewhere. Instead I had to be taken to lunch at Sheekey's, the very smart theatre-land fish restaurant. Kay came too and I already felt that I had let her down. I was absolutely numb with the effort of having spent the morning trying to read this play. It was something I hadn't had to do before. Ninety per cent of *The Beggar's Opera* is singing and in revue the scenes are so short and quick that you don't have to do a great deal of long-term learning of lines. I hadn't found *Hobson's Choice* as difficult as I had originally feared, either, because the bulk of the dialogue between the two sisters is in short one-liners and there are no speeches worth mentioning. I treated the scenes a bit like revue sketches and learned them that way. *A Public Mischief* was very different. It was a wordy play with speeches, with different tones, different qualities, comedy, crying, a bit of everything. And I was playing the lead. At that moment I was quite convinced that I was not going to be able to do it. When Harold announced we would have another read-though that afternoon, I thought I would die. It is just

about unheard of in the theatre to have a second read-through –
normally you go right on to the plotting. I knew it was entirely because
of me and I was mortified.

Back in the theatre, Harold said, 'Right, can we all concentrate this
time?'

I realised that he thought I hadn't been. Nothing could have been
further from the truth. Fear kicked in with a vengeance then and would
you believe that I was even worse at the second attempt?

I certainly don't think Harold French could believe it.

By the time I returned to my mother at the Eros Hotel I was almost
rigid with fear. I had this terrible ringing sensation in my head and I felt
as if all my nerve ends had gathered in my nose.

The rehearsals were a nightmare. I just couldn't get to grips with the
play at all. Halfway through the second week, with two and a half
weeks to the opening night, I started to get really ill. I didn't know what
was going on, whether or not I'd been to a costume fitting, if I'd been to
sleep, if I'd had a meal.

My mother kept saying, as she would, 'You can do it! You can do it!
Come on! Come on! Just sit and work.'

I couldn't. I didn't know where to begin.

Every so often Kay Hammond would come to rehearsals and I
would be even worse. I will always regret that I was in that state when
I had a chance to spend time with her and get to know her. George
Cole barely spoke to me for which I forgive him entirely. He must have
been horrified. He pretended that I didn't exist, which was fair
enough, when you were expected to work with someone as bad as I
was. The person who was nicest to me was the actor Robin Hunter,
Harold French's godson, who was also in the play. Robin was

extremely charming and very good looking in those days, and his support meant a lot. I felt that all the other actors were laughing at me, but Robin sent me up gently and laughed with me. That was about the only time I did laugh, because the rest of it was a total disaster. I was missing entrances. I was freezing up. I think they'd kept me on originally because they didn't think anyone could be quite that bad and reckoned I was bound to improve. Then by the time they began to fear that maybe I was never going to improve we were too close to opening for them to get rid of me.

The crisis came about five days before we were due to open in Newcastle where the pre West End run was to begin. Harold French suddenly said, 'You've got a very common voice, dear. Get rid of it before we open.'

In the context of the time he was absolutely right. I only had a slight northern accent – which I did get rid of but re-acquired a bit during *Coronation Street* I think – but at that time West End actors really didn't talk that way. This was the era of, 'Diddy, Diddy, there's been a frightful iccident. Hippy birthday, Diddy.' Actors tried to put on an 'air of seedy grandeur', to quote Noël Coward. They wore their smartest clothes to rehearsals, which led to many impecunious thespians trimming their frayed shirt cuffs and struggling for hours to try to remove the shine of well-ironed lapels and pockets. I have always thought that there was nothing worse than 'theatre grand', and I never had any part of that. Hence the way I spoke. I hadn't even been to acting school.

However, to be told such a thing so bluntly by my director was the final blow. I went totally to pieces and collapsed in a sobbing heap.

My mother could do nothing to help. In a panic she called Alec and asked him to come over immediately. She should probably have called a doctor, but that might well have meant me being ordered out of the show for medical reasons, so for Mummy that would have been absolutely the last resort.

Alec came straight away, and he was brilliant.

'It's no good,' I wailed, 'I just can't go on. There is no way I can do it. I just can't.'

'OK. But why? Is it because you can't learn it? Is it because of something else? Try and work out exactly what is wrong.'

Most agents I think would have given up on me at that stage, but Alec didn't. He was so good in persisting until he reached the core of the problem. 'What aspect of it is it that you can't face?' he asked. 'What is it?'

'I'm not sure,' I replied at first. Then I gave him, and myself, the key to it.

'I keep thinking I know the play,' I said. 'But I don't.'

In a way that was lesson one for a dyslexic. Unlike other people I couldn't learn from the written page without saying the words aloud again and again until they were stamped indelibly into my brain. The fear of forgetting is so much worse for a dyslexic to whom the written word is the deadliest of enemies, that I had absolutely no hope whatsoever of acting. I wasn't linking the words with attitude or emotion, they were just black squiggles on the page.

Alec sat with me and helped me to learn. He promised me that if it didn't work and if I felt the same in the morning, he would hand in my notice if that was what I wanted.

We stayed up all night. We went through it and through it and through it. He made me keep on and on saying the lines out loud. Then the next morning, he and my mother persuaded me to give it one more go. And so with my common voice and all my other handicaps, I just gritted my teeth and got on with it. It was one of those moments in life which could have gone either way. I had to put all the effort in the world into something impossible, or just give up. I have never been a quitter. But *A Public Mischief* was a very close call.

However, although I was far from as I should have been at that stage of rehearsals, I did get through that day's run-through much better than before. Then, when I got back to the dreaded Eros Hotel, Alec was there once more. 'You're doing it again,' he said.

So we worked all night, reciting every page three times. If I made one mistake I'd go back to the start and do it again. We did this for three nights, and by the time we travelled to Newcastle on the day before we opened, I had finally got it.

The opening night was a miracle. Something happened that was to become a pattern for me throughout my career, although with *A Public Mischief* the contrast was far greater than it was ever to be again, thank God. I had been a total disaster throughout rehearsals. On opening night I was fine. In fact, though I say it myself, I was really rather good.

Eventually even Harold French decided that maybe I wasn't all that bad after all. So I used to sit in the bar of the Turks Head, a big hotel where we were staying in the middle of Newcastle, with Harold telling me wonderful stories about my heroine Gertrude Lawrence, whom he had played opposite in *Oh, Kay!*, the musical created specially for her by P. G. Wodehouse and Guy Bolton who wrote the script, and George and Ira Gershwin who wrote the music and lyrics. Meanwhile, the producer, Martin Landau, had taken a shine to me as well and kept repeating, 'You're going to be a star, you're going to be my next big star.'

But on the final day in Newcastle before we were to move on to our next venue, travelling via London, we all most unwisely stayed up the entire night drinking and talking in the bar of the Turks Head. I really did absolutely nothing to help myself during that period of my life. At some stage Martin suddenly turned to me to announce, 'I want you tomorrow morning on a train call. I will have the press meet you at the other end as my new leading lady. We will take the papers by storm.'

Robin Hunter, with whom I had by now become great friends, and I found all this highly amusing. I was far too much of a mess ever to be a star. I was invariably covered in bits of glue, stick-on nails not stuck on properly, eyelashes falling off, a hairpiece called Esmeralda that kept going missing, and I always carried a plastic bag containing bits of food because I never seemed to have time to eat properly.

The following morning, possibly in anticipation of my promised launch into mega-stardom, I exceeded even my own standards of messiness. Having been up all night I decided that I would at least try to have breakfast like people in smart hotels do and not like a mixed-up chorus girl intent on starving herself to death.

I ordered – and I remember it distinctly – scrambled egg and bacon, which is always my favourite, honey, toast, cornflakes, milk and tea, made with proper tea leaves, not bags. All this was on a tray on the bed when Robin called me from his room. I leaned over to answer the phone and the tray slipped off the bed tipping its entire contents into my handbag. The whole bloody lot fell straight in. Dancers always have big handbags, and mine was no exception. I spent the next twenty minutes on the floor trying to salvage cheque books, money, make-up, and everything else.

Robin came down to look and naturally thought it was the funniest thing ever. I couldn't come close to cleaning it up. Eventually I had to set off for the railway station with my bag still full of this awful mess. I was sharing a cab with Robin and his godfather and they were tearing up bar bills that they hadn't paid and throwing them out of the window.

As I boarded the train back to London for my big press call, clutching a bag full of breakfast, I thought that things couldn't disintegrate much more. But they did.

The journey turned into about the most stupid of my life. The train left at 7.30 a.m., never my best time even if I have had some sleep the night before. That's the only excuse I can come up with for our behaviour.

Firstly, two rather butch ladies came aboard with us and one of them went straight to the buffet counter and asked, 'Could I have a tongue sandwich for my friend?' We all descended into giggling stupidity. This culminated in the purchase of a sausage, two scotch eggs and a cherry, which, with the help of a couple of cocktail sticks, we fashioned into a fair representation of male genitalia, promptly christened Fred and proclaimed the company mascot.

I remember Harry Bowers, our lovely company manager who was camp personified, flashed the thing through the window at some poor army cadet standing on the platform at Crewe Station. The little cadet saluted it. Naturally we all thought that was hilarious and proceeded to wreck ourselves by buying copious quantities of British Rail red wine. At some stage, somebody poured a bottle of red wine over me. Somebody else ran to the kitchen and found a tub of salt which they then threw all over me. It was supposed to remove the red wine stain. It didn't. It just added to the mess. So I arrived at Euston Station – a bedraggled creature covered in red wine and salt, carrying a bagful of breakfast, being propped up by Robin and all the others – to be greeted by Martin Landau and all the press. So much for his glam new leading lady. Martin was absolutely furious and I was deeply ashamed.

Photographs were duly taken of me desperately trying not to look too dishevelled while keeping the wine stains off camera. Strangely enough the pictures didn't turn out too badly.

We toured with *A Public Mischief* for six weeks before going into the West End, by which time I had almost started to enjoy it and to relax a little. It was in Blackpool that what was probably the inevitable happened. I had quite seriously fallen for Robin and in the Clifton Hotel, Blackpool, having drunk a fair amount and, despite him being married, we went to bed together for the first time.

The next day was Cup Final day, and we went to a pub to watch the game. I didn't drink any more because I never have a drink before going on stage and we had a show to do that night, but I still felt pretty peculiar from the various excesses of the night before. I had never drunk as much as we were putting away on this tour, not even in the south of France. I was trying to play with the big boys, and I had been to bed with somebody again – which always came as an emotional shock to me. I felt awful. I went on that night and I suddenly had an extraordinary experience. It sounds so stupid, but every time Robin came on stage I started to heave. I didn't know then, but it was the start of big trouble for me. I felt as if I couldn't speak. I was fine until Robin came on, then I started to have this reaction. I got in such a state that I passed out on stage, collapsing in a heap behind the sofa. Robin, ever the pro, just stepped over me and went on ad libbing with George Cole. George froze. He'd never seen anybody fall over on stage before. They dropped the curtains, picked me up, shook me, sat me down, and on I went. In fact I have hardly even been off during my entire career, which, considering all the things that have happened to me, is pretty amazing.

Later they called a doctor who said I had a kidney infection. This marked the beginning of a period of illness which was to put a real blight on my life for many years. Having actually started to heave on stage, the tendency I already had to be sick before performing stepped up to a whole new level. It became a compulsion. I would not let myself go on stage with any food inside me. If I thought there was, I would make myself sick – sometimes six, seven, or even eight, times a day. I never ate breakfast because I always felt too ill in the mornings. The only thing I ate much of was stale bread with salt on it. Sometimes I could eat a peach or something like that, but that was it. Even bacon sandwiches held scant appeal. All the time Robin was there, and his solution was, 'Come on, my old fruit, we'll go and have a drink somewhere.'

In his defence I must say that he had no idea that there was anything wrong with me. He had no idea of what I was doing. Bulimics are famously secretive. I'd get ready before a show, put on my make-up, and then go straight to the lavatory. I was in danger of ripping my voice to shreds. I knew that. But it didn't stop me. Nothing could. I was obsessed with emptying my stomach before I went on. I told nobody. As far as the management and the rest of the cast went, everything was fine. In fact, I seemed to be doing rather well. I was getting good reviews everywhere and the only indication that there might be anything at all amiss had been the night when I had passed out in Blackpool. However, I appeared to have made a swift recovery and there were no further incidents during performances.

Meanwhile, as I was busily destroying myself, my agent was having a dreadful row with George Cole's agent over which of us should have the number one dressing room at the St Martin's Lane Theatre. In view of only having just conquered my fears and short-comings to make it on stage at all, and all too aware of the horrors of pre-performance sickness, I did not feel able to become involved in this. And I can honestly say I have never been very interested in which dressing room I have. However, I did end up with the number one which led to the producer, Martin Landau, being confronted with me yet again in rather unfortunate circumstances.

Harry Bowers had a budgerigar called Sod, so named, Harry liked to explain, 'Because when he makes a noise in the morning we all throw cornflakes at him and yell "Sod!"' So when my name was put on the door of the number one dressing room the whole of the stage management went out and bought huge quantities of cornflakes which they came and hurled at me while yelling, 'Sod!'

Then, before I could do anything about the mess, Martin Landau appeared. Having previously met his new leading lady off a train looking the way no producer ever wants his leading lady to look, he now found her and his number one dressing room knee-deep in cornflakes.

I couldn't do anything right. Except perform, ironically enough. As always I became someone else on stage. The first night at the St Martin's Lane Theatre was a bit of a personal triumph. I got great notices including one that described me as being second only to Maggie Smith as a comedy actress. There's probably been a steward's enquiry on that since then, and I may well have been placed last, but I shall always treasure that notice, particularly under the circumstances.

Off-stage I was a total disaster area. I was anorexic, bulimic, generally neurotic, and frightened. I needed a minder, I needed my mother – but she'd disappeared, the way she was inclined to. I knew she'd be back, of course. She never stayed away for long. But I needed her right then. What I didn't need was Robin, the new man in my life, to say, 'I think if we have a good drink, you'll be fine.' That was not what I needed. I needed some sort of structure in my life. I needed a home. And I needed somebody there to look after me, to sort me out.

CHAPTER ELEVEN

❧

S omehow, I kept going throughout the West End run of *A Public Mischief* but as it ended I completely cracked up. The breakdown that had been threatening for months, if not years, took me by the throat and shook me rigid.

By this time, thanks to my mother, I had finally moved into my little third-floor flat in Bow Street. Mummy had furnished it, moved over all the things I already had in Endell Street, and made it really beautiful – albeit at the same time contriving to run me up a £3,000 overdraft, more than enough to buy a house at the time. But that was my mother. As far as she was concerned only the finest antique furniture would do for my new home, so she had completely ignored the budget I had left for her and spent a great deal of money on my behalf that I didn't actually have.

However, while lamps from Liberty illuminated every corner, it transpired that she had omitted to buy a number of more practical items. I had absolutely no crockery or cutlery, for a start. But there really was no way I could let that overdraft get any bigger. Mummy was, of course, undaunted and swiftly returned to familiar ways. Unbeknownst to me she began to eat regularly at Verbanella's restaurant and suddenly I miraculously acquired an entire set of their knives, forks, plates, cups and saucers.

One way and another, Bow Street was truly beautiful but it was also empty. Robin was a married man with a family. I had known that from the start but on tour with *A Public Mischief* I'd half-forgotten it. That, as all actors know, is frequently how things are. Indeed, there is a dreadfully cynical show-business expression that sums it up quite neatly, 'It doesn't count on tour or location.' Back in London, however, everything was different. Robin returned to live with his wife and having at last finished my flat my mother had gone home to immerse herself in her Disley hairdressing business.

A few days after *A Public Mischief* came off in the West End, I had to do a television show with Lance Percival. I felt nervous before going on, and went through my usual routine of being sick several times. I had a couple of sketches to do, which I got through without incident, even though I had this strange buzzing sensation in my nose and just felt generally unwell.

Back at Bow Street I thought I had better eat something so I made a bacon sandwich, my favourite, and a cup of tea. Then suddenly the buzzing sensation travelled right through my body. It was as if I were paralysed down the whole of my left side. I remember being filled with utter terror. I couldn't breathe. I thought I was dying. I slumped to the floor, my legs no longer able to support me. I crawled towards the window for air but couldn't get that far. I lay on the floor all night, curled up in a ball. I couldn't stand, couldn't breathe, couldn't see properly. I just lay there, frozen.

At about seven o'clock in the morning I managed to crawl to the telephone and call Robin. I couldn't think of anyone else who was near enough. He came straight over, but apart from lifting me into bed he couldn't really help. He phoned Alec, my agent, in Brighton and between them they decided that the best thing was to get me down there straight away. When we got there I remember Robin trying to make me walk up and down the beach before he took me to Alec's house.

Alec didn't know what to do with me either. I stayed with him for about a week during which he tried to sort me out by talking to me, and did his best to ensure that I ate and slept properly. Then to my horror, while I was in his home desperately struggling to regain my faculties, I was invited to play the lead in the American comedy *Any Wednesday*. The play was a really big deal at the time because its New York star Sandy Dennis had won the Tony award for Best Actress on Broadway. Apparently there was a team of thirteen or so producers who had to approve the choice of lead, and they'd all approved me. Mind you, they mightn't have wanted me if they could have seen the state I was in. I went on my knees to Alec, sobbing and begging him to say no.

To this day I have no idea how I was persuaded to let him say yes. But he did. So I had cope with my breakdown and the prospect of another daunting West End lead.

When I returned to London, I began to see more clearly what a lot of my problem was. I had never ever lived on my own and I think that is what triggered off my breakdown. If I hadn't been in digs with the chorus girls and boys I had always been sharing with someone. I think I would have been fine if I'd been able to eat and sleep normally, if I'd had any sort of normal family around, but I suppose my bizarre child-hood and the fast track I had taken into show business had caught up with me. As I lay alone in my bed in Bow Street, I used to see big hoops of light inside my head, cracking and whirling and keeping me awake.

I felt that the bed was levitating and whizzing around the room. In the end I was afraid even to try to sleep. I still wasn't eating and I felt sick all the time. The only thing I could get down was rice with egg and lots of salt and pepper. I more or less lived on that. I developed a far too intimate relationship with death. Every day, all day, I felt as if I was going to die. I would walk around London and be overwhelmed with the awful feeling that everybody else was fast asleep, and I was the only one awake. I wanted to scream at the top of my voice, 'Don't you realise you're all going to die!' Can you imagine? It was just lunatic. It was a terrible preoccupation. All I could think about was death. I kept telling myself it would go away, but it didn't do so completely for years.

Robin visited regularly, but I think he was bewildered by me. My doctor gave me drugs for the sickness and sleeping pills. They didn't touch me. I had built up far too many defences against sleep. If I slept I dreamed about death, and the dreams were much worse than my waking thoughts. Other than that he didn't really know what to do.

Mental problems are sometimes more difficult to treat than physical ones, and also, you can cover them up. Rehearsals began for *Any Wednesday,* and nobody I was working with had a clue about what I was going through. The play was a four-hander starring Dennis Price, Moira Lister, John Fraser and me. I shouldn't have been working at all, of course, and I was having my usual dyslexic problems. However, right from the start, my own difficulties and neuroses were somewhat overshadowed by all that went on around me.

On the first day we were all invited to a small cocktail party, which was quite the thing to do in those days. It was supposed to provide a chance for cast and management to meet and get to know each other. We duly assembled in producer Michael White's offices and I remember sitting on a very low sofa with Moira. Dennis Price, who went everywhere with a green bag that made bottle-sounding rattling noises, was on the other side of the room with his friend and prompt, Marcus.

We were making small talk, and Michael White asked what everybody did in their spare time.

I kept very quiet about what I did in my spare time because I was having a nervous breakdown and it didn't seem the sort of thing I should tell the management. Moira went on about how she liked to entertain. Then Dennis said, 'We do a lot of shooting in our spare time. Actually one of our hobbies is that Marcus shoots cigarettes out of my ears.'

I noticed then that he had a bloody great piece of sticking plaster on one ear so I nudged Moira, half-pointed at it, and whispered, 'Missed.'

Now Dennis was rather grand. He was a distinguished leading man, primarily in film, and had just begun to play Jeeves in the very popular sixties TV production of *The World of Wooster*. The thought of him walking round with a green bag of bottles clanking together and a special friend who shot holes in his ears was pretty unnerving.

I don't think Dennis had wanted to come into *Any Wednesday*. We discovered later that he usually had his passport in his pocket in case he couldn't cope with doing the play. Not very reassuring for the rest of us. I understand he had tax problems and was overworking terribly at an age when work starts to get harder rather than easier. You don't trust your memory so much as you get older, either, so he absolutely refused to put his script down during rehearsal. That was quite comforting for me because for once I didn't feel that I was the worst and most hesitant member of the cast.

Marcus – a big man who had once done a snake act in Soho – was Dennis's constant companion and so-called helpmate. At some stage Dennis told us that another of Marcus's habits was to hypnotise him. By then we other cast members were past being surprised.

'Oh yes,' we murmured politely.

'As a matter of fact he often sits in the box and hypnotises me while I'm on stage,' Dennis continued.

When you are in the throes of having a nervous breakdown, the prospect of your leading man being in a state of hypnosis does not exactly fill you with confidence. But I soldiered on.

On the eve of our opening there were two big problems with Dennis. He still refused to put his script down and he was still reading his part in beautifully modulated English which, as he was playing an American tycoon, was rather unfortunate. When they finally prised the script from his hands, he was told that he had to put on an American accent.

But on the opening night he somehow fluffed it. Early on in the play he had to say the line, '*Time* magazine says I have the ruthlessness of an eagle.' It came out, '*Time* magazine says I have the ruthlessness of Anna Neagle.'

'This does not bode well,' I thought. And it did turn out to be just the tip of the iceberg. On more than one occasion he came on stage and started doing the last act when he should have been doing the first. Then there was the Marcus factor. He would stare at Dennis from the box, and eventually Dennis would walk forward and yell, 'Zammadah!' which was his programmed response when Marcus hypnotised him. We were warned this would happen at precisely 8.20 p.m. so would be anxiously anticipating the moment. It took enormous control to carry on working properly.

Can you believe it? They were both absolutely serious too. There I was slowly going out of my mind, being sick all the time, and when I went on stage this was happening. It was a bloody nightmare. 'Who wants to be a leading lady in the West End?' I thought. To make matters worse I had my own first-night disaster, which caused me to miss two performances at the beginning of the run, the only time I have ever been off during my entire career. It was not because of my mental problems at all. It was actually due to being dropped from a great height. There was a schmaltzy scene at the end of the play where I was given a bunch of balloons. The director had the idea that because I was light and could dance it would be a wonderful idea for me to be lifted up above the stage with them. The plan was that I would go up about six feet as the curtain came down and then be lowered to the stage for the curtain call.

However, this was before safety regulations were as stringent as they are today and I was just hanging with one hand from a pulley concealed in the balloons. On the first night the stagehand who was supposed to be looking after the pulley went missing, to the pub probably. So somebody else rushed along at the last moment. They yanked on the pulley so hard that I shot way up into the air, where I was left hanging and sweating while the others came on to take their calls.

John Fraser screamed for me to be let down so the stagehand promptly dropped me with a wallop. Then as I started to take my hand out of the balloons – and there were about twenty of them – they had wrapped themselves round my wrist and I couldn't untangle them. At which point the stagehand decided to take me up again. I thought if I let go now my hand will be severed from my arm so I just hung on grimly. By the time he eventually dropped me, with another bang, I was in quite a bad way. My arm felt as if it had been pulled out of its socket, I'd hurt my back and strained my groin. I was determined not to give in to my injuries, despite how much I hadn't wanted to do the play in the first place. But the next morning they called a doctor who said, 'You can go on if you can walk across the room.'

Well, I couldn't. I really couldn't. So I was off.

I remember seeing the evening paper hoardings outside Bow Street announcing, 'West End star off.' 'Who's that?' I wondered. It didn't occur to me that it could be me. I wasn't aware that I was a West End star. I didn't think of myself like that at all. And, quite frankly, amid the madness of *Any Wednesday,* who would? I was just a deranged chorus girl having a nervous breakdown while surrounded by loonies.

Amazingly enough my notices were not as bad as may have been expected – indeed, although they were mixed, some of them were excellent – but the theatre did not provide its usual solace. There was no respite on stage from the madness going on inside my head. I could have had all my panic attacks on stage, I didn't need to go home.

Moira Lister became a great friend and is someone for whom I have the utmost professional admiration. She did, however, have a tendency to lose control over her laughter quite easily. She once told me that she'd been having problems in South Africa and went to a Belgian hypnotist, who turned out to be a one-legged ex-footballer – but that's probably another story. She asked him to hypnotise her so that she would enjoy her work and everything about it from then on. He did it so effectively that she had been unable to stop laughing on stage, so she'd had to go back to him the next day and he'd hypnotised her all over again this time saying, 'Don't enjoy your work quite so much. It is not quite so hysterical.'

But the legacy of this lived on. She has always had a smashing sense of humour, and every so often she was reduced to hysteria. Mind you, nobody in *Any Wednesday* could be blamed for that.

We had to play a word-association game on stage that involved all four of us responding to whatever word was thrown at us. At the end of it Dennis, whose character I was supposed to be having an affair with, had to say 'sex' as a response. This was crucial to the plot, because it was done in such a way that it made it clear he was still sleeping with his wife. Unfortunately Dennis used to say 'sex' on every line throughout the game which totally destroyed the object of it.

After a while he started filming a series of *The World of Wooster* at the same time as doing *Any Wednesday.* So he was working all day and all night and, on his one night off, I learned to my horror, did a shift for The Samaritans. I thought, 'God Almighty, if you were a suicide case phoning The Samaritans and you got somebody shouting "Zammadah!" down the line at you – well, you'd just do it wouldn't you?'

Meanwhile, the director, Frank Dunlop, a man very much at the top of his profession, was pretty hard on me. He and the producers knew how inexperienced I was so I think this was unfair. They shouldn't have hired me if they had different expectations. One night he walked past me in the wings and he pushed something in my face. Chopped onions. My eyes started to stream at once. I was wearing heavy mascara which ran, and practically blinded me. I don't even recall doing the first act. It really was terrific. We had Dennis yelling, 'Zammadah!' We had Moira with her perfectly understandable tendency towards hysteria under the circumstances. And now the director had stuck onions in my eyes. Just great.

It had been my dream to play leads in the West End, home of my heroes Gertrude Lawrence, Kay Hammond, and Noël Coward, for as long as I could remember. This was not quite how I had imagined it.

Extraordinarily, *Any Wednesday* ran for a year at the Apollo and then transferred, with Dennis still in it. The only way I can explain that is to say that audiences do trust actors on stage. They've paid good money to come to the theatre and take it for granted that what they see is what they are supposed to see. They don't realise that most of the time they're watching a load of damaged, fragile, ego-ridden idiots who don't have a clue. Sometimes they're not doing the right scene. Sometimes they're not even doing the right play.

One way and another *Any Wednesday* did little to help me in my struggle to keep my sanity and my health. I became more and more ill. Eventually my doctor sent me to see a specialist called Dr Beard. I walked in past a poster for something called *The Manic Depressive Society Revue,* and it occurred to me that I would have been rather better suited to that than a major West End play right then. When I got to the waiting room, two strange young men came in and started touching me and grunting at me. For a moment, I wondered what sort of place I had been sent to. It was, of course, a heavy-duty psychiatric ward where most people were in-patients. Eventually I was called in to see the doctor, a tall man whose face had been kicked in by a horse, which I somehow found quite comforting. He fired all sorts of questions at me. 'Age?' 'Marital status?' 'Sexual preference?' Naturally when he got to that last one I felt like screaming.

After a while he said, 'I would like you to come here as an in-patient for a while.'

I was horrified.

'I can't,' I replied quickly. 'I'm the lead in a West End play. I can't go into hospital.'

'All right, Middlesex Hospital, out-patients department, tomorrow morning. Nine thirty. There's a clinic. Do you want to see a man or a woman?'

'A woman,' I replied, for no particular reason, and I was duly referred to a psychiatric social worker called Miss Fowles to whom I owe a great deal. She kept me going, after a fashion at any rate, and I saw her regularly for four years. I continued this dreadful experience of living with death all the time. I continued to have these terrible panic attacks. The only thing I can say to anybody who suffers from them is that you do come through them, and you just have to keep telling yourself that you will. But at the beginning in particular, that is very hard to believe. With Miss Fowles's help, I at least began to unravel the cause of my problems. I had utterly dismissed the traumas of my childhood, pretending that they didn't affect me. I had also pretended that my confusion about my sexuality didn't affect me, and that neither did my dyslexia, anorexia and bulimia. I learned to cope a little better when I accepted that all these things had affected me deeply.

My mother was very worried about me, and turned up occasionally. She promised all the time that she would come to live with me in London but she kept going back to Manchester, which remained home for her and Caroline and where she still had her hairdressing business. Things with Robin were much the same. He was concerned, but he was also concerned about what was going to happen to his marriage and his two children. All my life I seem to have had people worrying about me from a distance, unable to be with me.

Mummy attempted to solve the problem by hiring Frank, a very camp man she'd met, as my cleaner and general helpmate. He would arrive every morning and make me a cup of milky white coffee with sugar. It wasn't something I usually drank but as I was still eating virtually nothing I was aware that it was at least giving me some sustenance. He'd encourage me to nibble a biscuit while he sat on the edge of my bed and told me about himself. Frank did offer a certain companionship, but unfortunately he had a tendency to start the day by describing his bowel movements that morning, which were always horrendous, in the most gross detail. He would also tell me repeatedly about how he had been buried alive with a lot of dead men during the War. 'Some of my best friends were there, you could see parts of them.'

As I was suffering from this death phobia thing it is possible my mother had made a pretty unwise choice to cheer and cherish her daughter. But at least Frank was with me, I suppose.

I was also living through the legacy of my experiences in the south of France. The lovely Ian was a frequent visitor to Bow Street, but his presence was not the lift it might have been because he too was in a distressed state and was going through a particularly tricky time with

Rudi, whom he was pursuing all over the place. He used to lean out of the sitting-room window of my flat, which was just opposite the stage door of the Royal Opera House, and when Rudi arrived he would scream abuse at him across Floral Street. This would be roundly and colourfully returned by the Russian genius. I met Rudi quite a few times with Ian, and witnessed more than one of the awful fights they specialised in.

Rudi used to be known as 'The Squirrel', and one of the things that Kay did for Ian at that time was to keep buying all sorts of gifts, a tea towel, a charm bracelet, anything with a squirrel on it, for him to present to Rudi. Sometimes, when relations were particularly bad, Ian would just leave them at the stage door and then come across to my flat.

On one occasion it was Rudi's birthday and Kay baked him a huge chocolate cake with a great squirrel on top and the message, 'To Rudi, Happy Birthday, love Ian,' iced on it. Rudi had just begun partnering Margot Fonteyn and was appearing with her at the Bath Festival, so Ian took off on the train for Bath clutching this cake, determined to give it to Rudi, whether he liked it or not. Unfortunately he picked the night that Fonteyn's husband, the Panamanian political activist Roberto de Arias, was shot in South America.

Now that, somehow, was Ian. It was typical timing. But it wasn't going to stop him. He duly stormed into Rudi's dressing room and presented him with this cake, even though Rudi had made it quite clear that he wasn't interested. Ian was being the petulant queen. Rudi responded as usual by being the temperamental artist and hurled the huge chocolate cake at him. It went all over the dressing room and all over Ian who left in tears with Rudi screaming after him, 'No more squirrels.'

This of course was duly related to me in Bow Street when a tearful Ian returned there in the early hours. The dramas of Ian and Rudi were all I needed in the state I was in.

It was quite extraordinary how many people at that time seemed to bring their troubles to me. Most of my friends had no idea at all just how bad a state I was in. I was programmed to get on with things, somehow, and that was what I did, particularly when it came to my work, which, whatever the difficulites, was always sacrosanct

CHAPTER TWELVE

⟡

A fter *Any Wednesday* ended in 1965 I did a lot more TV work and continued to struggle along with regular visits from Robin who was still living with his wife, and from my mother who came and went between Manchester and my Covent Garden flat.

Then one day everything changed. Up the stairs came Robin with his suitcase, much to my mother's horror. He'd arrived. He'd left his wife.

I don't remember ever being asked if I wanted him to move in. I think that he just took it for granted.

In many ways he did help me with my mental problems, although his methods were unorthodox! There was a pub game at the time called Shut the Box, which was a bit like a cross between checkers and shove ha'penny. Whenever I had a panic attack, Robin would say, 'Right. Shut the Box,' and drag me across the road to the pub where he'd make me play while he poured a couple of gin and tonics down me. Another thing he did was to make me run on the spot, which I can in fact recommend as a cure for panic attacks. He would also occasionally clout me and yell, 'Stop it!' Actually that is also quite good. But I was too ill for any of that to cure me properly. I began to see a succession of Harley Street specialists who all attempted to sort me out, including one doctor who considerably increased my tendency to panic attacks by telling me that I was the nearest thing he had ever seen to a hermaphrodite.

But at least I had somebody to share my home with. Robin and I were extremely good friends. He was also very funny, which gets my highest marking on the Richter scale of what is desirable in a partner. We communicated well together. We were a very good team. But Robin wasn't always a good influence and I found myself in a life dominated by the pub and the racetrack.

Robin came from an amazing theatrical family to whom I was duly introduced. His father was Ian Hunter who played Richard the Lionheart in the 1938 Errol Flynn blockbuster *The Adventures of Robin Hood*. The Hunters had lived half their lives in Hollywood, but when the Second World War started, Ian had done the right thing, like the English gentleman he was, and returned to Blighty to join the Navy. When I met Robin, his parents lived in rather grand style in Jermyn Street, St James's, surrounded by well-known and fascinating people, including some of the greatest show-business stars of the era, which to me was magic.

But Robin's mother, Cash, did not like me. I simply was not good enough for her son. Neither, however, did my mother like Robin. It was the clash of the Titans. After all, my mother had still been in the habit of sharing my bed when she came to Bow Street and I only had one bedroom. Also there was from the start a much greater sense of permanence about Robin's arrival in my life and home than either

Richard or Billy. I think she felt as if she had finally been usurped.

Robin never seemed particularly bothered by any of this. He was a man who had a lot of style. He always looked extremely smart and rather typically English. His clothes were rather honourable, well worn and of the highest quality. He had a favourite battered trilby hat which he used to wear all the time until it blew away over the Irish Sea one day when he was aboard a ferry. Then he just went out and bought another which he almost instantly managed to reduce to the same battered state.

Robin and I were very much a couple in the beginning and enjoyed each other's company enormously, so much so that we wanted to work together as much as possible. I think probably I behaved rather stupidly because rather than pursue my own career, which really needed looking after, I chose to work with Robin most of the time.

I still had plenty of TV work, such as *The Jimmy Tarbuck Show*. I was Jimmy's first 'tatty head' and I used to dance and sing on his show, songs like 'Kinky Boots' and 'Chim Chim Cheree'. The last was an absolute delight because this was before *Mary Poppins* opened and it was the first time it had been performed. I sang it with two kids sitting on top of chimneys.

But meanwhile I was settling into a new kind of life in Covent Garden and plotting to work with Robin. One of the first plays we did together after officially becoming an item was a tour of *Lord Arthur Savile's Crime*, based on Oscar Wilde's short story, which also starred William Hartnell, the original Doctor Who, and the veteran actress Elsie Randolph. She caused a modicum of concern from the start because she didn't want to wear her frocks, which were in keeping, shall we say, with her age – which was eighty. She wanted to wear mine instead, and I was the juvenile lead. The play is really about a wise butler called Baines who looks after Lord Arthur and has the ability to be extremely eloquent. William Hartnell played Baines, and when we began rehearsals my usual nervousness was enhanced by William, fluently doing the lot without his script, even at the first read-through. Off he would go, in charge of everything from the start with everybody else struggling to learn and him waltzing along as if he'd been playing the part for fifteen years.

So imagine the horror when the curtain rose on opening night and he was unable to say his first line. It was simply, 'Good morning, your Lordship.' But his version went, 'Good morning my Lord . . . Lord . . . Lord . . . Lady, Lady . . . Lord, Lady, Lady . . . Lord.'

The prompt called out, 'Lordship.'

'Yes, yes,' said Hartnell. 'Good morning my Lord . . . Lord . . . Lady, Lady, Lady, Lady . . . Lord . . . Lord.'

We couldn't believe it. The poor man was just unable to do it and proceeded to have a problem with just about every line he had, including a number of long speeches the whole point of which was their eloquence. At the end of these speeches somebody else would have a line like, 'Oh Mr Baines, sir, you don't half speak beautiful!' But unfortunately Mr Baines hadn't actually managed to say anything. It became a sort of farce. Robin, who was a great ad libber, was playing Lord Arthur Savile and virtually took over. He came to the rescue saying things like: 'Ah Baines, I think what you meant to say to me was . . .' And then he'd go into William Hartnell's speech.

Most actors in Hartnell's situation – and, believe me, it happens to the best – would just say, 'Look, I'm having a bad patch, I need to leave.' But not William Hartnell. He didn't want to quit and his agent didn't want him to quit. He seemed to be living in his own Tardis land. He would even dare to discuss the faults of other cast members. In the end the producers had to get Equity in to rule that things were out of control. But Equity insist on seeing three performances at totally arbitrary times before making any such ruling. In this case, that took about four weeks during which we just carried on touring.

There was also the scenario of Elsie Randolph and her obsession with my costumes to contend with. I would be frantically looking for whatever it was I was supposed to be wearing next, while Elsie would be skipping on stage carrying a parasol and wearing my dress. She was meant to be a frail old lady, but she was dark brown from sitting outside in the sun at her home in Worthing and was probably fitter than the lot of us.

I was, however, better prepared than most actors might have been for one little incident that occurred, because I had already had some practice. A few years earlier I had played opposite Leonard Sachs in Noël Coward's *Blithe Spirit* and when he screamed, 'Elvira' at me, his teeth had shot out and I caught them. So when the same thing happened to Margaretta Scott, who was playing my mother in *Lord Arthur Savile's Crime*, I knew exactly what to do. Her teeth flew toward me, and I caught them – rather neatly I thought. Whereas Leonard Sachs didn't even say thank you when I handed his teeth back – I realise he was probably embarrassed, but even so – Margaretta Scott, whom I adored, was absolutely wonderful. We both nearly died laughing when we got off stage.

Ultimately William Hartnell was removed and Dave King came in and took over, but the play never made it into the West End. I think we were all quite glad.

Not long after *Lord Arthur Savile's Crime*, I succeeded in getting named in two divorce cases on the same day. Both Richard and Robin's wives sued them for divorce on the grounds of adultery and cited me. The story of Robin and I made all the front pages, but I was spared from even more lurid headlines because I was named as Shirley Broadbent in Richard's divorce proceedings, and the press fortunately failed to put two and two together otherwise it could have been professional disaster for me.

The fact that there were two such proceedings in progress had already caused considerable confusion. One day when Robin and I were away and my mother was staying at Bow Street a man came to the door, wheedled his way in and asked, 'Is that the bed?'

To which my mother replied, 'Of course it's the bed. Why?'

'Is that *the* bed, where it took place?'

'What are you talking about?'

'Well, Amanda Barrie has been named in a divorce case,' he said. 'So is that the bed where *it* took place, *the act*?'

My mother showed him the door pretty promptly then. His parting words were, 'She'll be issued with papers.'

So she wasn't surprised when a couple of weeks later somebody else came to the door, asked if Shirley Broadbent lived there, and said that she'd been issued with divorce papers.

'Yes, we know,' said my mother, taking them from him. But when we looked at them later they were for Richard's divorce, not Robin's. It was quite a coincidence that they then came up at the same court session.

A little later, during the 1966 World Cup final which England so famously won, Robin proposed to me. He proposed as Gordon Banks saved a goal. I always thought it was a funny moment to choose.

First he shouted at Gordon Banks on the TV screen, 'I love you.' Then he said to me, 'Will you marry me?'

At least I assumed he was addressing me.

'Do you mean me or Gordon Banks?' I asked just to be sure.

Somewhat to my surprise I accepted his proposal right away. However, I did think that this was the moment when I should tell

Robin about Bernie and about my experiences in the south of France. His reaction was rather different to Richard's. I might have known it would be.

'Oh goodie!' he said. 'I've always wanted one on a lead. I've been looking all my life for a small fuckable chap who drinks.'

I took that as a compliment, which from Robin it most definitely was. And I suppose it is probably what a lot of men want. I suppose I was 'a small fuckable chap'. Certainly I used to quite frequently go to the Nags Head at six o'clock in the morning with Robin, when the Covent Garden pubs were open for the porters. I would stuff my hair into a large cap and do my best to look like a small chap because women weren't allowed in the pubs at that hour. Of course everybody knew exactly who I was. We were just paying lip service to the law, and I'd be there with Robin, tucking into a Covent Garden breakfast of black coffee, toast and dripping, and brandy. I should have been concentrating on my career, which was actually going rather well, but once again I was doing my chameleon trick and had turned into this 'small fuckable chap' who drank at dawn and was a total racing fanatic spending every spare minute running round Covent Garden chalking up bets. It was before legalised betting shops were introduced and we often used to bet with one of the stallholders who ran a book. Once Robin and I got a 20–1 double and the man couldn't pay out, so he paid us in vegetables for months. 'Sorry about that, Rob, but it was a big win, big win, and I just 'aven't got it. Now, 'ere's a sack of parsnips.'

We weren't best pleased, but we accepted it. That was how things were in the Garden. We didn't just bet on the horses either. Once we had Geoffrey Tate, now a famous Mozart conductor, and some of the Opera House singers in the pub and we decided to bet on who had perfect pitch. There was great rivalry over who could sing middle C. I actually could and won several times.

On another occasion, when racing was cancelled for a particularly long spell because of bad weather, we even had a book going on the condensation on the windows in the Nags Head. You had to pick a drop of water and follow it down to the bottom of the glass. First to the bottom won. Very serious betting that was.

Even in bed at night racing was much more of a passion for Robin and me than sex. Robin used to set racing quizzes for me. 'OK, what is the Spring Double?' he'd ask. 'Which Grand National winner was accused of only going around the course once?' and, 'Recite the winners of the Grand National for the last ten years in reverse order.' That was my party piece for years.

My mother was not overly delighted with the news of my impending nuptials. Robin had already invaded Bow Street, spoiling her dear little bijou residence with its delicate antique furniture and silk walls with his masculine presence. There was a dartboard over the kitchen table and holes all over the wall where we'd missed when playing darts while slightly pissed. There were piles of newspapers everywhere, so much so that the chairs were getting higher because there were so many newspapers underneath. The papers never got thrown away because Robin was always saying, 'No not that one, we've got to keep that one. I marked all the racing results on that one.' However it was he, at one stage, who remarked, with absolute accuracy, 'If this were a Chinese restaurant it would be condemned.'

Although I had accepted Robin's proposal we did not actually do the deed until the following year and the main reason we went ahead then was because there had been an unpleasant story in the press about us living together, which in those days was really not very good news.

We deliberately chose to get married on the same day that my brother Chris was getting married in Manchester. This was because, although my mother disapproved of Robin as a son-in-law, she would still have wanted to organise our wedding, probably on about the same scale as her own too, and that was something I just could not face. So by making the final decision swiftly and by choosing what was also Chris's wedding day we managed to avoid her even being there.

We married at London's Caxton Hall on 19 June 1967. As 'a small fuckable chap' I wore a trouser suit and one of those little jockey caps everybody wore in the sixties. Inside my cap were two miniature bottles of whisky, which Robin joked that he would need in order to get through the ceremony.

After the ceremony, with just a few friends and Robin's parents present, we posed outside for photographs, which virtually every national paper printed, before making our way back to the Nags Head for what was supposed to be just a quiet drink. But the good people of Covent Garden had other plans. A proper wedding breakfast had been laid out and everyone we drank with had been invited. From not planning a reception at all we ended up having a huge one. The scene was set from the start. There was a large man with dropsy, known as the Major, who was a bookie's runner but due to his disability he couldn't run anywhere. He also sold biros and French letters. He took it upon himself to go round the tables at the Nags Head and lay out a biro and a packet of three as a wedding present for everybody.

Later that night my brother and his new wife Edna called in to see us on their way to their honeymoon. They had had a traditional white wedding and a normal day of reasonable behaviour, and I think they were quite horrified to find all these drunks falling about in Covent Garden.

Robin and I, of course, did not have a honeymoon. We continued to work together as much as possible and I continued to have terrible panic attacks and be carted around from doctor to doctor. I never stopped working throughout though. Maybe it was the work that kept me going. I was still doing lots of TV. Robin and I did several plays at Richmond and elsewhere, and a particularly memorable pantomime at Watford which was written by the Goodies and also starred Maureen Lipman.

Covent Garden really became my life during that period. I live there to this day and cannot imagine ever moving away, although it was a very different place in the sixties when the market was still operating. It really was an extraordinary place then. Porters, writers, artists, the press, the police, the opera singers and the dancers from the Opera House, all used to come into the area and mix. In the late afternoons and at night the streets were empty because the place was full of warehouses, which closed down in the afternoon, and the people disappeared until the early hours.

If we were cooking in those days — and Robin was a seriously good cook — we never thought of buying vegetables. We'd just pop downstairs and find a couple of onions and a potato on the road. Everybody did. There was stuff all over the place. I'd frequently forage for Robin, I'd be looking for a pound or so of sprouts when I'd see a pile of lovely radishes in front of me. So I'd decide we might as well make a salad with those instead.

Leaning out of the window of Bow Street to watch the market arrive at night was one of the greatest privileges of all. There'd be this wonderful noise of the rollers and the men calling to each other. Right below our window this patchwork quilt would unfold, as open trucks full of marvellously coloured fruit and vegetables arrived. There'd be one full of carrots, bright orange, vibrant, another a small sea of green, full of cabbages and beans, then another full of flowers on its way to the flower market. The stall right below my flat sold melons and grapes and the stallholders would yell up, 'Go on, give us a cup of coffee, Amanda.'

I used to make the coffee, prop it up in a basket attached to a rope and lower it three storeys down to them. When I pulled it up the basket would always be full of grapes and melons. Nobody starved in Covent Garden then, even though I did my best to do so. If I was ill they'd say, 'Oh, Amanda's got a bad cold hasn't she? I've heard that chest. It's all right.' Then I'd find a sack of onions, a sack of potatoes, a sack of something else left by the front door, always too much to use.

Friday night was the big fruit night. They used to leave all the leftover fruit in the barrows and you could just go around and collect it. That is why so many people in the Garden used to make wine. Robin wasn't into that though, because it took too long to ferment. Richard on the other hand had made quite a lot in Endell Street, leading to occasional explosions in the attic.

There were no restaurants in Covent Garden then. Soho was the place to go out to eat. There were a handful of pubs and a couple of cafés, one in Endell Street and one in Floral Street. But there were all these extraordinary characters. It was like a village where we regularly met up with artists like Edward Burra, and drank with Jeffrey Bernard, who occasionally slept on our floor. I remember one night that Jeffrey, who was a legendary drinker, looked in a particularly bad way, even by his standards and Robin asked him what was wrong.

'Day didn't go all that well,' he remarked mildly. 'I was just about to be introduced to the Queen Mother at York Races when I was sick all over the floral clock.'

I have never been able to look at that floral clock since without thinking of Jeffrey being sick over it in front of the Queen Mum.

The people and their language were very special. Everybody had a nickname. There was one porter known as Mr Shovel Shit, for reasons I was never entirely sure of, all for the best perhaps, who had a particularly colourful turn of phrase. He was inclined to say, 'Do you know, Amanda, I could 'ave fancied you twenty years ago. Mind you, I was very untidy downstairs in my youth.'

What a wonderful remark. I had no idea exactly what he meant, probably also for the best. It was also Mr Shovel Shit who told me, in his inimitable way, about Times Annie. 'You never knew Times Annie, Amanda? I'm surprised at yer. I'd 'ave thought you'd been 'ere long enough to 'ave known Times Annie. She was one of the prostitutes who was around 'ere during the War and after. Mind you, you wouldn't 'ave been around them, would yer? Now most of 'em couldn't afford a room. But Times Annie was very clever, what she used to do was to purchase two or three copies of *The Times*, not to read but because it was very good quality paper. Then she'd go down among the potato sacks and we would 'ave our way wiv 'er and she'd 'old up the newspapers like a sort of screen around us. Hence 'er name, Times Annie.'

The porters used to pass around very badly spelled pornography in brown envelopes. It was so bad it was hysterical, even to a dyslexic like me. One day Mr Shovel Shit, clutching a brown envelope, said to me, 'Do you know Amanda, I'm going to go 'ome now. I'm going to take this piece of literature back to my wife Myrtle, I'm going to put 'er 'and on my almond rock and burst into fucking tears.'

Pornography, of a very amateurish kind, featured quite largely in the Covent Garden lifestyle, and a group of us once had this great wheeze of showing a blue movie on the side of the Opera House, which Garden people are not inclined to treat with quite the same reverence as the rest of the British population. Unfortunately we put it in the projector upside down, making an already bad bit of porn completely incomprehensible.

From Friday night until Sunday night the Garden belonged to us, no traffic, no people, no shops. Everything was closed. It seems hard to imagine now. The porters used to bring their wives in on Sunday for a drink in the Nags Head because it was their pub and they were like different people to how they were in the week, shouting obscenities at each other and screaming their bets across the bar. On Sundays butter wouldn't have melted. They were all dressed up and they'd be horrified if we swore in front of their wives. Mr Shovel Shit would always be there in his neat suit and trilby.

After one Sunday lunchtime session he said, 'I'll tell you a little secret, Amanda. My wife doesn't even like the idea of me coming into work in a cap. She thinks it's common. So, as far as she's concerned I come into work in my trilby. Well, what I've done is I've knocked a couple of bricks out of the side of my house, and I leave 'ome in my trilby but really I nip round the back, take my cap out of the hole in the wall and put my trilby in. Then when I come back I do the same thing the other way round.'

I think there were about 7,000 local inhabitants in Covent Garden back then, and it was a complete privilege to live there amongst them.

Around this time I starred in the show that never was. It was to be a revue with a difference – and it certainly was. It was directed by Peter Myers, a well-known figure in revue, and featured Leslie Crowther, David Kernan, Moira Lister, Sally Smith, me – and Robin of course. So the show had a fine pedigree and already had a West End slot. Nonetheless I had a bad feeling about it from the first day. I called my agent, Alec, who was also David Kernan's agent. 'Is there any way of insuring your salary against a show that never opens?' I asked.

'The last West End show which failed to open was in 1911,' he replied. 'Aren't we being a little pessimistic, Amanda?'

Rehearsals continued and were fairly chaotic, but that was nothing to go by because revue rehearsals always were. The first major problem seemed to be that the producers couldn't decide what to call the show. So they decided to call it the telephone number of whichever theatre we were at. The idea was that the name of the show was the number you dialled to book it. I never understood it, and neither did anyone much else, I don't think.

We rehearsed at the Ballet Rambert school at Notting Hill Gate. There was one sketch featuring a man allegedly interviewing someone on stilts. The person on the stilts was right up in the flies so the audience just heard his disembodied voice. The tag to this sketch was that the two stilts were supposed to fall apart so it looked like the man had been split in two. Not that funny, but it might have worked if the stilts hadn't had feet which meant they didn't look like stilts. I did point this out to various people, but they just said, 'Oh be quiet, Amanda!' 'Don't be silly, Amanda!' David Kernan, probably because he did have some very good, very funny numbers in the show, kept on saying, 'Please, please. You are being so negative. We're all so bored with it.'

So I decided to shut up, and leave them to it.

We trundled off to Liverpool, where we had just a week and a bit to get the show on. It involved a great deal of magic which is always difficult. The problem was that none of the magic worked properly. It wasn't the fault of David Berglas, the magician, who was a quite brilliant man. I think the whole thing was just too ambitious for a stage show, there were too many complex special effects.

I was in a sketch about a magician and his wife living in a home where everything was operated by magic. I had a wand which I waved to light the oven on the far side of the stage. The first time I tried, a huge ball of flame shot out of the end of the wand and landed at the feet of the chief fireman who was standing in the wings. He nearly had a fit.

Things proceeded to go from bad to worse. I also had to do a stunt scene in which I was supposed to be Amy Johnson flying backwards and forwards across the stage doing double somersaults on a wire. Needless to say, before we even got to the opening night, I was flown smack into a piece of scenery by some idiot in the flies.

The show opened with most of the cast being loaded into what looked like a big old water pipe, from which we were supposed to emerge into this little, tiny house – as if by magic. The trick was enhanced by mirrors. There was nothing wrong with the idea but the reality was catastrophic. We were pushed in one at a time like cannon fodder. Sally Smith and David Kernan went first, then me, then Robin. The problem was that we had to spend about fifteen minutes in there. People were having claustrophobia attacks and refusing to go in. David Kernan, who was very good looking, had bought himself a beautiful, very tight white suit from Carnaby Street. I have never seen an actor look so miserable at the prospect of him and his trendy suit being stuffed in an old tube for fifteen minutes, or more when things went wrong.

Ultimately on the opening night they failed to raise the curtain. There was just no way we could put on a show. Naturally enough, the audience out front demanded their money back and later they barracked the theatre from the street outside, something I have never seen before or since. My prophecy, unfortunately, was beginning to come true.

It was announced to the audience that we would try to open the next night, and that they could either have their money back or tickets to see the show another day. But we failed again by which time that fine performer Leslie Crowther was sobbing in the foyer while we all sat on the black-and-white marble floor trying to work out a way to pull the show together.

We got into the theatre at the crack of dawn the next day but we were still unable to open. This went on for three days, by which time the public, who had paid for tickets for a big West End-bound revue, were completely disillusioned and fed up with us. We were surrounded by quite hostile crowds, and ended up being more or less locked in the theatre. Cast and crew used to make a run for it across the road to a little café on the corner with people booing us and yelling, 'Amateurs.'

Ultimately, in a desperate bid to salvage the situation, the management decided they would ask an invited audience to see us open. This meant hijacking innocent people walking by the theatre, thrusting free tickets in their hands, and hauling them in off the street.

Eventually we did bring the curtain up – fleetingly – but it was a disaster. Nothing worked. However, we almost solved the problem by shooting the audience. One of the magic tricks involved a robotic tank, which we actually had to assemble on stage as part of a routine. Then it was supposed to point itself at a post office and say, 'It's a stick-up.' Instead of doing that it turned itself, firing, towards the audience, rolled straight down the front of the stage, still firing madly, and fell into the pit scattering the entire orchestra.

The cast emerged from their pipe to chaos and finally left the stage, crumpled, broken, dispirited and weeping. David Kernan, who had miraculously so far remained, on the surface at any rate, cool, calm and collected, suddenly lost it and ran up the stairs to rant and rave at the director. Unfortunately, as part of a routine, he was wearing a suit festooned with magic roses which kept exploding out of every bit of his body, including his flies. All his dignity was lost. You just can't take a man seriously, angry as he may be, when he has roses sprouting out all over him.

At about the same time that we were making this last pathetic attempt to save the show, the management apparently ran out of money and disappeared. We found a note pinned to the stage-door noticeboard, 'Gone back to London for the dibs.' Things got a bit desperate then. Landladies were complaining because they were owed money, and we ended up more or less barricaded in the theatre, incapable of doing anything else except eat meat pies smuggled in from across the road and sit up all night fiddling with disastrous bits of magic.

Ultimately an announcement was made over the tannoy system backstage. 'Everybody will now leave the theatre. Everything in this theatre is now confiscated and is the property of Howard and Wyndham's Theatres.'

The next thing we knew was that there were people running in all directions gathering up our things. I thought, 'No way, mine!' We'd practically lived in the theatre, so we had most of our clothes, make-up, everything, and it was all about to be confiscated. I grabbed three suitcases that had been used in a sketch, loaded all Robin's and my things into them, and threw them out of my dressing-room window into the street below, while Robin shot downstairs to grab them. I think we were the only people who got anything out that night.

The kids in the cast and most of the stagehands didn't even have enough money to leave the theatre. We were stranded. We had to call in Equity because we were being held responsible for the price of everything. I can still see a picture in my head of the man from Equity arriving on a bicycle to bail everyone out. I think we got £20 each.

So I really was in the first West End booked show not to have opened since 1911. And if only I had taken out that insurance I would have done very nicely, thank you.

CHAPTER THIRTEEN

❧

For the first few years of our marriage Robin and I were exceedingly happy, in spite of, or maybe because of, some of the crazy escapades we were involved in. People used to say that we were made for each other, and it really did feel like that. We had fun together, we laughed at the same things, and we usually agreed on important issues too. But when he suggested that we go to South Africa in 1969 to play *Cabaret* – I was to be Sally Bowles and he was to be Ernest – I didn't want to go. I was violently opposed to the apartheid regime as, in fact, was Robin. We were also aware that we could have Equity problems if we went there.

However, I was eventually persuaded to go because the production was supposed to be different and was supposed to help the situation. Hal Prince had refused to let South Africa have *Fiddler on the Roof* and

West Side Story until they had had *Cabaret*. They didn't want it, because of the obvious analogy between the story set in Nazi Germany in the thirties, and what was happening in South Africa in the sixties. Ultimately, however, they agreed and Prince insisted that there would be black Africans involved backstage, that young black Africans would have access to drama coaching and there would be racially mixed audiences. At least that is what we were told. Predictably perhaps, the reality turned out to be rather different.

When we got to South Africa every single clause of the contract was broken, through no fault of Hal Prince. Black and coloured people were supposed to be allowed to watch rehearsals, and all profits from the show were meant to go to African theatre, which it turned out barely existed. None of this happened. We were escorted everywhere by men with guns who told us where we could and couldn't go. We were forbidden from performing before mixed audiences after all. The wonderfully simple excuse was, 'We've only got lavatories for white people.'

Robin and I got ourselves into trouble from the start. I was ill, because my mother had flatly refused to give me smallpox, or any other sort of jabs, as a child and all these things are more dangerous and more likely to affect you badly as you get older. Because of this I was given only the tiniest of smallpox jabs before leaving for South Africa, and I thought all was well, but it took about ten days to kick in, coinciding nicely with our flight to Johannesburg. Robin thought the answer was to pour alcohol down me and I obediently drank my way there. I have always been a nervous flyer, so I didn't need much persuading. But by the time we got to Johannesburg I had virtually passed out and had to be carried off the plane. My arm blew up like a balloon. I had a temperature of 106 and a doctor was called.

I was so ill I missed the first few days of rehearsal, and when I did go in I was at my least tolerant. I loathed the South African director,

Tauby Kushlick, on sight although she was revered as a great theatrical personality over there. She may or may not have been talented, but she was totally heartless and ruthless when it came to dealing with other people. I thought her behaviour was appalling.

Half the people in the show were semi pro. Poor kids who had come from as far away as Cape Town would suddenly be told, 'You're too ugly, darling. I don't want you. Go away.'

I had a personality clash with her from the start. I don't think I have ever disliked anybody so much in my entire life. It all flared up into a full-scale row at the first-night party. A huge spread had been laid out which we tucked into until we realised that all our black stagehands had been banned and were in fact locked in a cellar under the stage. So Robin and I grabbed a load of food and drink and went off downstairs with it. Tauby Kushlick went absolutely mad when she found out.

Robin didn't like her either. A few days later when we were rehearsing a new routine and she was screaming abuse at us on stage, Robin just launched himself from the back of the stage and in three strides got to the front, leapt over the orchestra pit, and ran across the backs of the seats to where she was sitting nine or ten rows back, picked her up by the scruff of the neck and shook her. It was an extraordinary spectacle and Robin moved so fast that he got to her more quickly than I would have believed possible. More quickly than Tauby Kushlick would have believed possible too. She just gawped at him, petrified. For some reason all she said was, 'My son – he's a doctor.' It brought the house down. The entire cast collapsed. However, our popularity with the management sank to a whole new level.

One night we were on stage singing 'Tomorrow Belongs to Me', the Nazi youth song, when we heard the most terrible noise in the alleyway by the theatre. I remember that Peter Bridge, from the *Six of One* management, was out front and later commented, 'My God, wasn't that the most wonderful sound effect that they used at the end of that number.' By that time we had found out what had happened. Our stagehands had been accused of stealing alcohol from the bar – apparently about a teaspoonful or so had been drunk from a bottle – and the police had been called and had beaten a number of them to a pulp outside. There was skin and blood and bits of skull all over this alleyway. It was horrendous. 'That wasn't an effect,' we told Peter. 'That was the South African police at work.'

We never saw those stagehands again.

South Africa was an incredibly grim and brutal place, much more so even than we had imagined. Robin and I were about ready to throw in the towel and return home. It was, in fact, our remaining stagehands and the other black Africans that we met who begged us not to. We had followed Dusty Springfield out there and she had made her feelings clear publicly and had duly been sent back to England. The black people we met all said, 'Don't go to the press here. If you say anything publicly you'll just have to go and that won't do any good at all. You can do good just by talking to people, and by showing them that not all white people are like the whites running South Africa.'

We tried. I used to get meetings going in my dressing room in which I taught them about trade unionism, the way I like to think my grandfather would have done. I would get some cold drinks in and pass them around in shared paper cups. Once one of the black lads suddenly said, 'This is the first time I have ever drunk from the same cup as a white person.'

The whole trip was a very emotional experience. It was hard to stand by and watch some of the things that went on. On occasions, I have to say, Robin and I didn't. In our hotel bar one night we were aware of a group of Afrikaans men, nine or ten of them, ordering drinks from a young black waiter who only looked about twelve or thirteen. They were behaving horribly towards him. One of these unbelievable creatures, I wouldn't call them human beings, got hold of the boy by his shirt collar and started giving him this ridiculously long order.

'I want 3,000 vodkas and 2,000 gins and 500 tonics and I want you to bring me a pillowcase full of ice.'

The men around the table all thought it was hilarious. This poor boy was shaking with fear, not knowing what to do. After a bit Robin could stand it no longer. He went to the next table and said in his very upper-class English accent, 'Excuse me, my good man, I think you're having difficulty with your order. Do let me take it from you.' Then he put his arm round this kid. 'Now what did he want? 3,000 vodkas was it?'

Of course they backed down at once as bullies always do.

This incident was, however, just one of many which made it all too clear to us just what a terrible place South Africa was back then. I had to do a quick change in the wings as Sally Bowles and, as I would in England or anywhere else, I handed my cigarette in a long cigarette holder to one of the black props boys. A white South African girl in the cast just knocked it out of his hand, saying, 'You don't give a nigger anything like that. You can't let them touch anything you're going to put in your mouth. It's filthy.'

Never being one to keep my mouth buttoned I heard myself say, 'I'll give my fucking props to who I want.'

I remember walking in the streets and seeing the expression in black people's eyes. The place was a bomb waiting to explode. Yet there was this awful racist white minority, living a life of luxury sitting around their swimming pools, drinking themselves silly, blissfully unaware that there was anything wrong in the way that they were running their country, or that it just couldn't go on.

There was no television in South Africa then. I think TV might have brought about the end of the apartheid regime much earlier because it would have shown a little of what was going on in the rest of the world. Nothing was allowed to show black people being clever and successful. The film *Sweet Charity* was on at a cinema near to our theatre, but the black girl had been painted out of the poster and they'd jump-cut the film in order to remove her almost totally.

The whites would say the most extraordinary things to justify their belief that black Africans were not their equals. I heard someone say, 'You must never let a black man drive a taxi because they can't see straight, you see. It's proved. They can't see straight.'

'What about Arthur Ashe, then? He seems to see quite straight, doesn't he?' I replied. But you could never get anywhere. It really was like Nazi Berlin.

The black Africans we got to know began to realise, thankfully, that we were different to the white supremacists who were running their country. They even smuggled us into Soweto where I listened to an eleven-year-old boy playing Chopin. Only about a third of the notes on his piano worked, but he sat there with his long fingers playing this lovely music, even the notes that weren't there. He was a natural musician. I was deeply touched by him, and I have never forgotten that image.

Shortly after that we decided that, somehow or other, we would put on a show for a black audience whatever the consequences. We managed to find a venue in a Victorian church hall just outside the Soweto men's dormitory. We weren't allowed access to scenery, so Robin and I hung paper streamers everywhere. It was like putting on a kids' show at Christmas. Not everyone was in favour of this venture. The white South African girls in *Cabaret* came to me with a petition refusing to do the Soweto show. I am afraid I blackmailed them, saying, 'Thank you for your petition and the list of names. I will make sure it is distributed by Equity all over the world, and you will never work anywhere in theatre except here in South Africa.' I knew that they were all dying to get to England and America to be stars of the West End and Broadway. They gave in with alacrity.

Eventually we got to do the show. Just the one, I'm afraid, but it was something. The audience came in slowly, undoubtedly unsure of themselves since apparently most of them had never seen any sort of stage show before. We were several minutes into it before we had anything like a full house, but we ended up with the old hall absolutely crammed, with people climbing up onto bits of this English-style wrought-iron framed church hall in order to get a better view.

There were curious moments. When I made my entrance as Sally Bowles I got a huge laugh and I had no idea why. Afterwards it was explained to me that it was because Sally Bowles arrived with her luggage being carried by a white man which was absolutely unheard of in South Africa. There was another big shriek of laughter later, followed by a round of applause, when Sally was hit by Cliff, the leading man. The audience apparently found the spectacle of a white man hitting a white woman most enjoyable.

After that show, our situation with the authorities really became quite tricky, and we even wondered if we would be arrested. We started to find bars and restaurants, obviously alerted to who we were and how we were behaving, refusing to serve us. On our last night in the country we were demob-happy and quite foolhardy. At the Brook Theatre there were rows of photographs of people like Lewis Casson, Sybil Thorndike and Robin's father Ian, who had been born in South Africa. We didn't think any of them would approve of having their photographs hung in a place where people were being treated so appallingly, so I'm afraid we behaved like hooligans. We took them all down and smashed them. The next day we left the airport followed by a convoy of Africans in broken-down lorries who wanted to say goodbye to us. I remember them saying, 'When it happens, we'll try not to kill the good people.'

I wanted to go home to a country where you could announce to the world, if you wanted to, that you thought the government was crap. And yet I had learned just a little about what it was like to live in a monstrous police state and it had changed me a bit inside. Half of me couldn't bear to leave that day. I even considered giving up theatre and going into politics so I could do something really worthwhile for once.

I didn't of course. I returned to London where Robin and I wept unashamedly when we saw our first red bus. I did, however, make a resolution then, which I have always stuck to, which is that I will never stand by silently in the face of prejudice. If anybody, from a taxi driver to a lord, chooses to express views I strongly disagree with then I will not be quietly polite. I will state mine – and I thank God that I am lucky enough to live in a place where I am able to do so without fear.

I did not go back to South Africa, although I had hoped to. Robin and I found after our return to England that the South African government had banned us.

And South Africa continued in its monstrous suffering for another twenty years – until a man called Nelson Mandela who'd spent decades in jail somehow performed a miraculous transformation and one of the most evil regimes in history gave way to a fledgling democracy with hardly any bloodshed at all.

Which was something none of us who were on that tour in 1969 would ever have believed possible.

CHAPTER FOURTEEN

※

Going to South Africa initiated huge changes in the way that I thought about almost everything. I think it made me grow up a bit. I realised that those of us lucky enough to be born in a free country had almost a duty to make the most of our lives. Particularly if we may have been blessed with a little talent. I also realised that I had probably never fully appreciated nor utilised many of the chances I had been given, and suddenly I wanted to do so very much indeed.

Robin's company was seductive. He was Jolly Rob, he was fun, drinking with him was fun. But I no longer wanted my existence to revolve around pubs and having a good time on an all-too-often superficial level. I was determined not to waste my life. Robin was still able to drink and work. I could never drink and work and I was not prepared to get to the stage where an irresponsible social life overshadowed everything else.

So it was that soon after we came back from South Africa Robin and I started to go along different paths.

I had started to be offered really good work again. A production of Shakespeare's *A Midsummer Night's Dream* for the BBC's prestigious Play of the Month spot came first. I played Hermia opposite Lynn Redgrave's Helena. Edward Fox, Robert Stephens, Michael Gambon, Eleanor Bron and Eileen Atkins also starred. For the first time I realised that I didn't feel out of place in such company, indeed I felt quite comfortable. I also appeared in another Play of the Month, William Wycherley's *A Country Wife,* with Bernard Cribbins and Helen Mirren.

In 1971, I went into Noël Coward's *Hay Fever* with Judy Campbell and we became lifelong friends. I used to stand in the wings with Jonathan Kent, who went on to run the Almeida Theatre in Islington, and we couldn't take our eyes off Judy. We knew we were listening to a great star, and listening to her rendition every night of 'Hearts and Flowers' was a theatrical privilege. It is no wonder Eric Maschwitz wrote 'A Nightingale Sang in Berkeley Square' for her for the revue *New Faces.*

Not only was that another really good production, but off stage the three of us had the most enchanting time. It was probably one of the best times I've ever had on tour, and Judy is still my friend despite the fact that she infuriates me by getting better and better at the age of eighty.

Another production I was proud to be a part of in the early seventies was Joyce Rayburn's play, *Come When You Like,* at the Shaw Theatre, with Raymond Francis of *No Hiding Place* fame. During this play, Robin's parents, Ian and Cash, returned in a very bad state from where they had been living in Spain. Robin and I went to pick them up at Heathrow. Cash was carried off the plane on a stretcher and Ian walked straight past Robin without recognising him. It was no secret that most of their problems had tragically been caused by drink. This had a great emotional effect on Robin, and I began to worry that he might be going the same way. I also had reason to believe that he was having an affair. Certainly, without question, we were beginning to grow apart.

However, just as I was thinking that our marriage was becoming dangerously rocky, it was propped up in a most unusual way. A woman whom I shall call Sally came into our lives.

She was gay and used to get teased a lot, sometimes quite unpleasantly. There was a lot more prejudice against homosexuals of both sexes then and I have always believed that women suffered particularly.

Robin liked Sally a great deal. He made friends easily and was always quick to befriend people who needed support, as he had been in South Africa. Robin didn't have any prejudice against anyone and he was inclined to be very protective towards people who might be suffering from it.

Robin had a lot of gay friends and at first Sally was just another one. I suppose I was probably attracted to her from the start, but because I had been trying to bury that side of me for so long I didn't let myself think about it. She was just a friend.

Until one night when everything changed, and Sally became the first woman I ever slept with. I have changed her name because her personal situation is such that to do otherwise could cause her considerable embarrassment in her present life.

I was alone in Bow Street. I'd just washed my hair and was drinking a glass of Alka Seltzer – we got through a lot of that stuff back then – when the edge of the glass broke in my mouth and I swallowed a big chunk, harpooning my throat. I managed to cough really hard and the glass popped out but it had cut the back of my throat quite badly. I was pretty shaken up and just as I was recovering from the shock

Sally phoned to ask if Robin and I would like to go out for a drink.

'No,' I replied. 'Robin's already out and I've just had a near-death experience, actually.' I told her all about what had happened and she simply said, 'I'll come up then.'

Maybe because I was still in shock, that was when I finally threw off my inhibitions and started a relationship with Sally. It happened quite suddenly. It was about the first time we'd been properly alone together, and there I was having just nearly choked to death, with wet hair and no make-up. If anyone likes me in that sort of state I'm inclined to be so grateful I'm hooked straight away. Also, I suppose a part of me was waiting for it to happen with someone. There simply hadn't been a likely candidate since Ginette, and of course the frightened part of me had been actively trying to avoid it. But I just fell for Sally and I could do nothing to stop it. There was a certain relief for me in finally going to bed with a woman, and it was a very good feeling to be with Sally.

I have come to realise as I have grown older that it is the person that matters. For me, some people are just more all right – in bed and out of it – than others, and it doesn't particularly matter whether they are male or female. You can't compare one person in your life with another.

In many ways, I remained this 'small fuckable chap who drinks' to Robin. But whereas he had a complete lack of fear about both work and life in those days, and could waltz through a first night with no nerves at all, I could not. It wasn't just nerves. I took work more seriously and certainly always felt that, in order to succeed at all, I had to work much harder at it than he did. But already, even though Robin had so much talent and had played leads in the West End years before, he was beginning to fall behind such contemporaries as Nigel Hawthorne and Paul Eddington. His lifestyle didn't help, but neither did the fact that he wasn't really a fighter in his work. People who find things as easy as Robin did, certainly during the early part of his career, never learn to fight in the way that the rest of us do. Although we had so much in common, our approaches to our work couldn't have been more diverse, and Robin used to get quite cross with me over both my pedanticism and my extreme nervousness. More than anything, Sally fulfilled an emotional need for me at the time. I turned to Sally for understanding, and I got it. She helped me cope with all my various insecurities, and was particularly supportive about my work.

I told Robin about Sally almost straight away. I could have imagined doing nothing else. I didn't have any secrets from him. He was not at all fazed. In fact he made it quite clear that he rather liked the idea. I never cease to be surprised that the idea of two women together, and of perhaps actually joining in, seems to be the fantasy of so many men. It was certainly a fantasy of Robin's.

Sally, who like many gay women had once been straight, used to meet us most days in the pub, and Robin was always terribly affectionate and good with her. She worked in central London but was living out of town and used to drive in and out. Then one day she'd had too much drink to drive. She ended up staying the night at Bow Street. It seemed a bit daft to start trying to sort the settee out and make all that mess with bedclothes, and it felt like a perfectly natural move for Sally just to crash with Robin and me.

I know that the idea of three in a bed is a big turn-on for a lot of people, even if it is taken no further. And of course I was excited by the idea at first or I wouldn't have gone along with it. But is also seemed like a kind of solution, albeit a bizarre one, to my various sexual and emotional dilemmas. I still loved Robin, the man who for so long had been my best friend as well as my husband, and the way in which we were growing apart distressed me greatly. I was worried that be might be being unfaithful to me and I think it did occur to me that by allowing another woman into our relationship this might prevent Robin looking elsewhere. After all, there was no doubt that I found sex with Sally more erotic and satisfying than I ever had with any of the men in my life, including Robin.

I think Robin knew that too. He had previously commented after he had been drinking, that I was frigid. I wasn't, but my sexuality had needed awakening, and Sally had done that.

Therefore the sex between the three of us, the details of which I will leave to the reader's imagination, was, to begin with, quite interesting. And the fact that Robin, Sally and I intrinsically liked each other so much added greatly to that.

The three of us ended up more or less living together in my little flat which – when it became known around the place – led to saying other men to Robin, 'Aren't you lucky?'

He rather liked that and thought it was one big joke. In a way people's reaction to us was a joke because, as is so often the case, things quickly became not at all how they seemed. The friendship between the three of us endured, but the eroticism that was orginally between us did not last long.

I am sure that everybody who knew about us assumed we were indulging in one great everlasting sexual orgy, and indeed we were once nearly exposed in the press, which would have been deeply embarrassing at the time, but the reality wasn't like that at all. Except at the very beginning it was surprisingly innocent and very giggly. When we went to bed Robin had often drunk too much to do anything and fell asleep snoring loudly. I was usually exhausted because I was invariably doing eight shows a week and just lay there wishing I had more room in the bed.

I should also mention that it was during the time that Robin, Sally and I were the odd threesome that I acquired a little Yorkshire terrier called Katie Cupcake who liked to sleep on my head. I can assure you that when still fighting off a complete nervous breakdown and prone to panic attacks, in a state of permanent exhaustion playing the lead in the West End, sharing a four feet six inches bed in a tiny flat with two rather large people and a dog intent on smothering you, it is actually quite difficult to experience much rampant sexuality. You just don't have the energy.

What I remember most of this time with Sally, Robin and me, was the enormous fun that we had and the support that we gave each other. It was like a permanent party. We were a group already when we went anywhere.

If two people live together there are always grumpy periods, but add an extra one and with a bit of luck at least two will be all right so they'd be saying, 'What's the matter with her – or him?'

Incredibly, our threesome lasted seven years on and off. I can recommend it as a way of living if you have the right three people, I really can. And, strange as it might seem, if Sally had not entered our lives I really do not think Robin and I would have stayed together for nearly as long as we did.

While all this was going on, and I was living what must have seemed to be this extraordinary Bohemian life, I continued to work extremely hard. In fact work has been the one constant factor in my life. Whatever has been happening in my personal life, whatever state I've been in mentally and physically, I always seem to have just kept on working through.

I was becoming a lot stronger mentally though. The psychiatric treatment I received at the Middlesex Hospital helped, and I do think the experiences of South Africa made me less self-obsessed, and I hope this was reflected in my work. Unfortunately, I was not in a position to concentrate solely on really good quality work, even though I was being offered plenty of it. A sorry side of show business is that the best work is often the worst paid.

Robin was appearing at the Players Theatre, which rarely pays well, and also trying to launch a writing career. This started very promisingly and there was certainly no doubt about his talent. However he didn't really persevere and his early promise was never fulfilled.

I, therefore, was the major breadwinner and not in a position to pick and choose my work in the way that I might have liked. I was also still sending my mother money regularly, as I did until she died. Neither her hairdressing business nor anything else she became involved in ever seemed to bring in sufficient funds.

That was how, in the early seventies I went into a children's TV series called *Hickory House*, made in Manchester by Granada. While filming, I used to stay with my mother in her Disley cottage, where we still shared a bed.

Alan Rothwell, who had also been in *Come When You Like* in the West End and who went on to play footballer David Barlow, younger brother of Ken, in *Coronation Street*, was more or less in charge of *Hickory House* and asked me to present it with him. Unfortunately the show was a complete disaster for me. I seemed to do nothing but get myself in trouble with the Lancashire Education Committee.

We didn't have enough rehearsal time and *Hickory House* was always over- or under-running. After just half a day's rehearsal we'd end up having to ad lib our way through. There was one occasion when we had made two little boats, just like on *Blue Peter*. But I don't think what happened next was the sort of thing that happened on *Blue Peter*. Alan asked me what I was going to call mine just as it began to sink.

Naturally enough, I feel, I replied, 'The *Titanic*.'

This went down almost as well as the ship herself, because you weren't supposed to make cracks like that on children's shows.

Also, I was expected to read stories, the very idea of which terrified me because of my dyslexia. 'Of course you can read this kind of thing,' they assured me. 'It's only kiddies' stuff.'

However, my attempt at reading *The Little Red Hen* ended in disaster. I rehearsed it and rehearsed it, I tried and tried, but dyslexia ruled, K.O. The production team thought I was just misbehaving and I was never asked to read anything again.

My most serious crime, however, was one which I still think was quite ridiculous. There was a wall around Hickory House, and one day, in order to pad the show out because we were under-running again, I jumped onto the wall, hopped about a bit, and jumped off the other side. The Lancashire Education Committee promptly insisted on a meeting at Granada to which I was duly summoned. They said I was encouraging children to climb on walls and gave me a telling off.

'I don't think children ever need encouragement to climb walls,' I replied.

'Well, seeing you do it is a very bad example,' they continued.

'No it's not,' I told them indignantly. 'I did it extremely well. If I taught them anything I taught them how to climb on a wall properly.'

On the other hand, they had failed to notice that the *Hickory House* glove puppet, Humphrey Cushion, had this most extremely phallic nose which always seemed to look both highly suggestive and highly inappropriate to me.

There followed, thankfully, another opportunity to do some rather good work. I had a role in a most prestigious production of Shakespeare's *Twelfth Night* at the temporary theatre on the site of the bard's old Globe which has now been so splendidly reconstructed, largely due to the efforts of director Sam Wanamaker, father of the wonderful actress Zoe, whose dream the whole project was. It was there, on such hallowed ground, that I chalked up another memorable first.

The play was directed by Michael Attenborough, son of Richard. Alfred Marks played Sir Toby Belch. I played Maria and I stopped the show. Literally. But I did have good reasons.

The clue is in the name by which this theatre was known – The Plastic Bucket. It was open-sided but partially covered by a tent, which looked like a kind of mini Dome, and was a total water trap. One day we had torrential rain. The tent had filled with gallons of water. There we were in our costumes and wigs and the entrances to the stage were like Niagara Falls. There were sheets of water coming down all over the place and a nutty girl was fiddling around with an electrics board that was running with water. It was all getting highly dangerous. The stage was painted, and when stage paint gets wet it becomes Torville and Dean land. Also, people had to enter on bicycles. I have no idea why directors of Shakespeare want to put people on bicycles, but they often do, and this production was no exception.

I looked up, and there on the fast-collapsing tent-like roof, which you could see through, was this great man of the theatre, Sam Wanamaker, in his underpants, baling out with a plastic bucket. Hence the theatre's name – apparently this spectacle was a regular feature. It was, however, like picking up grains of sand off the beach. There was no way Sam and his bucket were going to do any good. But the sight of a half-naked Sam Wanamaker doing this sort of extraordinary trampoline act above people's heads is something I shall always cherish.

However, it suddenly became very clear to me that not only were our costumes and wigs going to be ruined, not only were we all in danger of breaking our legs on a treacherous stage, not only was it impossible for the audience to hear us, but the roof was about to collapse too. So I just walked forward on stage, held up my hands and said, 'That's it. We're stopping. It's not safe to carry on.'

The roof did hold out, just, and the next night we were back on. But I know it did finally collapse not long afterwards.

Making any kind of open-air theatre work in the UK is a triumph, and there were so many problems with the Globe in the early days that is a great tribute to Sam Wanamaker and all concerned with the project that they persevered and made the theatre into what it is today.

I did find it a great thrill to work there. There is something special about performing outside, and something even more special about standing in the same spot where actors were actually playing in Shakespeare's time. It used to make me laugh to think that Shakespeare's actors were probably muttering and grumbling about the same things actors grumble about today. I could almost hear the dialogue drifting on the breeze.

'It's better than the last bit of writing he did, but there isn't a lot to work on.'

'I'm supposed to be a comedian and he's not written anything for me. I'm not working for him if he keeps on like this.'

'This costume doesn't suit me at all. Wardrobe hasn't tried. I looked far better in *A Midsummer Night's Dream*.' I swear to God, thespians will always be found mouthing exactly the same words. There is an extraordinary timelessness about the theatre.

In 1974 I made another brief foray into the world of films. I was given a part in the Disney film *One of Our Dinosaurs is Missing*, which was released the following year and centred around a secret microfilm that is smuggled out of China and hidden in a dinosaur's skeleton in the Natural History Museum.

I nearly went missing too – permanently.

It was another film with an impressive cast including Peter Ustinov, Derek Nimmo, Roy Kinnear, Bernard Bresslaw and Helen Hayes. I played Joss Ackland's wife and in one scene he took me out for a special dinner at a Chinese restaurant where he presented me with a rather unusual birthday present.

'Happy birthday darling, I bought it for you,' said Joss as a dinosaur appeared in front of me.

Now the creature concerned, a 60-foot high replica, was supposed to trundle along on a kind of track and stop a foot or so away from me. It didn't stop, though. It just came trundling on until it smashed into me. The set was pretty solid, but everything was smashed to pieces including the table in front of me and the chair I was sitting on. There was an awful splintering sound and I ended up stuck under the table with this dinosaur, still moving, on top of me. It was actually extremely frightening. I suffered concussion and quite a few bumps and bruises, but it would have been even worse if two of the extras playing Chinese waiters had not reacted very quickly and pulled me out from the wreckage.

Nowadays an actor would probably sue for compensation. That didn't occur to me. But I did get a bunch of flowers from the dinosaur.

It was also during the early seventies that the struggle to preserve Covent Garden took place. It was about the same time that Les Halles, the inner-city marketplace in Paris, was flattened, and those of us who were part of the Garden and loved it, were determined that the same thing was not going to happen in London.

Our beloved fruit and veg market moved to Nine Elms in 1974, but the battle to preserve its old home for our capital city began long before then. All the diverse characters of the Garden got together, and boy, did we fight. We battled for every brick of it, and to this day walking around Covent Garden as it is now, I feel a certain pride that I was part of that struggle.

The people who lived and who worked in the Garden were not opposed to moving the commercial operation. We realised that such a central site was no longer feasible, but we were not prepared to let its history and architecture be destroyed.

The Covent Garden Community Association was formed. I was asked to become involved because I was quite well known, but I would have done all that I could in the fight in any case. It began in a very small way with the Association seeming something of a David against the Goliath of the big-business organisations that had control of most of the property in the area. We staged candlelit processions, and I helped organise the first big demonstration, a public meeting, in the piazza. I managed to get several public figures to speak including the broadcaster David Jacobs whose father had been a porter in the market. However, I didn't realise that I was going to be called upon to make a speech too. It was the first I ever made in my life, and I had to call on both my grandfathers' genes and Robin's support in the wings. I sent a message to the Greater London Council via Eliza Dolittle, 'You think you're going to get Covent Garden. Not bleedin' likely.'

Everybody in the community did their bit, including many of those involved in London theatre. Dame Peggy Ashcroft was a great supporter. The Players Theatre put on a show to raise funds. We were determined that bureaucracy and big business would not destroy our community. The GLC insisted it would be wonderful to have parks in Covent Garden for people to sit in, but they were intending to destroy people's homes to make way for them.

At one point we actually managed to steal their so-called plans for redeveloping the Garden. But there were no such plans, not really, just plans to flatten the place. Like everyone else, I was angry. The big landlords were offering people £30 to get out of homes their families had lived in for generations. These were people who didn't realise that they could say no, people who, because of their pride, refused to admit that they were in trouble. I arranged for some of them to be interviewed on *Panorama,* and gradually the truth began to come out.

Strange things happened during the fight. A building in Long Acre went up in flames shortly after it was ruled that it's beautiful old façade could not be touched. It burned down on a summer's night and I remember looking out of the window of my flat and thinking how heavy the fog was for that time of year. The street was full of smoke, of course, not fog, and it wasn't until the next morning that I realised how close that whole area had come to being burned down.

Against all odds, the Association ultimately won the day. We awoke public awareness to the planned destruction of this rather glorious part of our national heritage. The wonderful old buildings of the Garden were saved, and quite a lot of new council housing, some of it very imaginative, was built in the area for the people who belonged to that very special community.

I remember walking through the piazza just after all the boarding had been taken down, and there was a man in a long coat with a greyhound at his feet, standing alone in the middle, playing a flute. It was like something out of a seventeenth-century print. It made me cry because I thought it was every bit as important that we managed to preserve so much of the spirit of Covent Garden as to have preserved its architecture.

That spirit lives on, as do the characters. At one point when Robin and I were going through a particularly bad patch I was spotted in tears by an elderly neighbour who was one of my favourite Garden characters.

'Come on, Amanda,' she said. 'You can't cry. You're market.'

Now that was a great compliment and I still remind myself of it if ever I am feeling upset about anything.

To this day market people retain a unique way of looking at things. I have a lady who 'does' for me, called Catherine, who is of Irish descent, whom I once asked to buy me a *Daily Mail* and an *Evening Standard*.

'I couldn't get a *Mail* so I got you two *Standards*,' she informed me on her return. And that, I can assure you, is actually far more typically market than Irish.

I could not do without Catherine, however. Just as I could not do without my neighbour Annie, who guards me with her life against all evils both imagined and real, and to whom I invariably turn when the going gets tough, nor my dear friend Beryl, who is always there when I need her.

Like me, Beryl does not have a very high opinion of her own appearance. She once asked me how I'd got on in rehearsals, and I replied that I was too ugly that day to have an opinion.

'I know what you mean,' she replied. 'I felt too ugly today to go through the front door of my office, so I went round the back.'

Then there is Mr Kipps, who manages to stock almost everything you need in his small general store and somehow contrives to survive in spite of the nearby presence of giants like Tesco and Marks and Spencer.

I am lucky enough to live in 'old Covent Garden', at the heart of this community, unlike any other that I have encountered, and among such a rich variety of people who continue to make the place so special. I have never wanted to live anywhere else.

Playing a part in the saving of Covent Garden was one of the best things that ever happened to me. Another of the best moments of my life came shortly after when I was invited to play the lead role in *Oh, Kay!* in 1975.

The show was the one that was written for Gertrude Lawrence by P. G. Wodehouse and Guy Bolton with music by the Gershwins, and which Robin's godfather Harold French had appeared in with Gertie.

She had been my heroine since my schooldays. I even owed my name to her. I still keep a framed photograph of her by my bedside, which I always take to my dressing room when I am working in a theatre. I was, of course, even more nervous than usual of a new role, because I was stepping into Gertie's hallowed footsteps and that meant so very much to me.

The way in which it came about was the culmination of a series of incidents dating back fifteen years, to when I had met John Law in Scotland. Some might dismiss them as coincidences. To me, and forgive me if I sound fanciful, it was always much more than that. There was more than an element of destiny about it, and often in my life I have felt Gertie's presence quite strongly.

On that first occasion John Law suddenly presented me with a sheaf of cuttings from his newspaper library. They were Gertie's obituaries. John was working night shifts at the time and he told me that he suddenly got the urge to look them out for me. 'I've no idea why,' he said.

Then we realised that he had collected the cuttings at three o'clock in the morning on 6 September, which was not only the anniversary of Gertie's death but also the exact time that she died.

I learned a lot about Gertie from those obituaries. And after that, I always seemed to be meeting and working with people who told me things about her. Harold French, when he was directing me in *A Public Mischief* in 1964, actually said that I reminded him of Gertie, which of course flattered me greatly. Then one night in 1975 I opened a cupboard in the bedroom of my flat and as usual a pile of things flew out, including a programme for *Oh, Kay!* While I was looking at it, Robin, who was in the sitting room, put on a record of Gertie singing 'Someone to Watch Over Me', which I had never heard him play before and didn't even know we had a copy.

The following day I was interviewed by a journalist at the Nags Head who, completely out of the blue, asked, 'Have you ever thought of doing *Oh, Kay!* the musical?'

So it was, with my head full of Gertie and *Oh, Kay!*, that I went with the producer Marion Davis, with whom I'd worked before, to meet Guy Bolton and discuss a play he had written about Churchill. On the way I stopped off at Robin's office in Bond Street and by chance picked up a book which just happened to be *Bring on the Girls,* which Guy had written with P. G. Wodehouse. It is the story of their time together writing musical comedy. I flipped it open at a page which related an incident during the first night of the original *Oh, Kay!* in 1927 when a dog had run on stage while Gertie, somewhat appropriately, was singing the chorus of 'Do, Do, Do – What You've Done Before', and had peed on the footlights. Naturally I could not resist asking Guy Bolton about Gertie, as I always did anyone whom I met who had known her. But Guy was rather a gruff man, totally disinterested in the past, and he just said shortly, 'What do you know about Gertrude Lawrence?'

Without pausing to think, I rattled off the dog story that I had just read in his book. At the end of it Guy simply asked, 'Do you want to do her play?'

It was an extraordinary leap of faith. He didn't even ask me if I thought I could do it. I said 'Yes' at once, and worried about it later.

Oh, Kay! had never been revived in England since Gertie's day. I don't know that my playing it was any great contribution to the theatre, but it was certainly very special to me. I found it both nostalgic and therapeutic. Once again I got some rather splendid notices. A particular favourite was from Felix Barker in the *London Evening News*, which began:

Where has Amanda Barrie been all my life? Not idle, of course, but probably denied her full chance with fugitive films and fleeting TV shadows. Last night this enchanting actress with the Betty Boop eyes and mock-vacant manner landed slap-bang in my lap – in all our delighted laps at The Westminster – with what was surely the performance of her career . . .

And it ended:

Sweeping the evening along Miss Barrie switches with delicious ease from sentiment (Someone to Watch Over Me) to eccentric comedy, as the bogus parlour maid with a frill cap which, in an emergency, she pulls down over her head like a visor. Never have I seen an actress come so near the gentle ineffable charm, to say nothing of technical accomplishment – that musical stars possessed in the inter-war years. Very much *Oh Kay*, Miss Barrie.

But the 'notice' I am most proud of came in the form of a letter from the great man himself, P. G. Wodehouse, who had apparently heard nice things about me in the play from Guy Bolton. 'I can see from your photograph that you must be ideal in the part,' he wrote from his home in Long Island, New York. And he signed his letter, 'Lots of love, from Plum.'

I was knocked out to receive a letter from him, and even more so by the fact that he signed himself 'Plum', a nickname that I understand he normally used only within his circle of close friends.

I have to say that while I would never have presumed to suggest that I was like Gertie in any way on stage, several people pointed out to me that I did a number of things exactly the same way that she had done them, even though I didn't know that. Gertie's chauffeur came to see the show and afterwards he asked me what had led me to come to the front of the stage and kneel down when I sang 'Someone to Watch Over Me'.

'I have no idea,' I replied. 'Why?'

'Because that's what Gertie did,' he said.

I hadn't even known that. I'd just done it.

As I opened in *Oh, Kay!* something else of profound importance happened in my life. I acquired Katie Cupcake, the dog who was to sleep on my head. She had been found abandoned and taken to Bow Street Police Station. A policeman we knew came into the Nags Head one Sunday lunchtime, obviously saw me as an easy touch and said, 'Amanda, please will you take this little Yorkshire terrier because the last dog we had went to Battersea Dogs' Home and I can't bear the same thing for this one.' They tied her up outside the police station, then they cut the string, pushed her down the steps, and said, 'Oh look, Amanda. The dog's escaped. You'd better catch her.'

Apparently the time they were allowed to keep her before sending her to Battersea had expired, and by arranging for her to escape she obtained another eight days' grace before a decision had to be made. And by then Katie and I had bonded. Indeed, we became glued together for life.

She was a very nice dog and, rather like me – in spite of or perhaps because of, spending so much time in the country when I was growing up – was completely a town animal. She didn't like grass. She much preferred concrete and had a dislike for anything to do with the countryside. She liked pubs, and would happily sit on my knee for hours sucking iced vodka, if I'd let her. She also loved the theatre. She would come with me and curl up in my dressing room. She knew instinctively when we had two shows in a day – she wouldn't even bother to get up after the first one. Every so often she'd toddle off to visit the people she liked, but she'd always return to my dressing room well before curtain-up.

She appeared on stage several times, too, which she thoroughly enjoyed. Unfortunately though, she never quite got the hang of the fact that a show had come off, and if we walked past a theatre where I had recently played she would shoot in to see if anybody she knew was about. People would open their dressing room door to see this strange Yorkshire terrier galloping through their theatre with me in hot pursuit.

I'm not quite sure how she got her name. She started as Katie and it grew into Katie Cupcake. I think it was just another of those inexplicable Covent Garden nicknames. Her official title was even more ridiculous. She was Katie Cupcake FBC. It stood for Fur-Bearing Cockroach because one of the locals at the Nags Head had looked her up and down one evening and remarked, 'That's not a dog, it's a fur-bearing cockroach.' Poor Katie! The name stuck.

She was a real Covent Garden dog and she was very popular in the neighbourhood. Old ladies used to walk past us and say, 'Goodnight Katie,' without bothering to address me. But then, she was very good with people and would trot off periodically to talk to all her friends.

I had her for twelve years. She eventually died after an operation that went wrong and I was absolutely devastated. I know it's terrible to say this, although anyone who has had an animal they were really close to will probably understand, but her death probably hit me almost as hard when it happened as the death of both of my parents. Even my mother.

I was devoted to Katie Cupcake and I continue to owe her a great deal. She helped me through an awful lot of scenes in *Coronation Street,* even the later ones when Alma was dying. It was easier somehow to think about my dog than about a person. And whenever I had to cry on camera all I had to do was think about my Katie and the tears would always flow. As a tribute to Katie, and to my mother, I managed in one of my final scenes in the Street to get a props boy to place a framed photograph of Connie and Katie in shot – in a rather poignant scene in which Alma looked through a box of old photos shortly before she died. So both my mother and my dog have appeared on the show which played almost as big a part in my life as they did.

CHAPTER FIFTEEN

~

Holidays have not played a great part in my life. I have taken very few. However, those that I have had do seem to have been quite momentous. First there was the south of France, with its extraordinary legacy, then there was Spain with Robin and Sally.

Following a stay in hospital in the UK and then in the actors' rest home, Denville Hall, in the UK, Robin's parents had recovered their ability to function and fend for themselves – up to a point – and returned to Javea on the Costa Blanca. Robin suggested we all visit them there for a holiday, and, although I can hardly believe it now, Sally and I agreed that this would be a nice thing to do. My fear of flying was quite bad at the time, so we ended up driving there in Sally's car, which was allegedly better than ours – a left-hand drive Morris Minor known as Egg Fart partly because its registration letters were EGT and partly because it was yet another of those inexplicable Covent Garden names. However, the journey to Spain was so terrible and so long that at least it made me determined to conquer my fears as best I could and learn to cope with air travel in future. Sally's car broke down twice, once on a major highway halfway up a mountain with a precipice to one side, and secondly and terminally just a few miles out of Javea.

We were, therefore, exhausted when we finally arrived by taxi at Ian and Cash Hunter's home to be greeted by a strange vision, which I got quite used to over the ensuing few days.

My dear father-in-law Ian, this once very famous actor who had been Richard the Lionheart, was wearing a Simpson's silk shirt and nothing else. That was his attire in Spain. His 'almond rock', as Mr Shovel Shit would have said, and all his other bits were in constant danger of being on full display. He was also carrying a little Dorothy bag.

'Would you like a drink, my old darlings?' he enquired.

I just wanted to go to sleep, but we had a drink of course. And another one. And another one.

However, we'd got there, and Ian and Cash's hillside villa was lovely, with spectacular views. Let the holiday begin, I thought. We're going to have a good time from now on. We can just relax and sunbathe. I should have known better!

Unfortunately Robin's parents had reached a stage where they were beginning to fall apart once again. They were getting on very badly, and drinking extremely heavily. Robin's mother, whom I disliked very nearly as much as she disliked me (I suppose I should have known that might make it difficult to have a good holiday in her house) used to do awful things to his father like mouthing words so that he thought he was going deaf. Perhaps understandably, Ian had become quite paranoid about her. Once while we were there he got into their car and he started yelling, 'Look what she's done now. Look what she's done. She's even removed the steering wheel!'

She hadn't. He'd just forgotten that the car was left-hand drive.

It was very sad. All the time Ian and Cash were fighting and hitting each other over the head with shoes they would call each other by pet names. Part of the problem, I think, was this extraordinary expat community which existed on a constant round of cocktail parties and other drinking sessions at everybody's houses.

Robin fitted into the community like a glove. One of his party pieces was to swim in other people's pools with his corduroy trilby on and a cigarette in his mouth. He was a very good swimmer, but he didn't like being in the sun. So when we went to the beach he spent the whole of the time under a green plastic awning drinking Scotch. Even if he went for a swim in the sea he would keep his trilby on, and would just drift off waving. Talk about English eccentrics abroad! I think I had the whole package in one household.

One evening we were dragged along to one of these dreadful expat soirées by Ian's parents and Cash took it upon herself to introduce the three of us to our hosts as we walked in.

'This is my beautiful son,' she said, 'that thing behind him is his wife, and that's Sally. She's a lesbian.'

As a conversation stopper, I've yet to witness anything to beat it. The whole party came to a silent halt. There was nothing to say really. The evening that followed was not a great success. Sally was deeply upset. Her sexuality was something very private. It was not something she ever talked about. There was nothing about her, in my opinion, which gave a clue, and the three of us had, I'm sure, not done or said anything while in Spain to indicate that our friendship was anything other than conventional. But Cash had noticed something. Maybe it was because she was Robin's mother, that something odd struck her about our relationship. I have no idea.

The routine, however, was not allowed to falter. The next night we went to another party, in a beautiful converted windmill. After a bit I became aware that Sally, who had been extremely unsettled by the events of the previous night, was missing. I went looking for her outside. The windmill was quite isolated on top of a hill. I could see her on the horizon, and she seemed to be shouting something into the sky. I thought it best to leave her alone and I went back in. After a while Sally followed me into this very gathering which, on the surface at least, was extremely civilised. She was still shouting what turned out to be, 'I'm a lesbian, I'm a lesbian,' causing a number of eyebrows to rise. She'd come out all by herself. Yet another party was brought to a complete stultifying stop. I still have no idea why Sally did it.

The whole trip was a total disaster from start to finish. And people wonder why I am less eager than most to go on holiday. I will never forget Cash's introduction at that party. 'This is my beautiful son, that thing behind him is his wife, and that's Sally. She's a lesbian.'

It was truly, wonderfully horrible.

It was fairly remarkable that Sally, Robin and I stayed together after that. But we continued to maintain our funny little world for some time. The crisis came in 1976 while I was in *Absurd Person Singular*, the Alan Ayckbourn play, at the Vaudeville, with Paul Eddington, Millicent Martin and David Baron. It was the first time I had worked with Paul Eddington, which proved to be a joy. And for once, instead of this being a short-term experience – which is what usually happens when you find yourself working with someone you really like and respect, the show comes off and that's that – Paul and I were together for a year playing husband and wife in *Absurd Person Singular* and shortly afterwards went into the Michael Frayn comedy *Donkeys' Years*, at the Globe Theatre in Shaftesbury Avenue, for another year.

I also enjoyed working with Millie Martin. We had a particular bond. We both had Yorkshire terriers which we took to the theatre with us. One night her dog toddled downstairs with me, hidden beneath the long skirt I was wearing, and very nearly made it on stage. I noticed her just in time.

Everything about *Absurd Person Singular* was pretty good. Alan Ayckbourn directed the play himself, for the first time. It had previously been directed by Eric Thompson, creator of the *Magic Roundabout* and father of the actress Emma, at the Criterion, Piccadilly. I found it quite wonderful to work with Alan. Also I was probably performing at my best around that time which was in no small way due both to working with such a class act as Paul, who was just becoming really well known on TV in *The Good Life*, and appearing in such an exceptional play. Some nights the laughter went on for so long that on stage we had time to have a chat about it. I remember Paul saying to me once, 'When on earth are we going to get laughs like that again?'

There was however one matinee when the laughs did not come at all. And that, I'm afraid, was down to my mother. She was so determined to help us out that she kept laughing extremely loudly before we had finished our lines, thus absolutely killing the laughs for the rest of the audience. Paul and the others began to ask who this dreadful woman was. I had to confess that I thought it was my mother and send the theatre manager to tell her that we really didn't need her help.

But then in the second act she did something that she always did when she came to see me on stage – she lit a match so that I could spot her and see her face. Unfortunately this was at the time of a lot of IRA bomb scares in London and she was promptly grabbed by security and dragged out of the theatre. Fortunately I managed not to see this incident or I am not at all sure that I would have been able to continue.

Meanwhile, my home life was getting worse by the minute. It was a kind of general deterioration. All three of us were inevitably beginning to go in our separate directions. Sally gradually drifted away, staying with us less and less and going back to her mother more and more. The one part I didn't want to play in real life was Zelda to Robin's Scott Fitzgerald.

Big drinkers invariably want their partners to drink with them, and it's all too easy to fall into the trap. But I was playing the lead in the West End. I would have a drink after the show, but that was it. I never touched a drop during the day. I couldn't have done, I wouldn't have been employed. Meanwhile, Robin was still working at the Players Theatre occasionally, but that was it.

At this point a beautiful young woman, whom I shall call Mary because yet again it would cause her embarrassment to have her real name revealed to the world, joined the backstage team of *Absurd Person Singular*. Now, her looks actually meant nothing to me. I fall in love with what people are, not their gender and not their appearance. I want to put that in letters six-feet high and stamp it on everything, including my passport, because it simply is not a matter of, if you happen to be gay, seeing a woman in the theatre and going for her. Not for me it isn't, anyway. Mary, who was the sort of person who should have been on stage not working behind the scenes, seemed to spend a great deal of time around the part of the wings where Paul Eddington and I were usually waiting to go on. I actually thought she had taken a shine to him. It never occurred to me that the person she had fixed her eyes on was me.

Then one day, during the interval between the first and second act she came into my dressing room, hurled herself at my feet and informed me that she was in love with me. I tell you, between Act I and Act II that's quite a thing to be confronted with. I've found that people who have been interested in me have invariably been persistent and I am a pushover for persistence. If anyone reading this wants to seduce someone and is encountering resistance, hear what I say. Persist. I always think, 'How awfully nice it is of them to fall in love with me.' It isn't that it has always been returned but persistence is a bugger. Certainly in my case, the odds have always been that I will give in. However, this time I said, 'No.' But like an idiot, I told Robin. Now Mary was one of those people who could stop traffic. And when I continued to say no she actually set about him I think, she saw him as a way to me and he was very taken with her, almost any man would have liked Mary as a feather in his cap.

The three of us started to go to Rules every night, and it seemed to me that Robin thought we might have a substitute Sally on our hands. It certainly wasn't the way I was thinking. But at that time I seemed to have no control at all. I know I should have had, but I didn't. I just worked too hard. I was too tired to sort my life out. Things just happened around me and all too often I went along with what other people wanted. What developed between Robin, Mary and me was just part of that scenario.

One night they took the piss out of me so much that I just said, 'OK! I give in. Take me to bed. Do what you want.'

So we all went back to Bow Street and I just lay there like a stone. I was barely aware of what was going on. It was completely unimportant to me. With those two together the only desire I can ever remember having was for more sleep. I was working so hard I didn't care about what I was doing. I'd given up and I was on a downward slide.

I went along with this new threesome for a few weeks, mainly because Mary, who was very bright and clever, was extremely kind to me in all sorts of ways. But she still pushed. It was always me she was interested in and she always used to be trying to see me at the flat when Robin wasn't around.

It was all very different to the way things had been with Robin and Sally. We had been a little team. The thing between Robin, Mary and me had nothing to do with being a team, and nothing to do with caring. It wasn't an emotional bonding. It was something that had been manufactured. It was out of my control and I didn't like it at all. With the wonderful benefit of hindsight I can't believe that I ever allowed myself to get involved in the situation.

I did love my husband. Until the drinking became a problem, we'd had a very good marriage and a very funny one with a lot of laughs. And curiously enough, Sally had been part of that, not a destructive influence at all. But I suppose it couldn't last for ever. Few conventional relationships do, do they? Ours always had the odds stacked against it.

Meanwhile, Robin started to turn from a tall, handsome, fit man into a physical wreck. He was a great cook but he more or less stopped eating. He grew thinner and thinner. Once during *Absurd Person Singular* I was about to leave for a matinée when he keeled over and dropped to the floor virtually unconscious. Thankfully Robin recovered from this scare.

He had no interest in trying to stop drinking. You couldn't even talk to him about it. Robin had always been a grasshopper, hopping through life, always the person who made people laugh, always the one who shone. When things turned the other way for him he just couldn't cope with it at all. His lifestyle, which had been so much fun initially, demonstrating how you could find somewhere to drink in Covent Garden and Soho at any hour of day or night, was no fun at all any more, especially when I was watching this rather special man seeming to deteriorate in front of my eyes.

I suspect that underneath it all, Robin was as frustrated by his condition as I was. He'd gone from being Jolly Rob to someone who could still laugh in front of people but who would change completely once he'd shut the front door back in the flat.

Everything deteriorated, as things are inclined to around drink. My mother's lovely little flat turned into somewhere I didn't care about. It became just somewhere I crashed out. I always like to make my home as special as I can and to take care of my surroundings. I stopped doing that at that time. I was frightened to ask anybody up. Suddenly I was living with a man with a hairline emotional trigger. He developed another side to his personality. There were still glimmers of the old Robin, the man I had loved so much, but these were becoming more and more rare.

I remember once, when I was still in *Absurd Person Singular,* going along to the theatre one day and I was so upset about what was happening between Robin and me that I just leaned against a parking meter outside the stage door and broke down. I thought I was going to be unable to go on, but I did of course. As always. I was, however, totally exhausted and there didn't seem to be anywhere to rest.

I so desperately wanted to have a rest from all the emotional turmoil that was surrounding me. The whole point of me ever having a relationship with anyone was *not* sexual, *not* physical. It was all part of my desperate desire for some sort of home. That's all I ever wanted really, a home and someone to go home to, somebody to share my life with. I didn't want anything else. I don't think I had realised when I was sent to boarding school, and my home and my mother kind of

▲ Me as Cleo. Don't know the name of my guard dog.

◀ No wonder we couldn't stop laughing. Me dressed as a daffodil, Dora Bryan as a primrose, and Dickie Wattis as a bluebell, in the revue *Six of One*.

▼ Me, the cover girl – and it was *Tatler's* very first in colour.

12 AUGUST 1964   2s.6d.

tatler

& BYSTANDER

present laughter

◀ This is the picture of my mother and Katie Cupcake that I managed to get on screen in *Coronation Street* when Alma died. Mummy and Katie were wearing red-white-and-blue ribbons in honour of the Queen's Silver Jubilee.

▶ With the legendary Red Rum, my all-time favourite race-horse.

◄ Typical Mike and Alma. What a couple!

► In the caff with Gail – some of my happiest times in *Corrie*.

▼ Happy Christmas to the nation from the cast of *Corrie*. Pity the drinks at the Rovers are only pretend.

(H. WALKER/SUNDAY MIRROR ▼)

(◄ ▼ GRANADA)

◀ We toasted the future – but Ken and Alma were not to have one.

▶ With Curly and wearing that dreaded overall, I was employee of the month – but I never got the hang of the tills.

▼ Fighting for my life with Don Brennan, I've never liked minicabs since.

◀ Alma and Audrey out on the town. Note the name of the shop.

▼ The end of an era. Alma and I prepare to say a final farewell to *Coronation Street*.

▼ Will the real Alma please stand up. When I left *Coronation Street* the cast and crew presented me with an album of photos in which they'd all dressed up as Alma. Frankly I think most of them looked more the part than me. Clockwise from top left: Bill Roache, John Savident, Kevin Kennedy, Sue Nichols and Helen Worth.

▶ Life after the Street.
Me as myself.

▲ Cor! The artist Maggi Hambling, who did a series of drawings of me, called this one 'Amanda seated – legs apart'. I have nothing to add.

disappeared, how much I had been affected. My driving force was not about a great physical falling for men or for women. For me there was no amazing sexual thing about having three in a bed. It was, 'Oh look, I've got a family.' And certainly that was the way I felt about Sally, Robin, Katie Cupcake and me. They were about as close to a family as I ever got. I know it sounds ridiculous, childish even, but that's how it was.

So when things really started to fall apart between Robin and me, I was distraught. I was terrified of being on my own, and of what that would do to me. At that time I was still always about three breaths away from a panic attack.

I don't intend to chronicle in detail the sequence of events which led to the eventual breakdown of our marriage. It all remains too painful, for me, and I'm sure for Robin too. Suffice to say that I felt as if I were being dragged down, and that the only way I could hope to survive was to dive off the sinking ship of our life together and swim for the shore.

By then I knew for certain that Robin was involved with somebody else. I still remember how alone I felt and although I did not actively set out to look for another man it was not surprising that while I was in *Donkeys' Years* I began to have an affair myself. I suppose I needed solace. I started a relationship with a classical actor, someone else I need to protect because of the road his life has taken, and so I shall call him John.

He was an antidote to all that was happening at home. Maybe the thought did occur to me that he could be somebody who might help me find a way out, or at least be there for me, if I could gather up the courage to leave Robin. My affair with John, who was also married, went on for about six months while I was still with Robin. Unlike Robin and me, John and I were not compatible at all except in bed. It was one of the very few relationships in my life – probably the only one actually – that was physical rather than emotional. I was therefore in an even greater state of exhaustion than ever and I was, as usual, doing eight shows a week.

Robin knew something was wrong, of course, and eventually found out about John. But the strange thing was that it didn't break us up, even though I half wanted it to. The peculiar friendship that we had, and still do have, remained solid. Robin just admitted he'd been having an affair too. He hadn't realised that I knew. Then he said, 'So shall we just get on with what we're doing because we don't want to lose our lives together do we?'

Of course, John, although he was still living at weekends with his wife in the country, started to demand that I force Robin to leave. I still couldn't do that. So I decided I would leave my own flat. For the next six months, I slept on people's floors. There followed a particularly mixed-up period, even by my standards. I was not in a show for once and I was just doing bits of TV so I could move around fairly freely. I knew that I had to get out of Robin's way, John or no John, and I didn't want him to know where I was.

I used to stay with my mother in Disley some of the time. We had an arrangement which made things a bit easier for me. It was just the kind of thing she was brilliant at. Robin would call her and she would say, 'Amanda's just popped down to the village. I'll get her to ring you as soon as she comes back.' Then she'd call me wherever I was staying. 'Ring Robin, but don't do it for another seven minutes because I said you'd gone to the bread shop.' And so I lived this unbelievably complex life that you couldn't work out in a detective story. British Telecom were the big winners. It was before the days of ring-back and number displays, so poor Robin would assume he was talking to me in Manchester when actually I was probably just around the corner from him.

Not being together calmed things down and our telephone conversations were rather nice. After a bit he started begging me to return.

He would say, 'Just come home. Come back. I want to read Pooh to you.'

I got terribly, terribly upset over this. Early in our relationship Robin had read the whole of *Winnie the Pooh* to me because my reading was so bad and I had never read it. I realised that I did want to hear him read me Pooh and Piglet again. I did want to go back to Bow Street with him for those laughs, that closeness we had. I did want to have the things that Robin did for me and nobody else could, the quite extraordinary things, like the sweet little notes he used to write me which consisted of explanatory drawings rather than words. I just wanted Robin and me to be how we had been before his drinking took such a hold.

So I went back for a time. But he changed from saying, 'I want to read you Pooh and Piglet stories,' to, 'I want you as my lover again.' And I don't think you can ever turn the clock back in that way. I knew, I had known for a long time, that I was going to have to face properly finishing it with Robin eventually. We started having terrible rows again and I started sneaking off back to Disley with my mother whenever I could while John still lurked in the background.

Ultimately Robin did leave Bow Street and I will never forget him going. It was that image, like Jeffrey Bernard in the play *Jeffrey Bernard is Unwell*. And it hit me hard. He left very quietly clutching the same small suitcase he had arrived with so many years before – a very old and honourable suitcase that had once been his father's – around which he'd wrapped a tie to hold it together. I looked out of the window and saw him walking slowly up the street. I knew how much he loved our flat, loved Covent Garden, and the silly little structure we had kept going for so long. It really crucified me to see him go.

As I write now, however, I am pleased to be able to say that Robin, who has more recently survived a terrible cancer ordeal, did eventually pull his life together in many ways, with the help of a partner for whom I have the greatest admiration.

John more or less moved into Bow Street after Robin departed. But only during the week of course. At weekends he went home to the country and to his wife. He always said he had told her about us early in our relationship, but I later found that not to be the case.

At that stage I did have an immense, out-of-control infatuation with him. Certainly with John I made up for all the physicality I'd previously avoided. He was extremely highly sexed and I joined in wholeheartedly, perhaps because of my fear of there being something wrong with me. I think I set out with John to prove that there wasn't. I also threw myself wholeheartedly into his other interests. John was a devotee of Subud, whose creed involved meditation and passing into various states of consciousness. I ended up joining it too. With Richard it had been fishing and carrying maggots about, with Billy, digging up marijuana plants and with Robin, betting on the horses all day and drinking Covent Garden dry. Now with John I was walking around in Indian robes while I tried to find myself. My friends laughed themselves silly because they'd open the door to the flat and find me sitting cross-legged on the floor, wearing my robes. I thought the first time my sister Caroline saw me like that that she was going to die laughing. However I entered into it absolutely, and I did come to believe in quite a lot of what Subud was about, which was primarily a different way of living. One of their sayings was, 'Don't give me what I ask for. Give me what I need.'

They made you think things out. At the time I don't think I could have told you which colour I preferred, which music I preferred, if I liked art, or if I was interested in anything at all. I had nothing but the theatre, full stop. But while I was involved with Subud I came to realise that I had a passionate interest in art and antiques that had been lying dormant. I started to get up in the middle of the night and look at art books. It was about self-awareness. And one thing I found out, partly through the teaching, and partly just through living with John, who, ironically, had introduced me to it, was that Robin had actually completely spoiled me for other men.

John and I had all the ingredients of a bad relationship. We rarely talked and when we did he had only one topic of conversation. Himself. Robin and I had all the ingredients of a good relationship. We had been very special together. Robin was by nature extremely endearing, funny, nice and kind. I have never had much doubt in my mind that if alcohol had not intervened so devastatingly we would still be together. Certainly that would have been my desire.

CHAPTER SIXTEEN

❧

In 1978 my father died. He was sixty-six, the same age that I am as I write. It was particularly sad for me because we'd only just made friends, really, following decades of estrangement. After the peculiar emotional distance between us dating back to my childhood, my father remarried and his second wife decided that she didn't want to see me. Apparently she said that I reminded her too much of my mother. I did suggest once that he told her that I was his daughter, not someone he was having an affair with, but it made no difference. I barely saw my father throughout my adult life until six months before he died. He did not even meet Robin.

We had kept in vague contact, indeed when I was researching this book I came across letters that he had written to me over the years, all of which were very caring. Maybe because of my reading difficulties, I had not really been aware of them, or the message they put across, before. But when my father finally came to London to see me it was a very emotional meeting. We talked properly for the first time ever. It was extraordinary to think that I had seen him only a handful of times since I was thirteen and these had always been when I happened to be working in Manchester and then I'd only seen him briefly and in the company of others.

I remember vividly him sitting holding my hand in my flat. It was the first time, I think, that he ever held my hand. I also saw him cry that day – for the second time in my life. He told me that he and his wife had travelled to London thirteen years previously to see me in *Any Wednesday,* but they had made no attempt to contact me. I hadn't even known they'd been in the theatre. I found that very upsetting. At least I realised that day that he had cared for me. Life had driven a wedge between us, that was all. I think we may have been on the verge of finally becoming close, but it was not to be. My father was already a very sick man. He had a little cyst in his throat, went into hospital to have it removed and never came round from the operation. The strain on his heart had been too great.

I rushed up to Ashton, to where he still lived, and straight into another of those inappropriate farcical situations that seem to have always plagued me, particularly when my mother, who was already there, was involved.

We were taken to see my father lying in his coffin, something I was not at all keen to do but it seemed to be expected. Mummy, over the top as ever, rushed into the chapel of rest and crashed into his coffin on its trestle, nearly tipping my father onto the floor. Then, afterwards, to my bewilderment, the undertaker asked, 'How did you find him?'

'He's still dead?' I replied.

'But doesn't he look well?'

'I've seen him look better,' I said mildly.

'Ah, but doesn't he look rested?' continued the undertaker. 'Do you know, I think he's dropped ten years since he came in here.'

It was like something out of Alan Bennett. I couldn't believe it.

The farce continued on the day of his funeral. I stayed overnight with my mother and Caroline in Disley. Absurdly, none of us could find anything suitable to wear and we were up until five in the morning drinking tea, eating bacon sandwiches and desperately trying on various outfits. Eventually we set off rather jerkily over the moors in my sister's old car, with Caroline, who had only just passed her driving test, at the wheel. The car broke down and we arrived at the crematorium desperately late to be greeted by my brother Chris, who was frantic, wondering where we were. Then we rushed so much that we went into the wrong funeral and had to be escorted out and redirected. Throughout the service my mother's loud sobs at the back of the chapel could be clearly heard as she let everybody know that she was there.

Despite the chaotic way in which we saw him off, there is no doubt that my father's death upset me considerably more than I would have expected. That one special day in London had changed things. It was doubly painful that he died just as we may have been able to develop a proper relationship at last.

I was coping with emotional turmoil in other parts of my life too. Things were not going well with John. Although I knew I could not have gone on with Robin, I missed him and worried about him. Unsurprisingly perhaps, with all this going on, I did not feel that I was at my absolute best professionally.

In 1979 I went into a show called *The French Have a Song For It* with Helen Shapiro. It had been a huge hit at the King's Head pub in

Islington but then transferred to the Piccadilly Theatre where it was a huge flop. The show never worked for me, largely because I don't speak French and so could never get the hang of the songs. I had people leaving the theatre because of my French, and I was always getting laughs when I shouldn't. My pronunciation turned lines like, 'He got up and went out into the night,' into 'He washes himself.' Or worse.

Helen Shapiro and all the rest of the cast were lovely, but I never did conquer the French.

I recently came across a review of the show by the critic Jane Ellison who wrote rather ambiguously: 'Only Amanda Barrie comes through with credit, gazing around her with frantic grimaces as though signalling to us that her appearance in the show is attributable to a temporary fit of madness.' I am still trying to work out whether that was a good notice or a bad one.

Straight after that I got the sack for the only time in my life. I had a small part in the film *Quadrophenia*, set amid the sixties craziness of Mods and Rockers staging bank holiday weekend battles in sleepy seaside towns. It was based on the record album *Quadrophenia* by Pete Townshend of the Who, and starred Phil Daniels and Michael Elphick with Sting as a pill-popping, fashion-mad Mod. I'm afraid I only lasted two days. On the first day I had to film at the crack of dawn somewhere in the wilds. John had kept me up all night having some crazy argument about Vanessa Redgrave so when I got on set I couldn't keep my eyes open. I was told that I was being dispensed with because I was miscast, but I have never believed that was the truth. I really do think it was because I was too exhausted to work properly and was therefore very bad. It's a little episode I have always regretted. I believe that I made a complete pig's ear of *Quadrophenia*, largely because of the mess my personal life was in at the time, and lost an opportunity to feature in what became quite a significant cult movie.

One way and another I suppose it was inevitable that John and I couldn't last. It wasn't just that he was a bad substitute for Robin. I also didn't like the way in which I felt he was using me. John in Bow Street never felt right. Even Katie Cupcake, who had adored Robin, didn't like having him around. The crunch came when John arrived at the flat one day absolutely ashen and snorting with terror, and said, 'My wife has found out.'

'Found out about what?' I asked him.

'About us,' he said.

This was a shock. Early in our relationship, he had told me he couldn't leave her, not completely, but that he had been honest with her about me, so I felt able to carry on with it. I never put pressure on him to leave her, because I would never pressurise anyone into doing anything they weren't comfortable with.

'But you'd already told her,' I said, realising the truth as I spoke.

'Not that you and I went to bed together,' he responded.

I watched him quaking with terror because his marriage might be under threat, and it dawned on me finally that he'd been on to a rather good thing. He was appearing at the National Theatre on the South Bank, an easy walk over Waterloo Bridge from his rent-free digs in Covent Garden. I felt that I had been treated like an unpaid landlady with sex thrown in. I didn't do anything about it straight away, but from that moment on I began to hate John. Every day he used to walk across the road to the public phone boxes opposite and phone his wife. I remember going past with Katie Cupcake one Sunday and he was roaring with laughter into the receiver.

Now, I am somebody to whom laughter is very important. There had been very few laughs with John as far as I was concerned so I was quite hurt by this scenario. I waited for him in the flat and when he returned I confronted him about the whole sordid set-up. He completely lost his temper, kicking in the sitting-room door. I think he realised he wasn't going to be able to have the best of all worlds any more, and he was not pleased. The landlady was playing up.

As usual, I turned to my work to bail me out. I was offered a tour of Noël Coward's *Blithe Spirit*, and I took it in order to get away from John. He, however, had decided that he wanted me rather more than he had realised, once I started to pull away from him. At one point I was playing in Peterborough and John announced that he would come to collect me after the show and drive me back the sixty or so miles to Covent Garden in the middle of the night so that I could sleep with him there before finding my own way back on the train for a matinée the next day. Like a bloody idiot I agreed.

At this point, I was given some very good advice from the psychiatrist I was seeing at the time, a lovely man called Louis who told me something that makes sense of a lot of people's otherwise unfathomable relationships. 'Always remember, Amanda, that when someone tells you that they love you, they may well do so, but they don't necessarily mean the same thing that you do by love. Next time, you tell John to come up to you wherever you are playing, take you out to dinner after the show, and book you both into a good hotel.'

So I gritted my teeth, and told John exactly that. He did it just once. But although he booked us into an excellent hotel he typically drew the line at taking me out for an excellent dinner as well. Instead he had the nerve to unpack his wife's foil-wrapped sandwiches.

I think it was then that I realised we had definitely reached the end.

There was another factor. By then I had met Heather Chasen, who was playing opposite me in *Blithe Spirit*. Previously I had only known her from a distance as a very fine actress with an impressive theatrical track record. She had also starred in the long-running radio show *The Navy Lark*, and played the vampish Valerie Polard in *Crossroads*. She was an extremely beautiful woman, but I did not know just how good she was to be with. Heather was, and still is, a great English eccentric. She is very funny and very nice.

On our first day in rehearsals we left the building together and I noticed her clocking this rather attractive woman walking by. I just said to her, 'I saw that,' and we started to laugh. That thing that good shared laughter does to my heart happened right then.

I had heard the usual kind of rumours that you get in the theatre, that although she had been married Heather might well be interested in relationships with women. It was an open secret. Heather had been married and had a very beautiful son, Rupert, who because of his looks was chosen to play the particularly beautiful schoolboy Bobbie Phillips in the film *If*. Like so many people, Heather has had a mixed life. Like myself, and so many others, she is a perfect example of someone you cannot label in terms of her sexuality. Most of us are fairly complex creatures, both physically and emotionally, but the world has an obsession with putting labels on people. My attitude is how dare anybody label anybody else.

It wasn't long before Heather and I paired up. It was never a great physical relationship, that wasn't what we were about at all. Heather looked after me and we laughed a lot. I quite quickly came to love her wholeheartedly. I switched almost overnight from being in a relationship that was almost entirely sexual to being with somebody who more than anything wanted to make me a home, as I had always wanted. I just adored Heather. So much so that I decided to tell John about her straight away.

I thought the shock was going to kill him. He was fighting for breath. It was a near-fatal blow to his ego. The thought of me leaving him for a woman was almost too much. That any woman could prefer one of her own sex to a man was beyond his powers of understanding. That *I* should prefer another woman to a stud like him was, for John, quite unbelievable.

So John departed. Ironically, shortly after we finally split, he wrote me a letter asking me to marry him, a commitment I might once have welcomed in spite of the minor encumbrance of his wife. As things were, this seemed like an empty gesture far too late. I never replied and I never saw John again.

The most telling epitaph to our relationship came from my beloved Katie Cupcake who, being the exceptional, extraordinary, intelligent creature that she was, seemed to know at once that John was no more. I had taken her with me on tour, and when we returned to Bow Street, now a John-free zone, she shot through the door, ran into the sitting room, the kitchen, the bedroom and the bathroom before coming back to bark at me. She proceeded to whizz round and round my tiny flat as if she was a greyhound in a race, negotiating the corners so fast I don't know how she kept on her little feet. If only the horses I've backed over the years had run half as well as my Katie Cupcake did that night I'd be a far richer woman. She jumped on the bed and pulled all the bedclothes off with her teeth. Then she rolled backwards and forwards all over it, and throughout she just kept on barking, something she didn't normally do, and wagged her tail so much it was a wonder it didn't drop off. I could only assume that she was making a public statement of her delight at John's departure and that her antics were in celebration.

While Katie Cupcake was doing her thing, I had done what all old chorus girls do when they get home to roost. I'd taken my clothes off and gone foraging for food. There was a cold chicken in the fridge. And so, once Katie had settled down a little, the pair of us ended up sitting on the floor in the living room, me with no clothes on, her with her tail still wagging for England, and together we ate the entire chicken.

The next period of my life was one of the happiest. Heather and I had a very jolly, silly life. We shared our time between Bow Street and her mews house in West London.

Heather was not just immensely talented and immensely amusing, she was also a tremendous home-builder. She looked after me like nobody ever had before. Actually, at times it could be embarrassing. I remember arriving home at the mews after a show one night when Heather had some visitors. Nonetheless she greeted me with, 'Now, I've run your bath, dear. So just get into it, and I'll bring you a hot drink. Then you can try on the dressing gown I bought for you today. Oh, and I've got you a new comb. It's on the table in the bedroom.' She was very dear, very funny, quite idiotic, and she never failed to let me know how much she cared about me.

Once I was walking through Soho on my way to the theatre, thinking that my dog was safe, because she was at home with Heather, and that I was safe too because I knew Heather would be home when I got back, and that we would drink tea together and be together all night. I said to myself, 'I don't want much more than this, I really don't.'

One of the reasons I think that I felt so safe with Heather was that when we met she didn't drink at all, having had a problem with alcohol earlier in life. During the bulk of the time that we were together neither did I. I gave up alcohol for almost seven years. I did it primarily because Heather was my partner. I loved her, and if she didn't drink I didn't want to. But also I think, after Robin, the total absence of alcohol was truly a great relief.

Heather and I shared a crazy but delightful relationship. At one stage we were both playing the lead in different productions in the West End, yet we never seemed to have any money. As far as Heather was concerned, it may not have been unconnected with the lifestyle to which she aspired. She always dressed beautifully and was incredibly stylish in every way. I will never forget having tea with her one day in what was then one of the smartest places in town – Sagne in Marylebone High Street – her suggestion after she had been to the bank manager in order to get an overdraft. She'd been given £40, which in those days was a big deal, for an actress anyway, so we were celebrating with Katie Cupcake, whom I think Heather loved almost as much as I did.

'I do think one should always wear silk and cashmere, dear, don't you?' remarked Heather casually as she summoned a passing waitress to enquire, with the manner of one accustomed to being instantly obeyed, 'And could I have a little more cream for the dog.'

In our financial situation sackcloth and ashes and a cup of water would have been more appropriate, but Heather has never allowed herself to become bowed down by the tedious practicalities of life. So it was, impecunious but ever optimistic, that, as we were both interested in antiques, we ended up with a Sunday stall at Camden Lock. We spent two nights, or rather the early hours of two mornings after our shows, constructing our stall, and then every spare moment buying junk which, along with the fair amount of clutter we already owned between us, we would then sell on as antiques.

Heather, naturally, was rather grand about buying things. In the lowliest of venues she would behave as if she were buying at Asprey's. She would stand very straight and peer imperiously at everything through a gold monocle. It wasn't an affectation, she did have bad eyesight but she is the sort of person who would be at home walking around a supermarket peering at the price of Flora margarine through a gold monocle. People were inclined to look at her a little askance, but that never stopped Heather. At home in the mews she would greet callers with a rather regal cry of, 'Enter.' Although she was emotionally a home-builder, the mechanics of running a home without getting buried in debris and dogs were quite beyond Heather who muddled along in an unbelievable mess. I did my best to sort a lot of that out for her and redesign her home so that, for a time at any rate, it became at least very nearly the kind of place in which you could justifiably utter, 'Enter,' so regally at your visitors.

We thoroughly enjoyed our stall at Camden Lock which, rather surprisingly in view of our other commitments, we kept going for two years. I grew to love the company of dealers and made many good friends among them. On Saturday nights we managed about four hours' sleep after the theatre, if we were lucky, because we were up at four to get our stuff ready in Heather's garage, no matter what the weather was like. In the winter we were invariably frozen even before we got to load up her little car. Looking back I think we must both have been out of our minds, staggering off to Camden Lock in the middle of the night with bits of furniture on our heads after doing two shows in the West End. But it quickly became a way of life.

Heather had an incredible eye and could, I believe, have been the most wonderful antiques dealer had she wanted to be. However, she was also a compulsive buyer who couldn't ever leave anything alone and I think we bought more than we sold, making it rather difficult to make a profit. She also didn't like parting with things. 'Oh darling, this piece is far too nice to let go. I really think we should keep it,' she would say.

Through Camden I began to learn from all sorts of people about art, antiques and selling. And about finding things too. I have always had a great penchant for skips. I can't walk by one without peering into it and having a bit of a root about. I remember one day we were driving along Harley Street and I spotted a pair of old crutches, Edwardian with inlaid mahogany. They were beautiful. I yelled at Heather to stop the car, got out and put them on the roof rack. Then, after another block or two, I was yelling, 'Stop! Stop!' again because I'd seen some really nice lampshades in another skip. That was a particularly good Sunday morning. The first thing we sold were my crutches, and we instantly made about seventy quid on something I'd just picked up in the street.

I found that I'd got a real love of the whole business – not for the 'antiques' in inverted commas that are sold at Olympia or in posh shops in Mayfair, because I often find them pretty horrible, but for all kinds of objects that have been damaged and restored, things that you can use in order to make your home look and feel better.

It was also at Camden that Heather and I met Rachel McKay, who became my very best friend in all the world. Indeed, she became more family than friend and still is. When we first encountered her at the market she was sitting quietly in a corner selling beads.

She was the one who rescued us when Heather's car was stolen, a story that is pretty darned typical of Rachel. We heard the poor little car being driven away in the middle of the night. It was too late to do anything about it, and we were deprived of our only means of transporting our goods to and from Camden. Rachel promptly volunteered to drive us. When she did I said to Heather, 'Poor girl, we must pay her.'

'I think you'll find that she's actually rather grand, dear,' responded Heather, who was always much more aware of that sort of thing than I was. And it did indeed turn out that Rachel came from this rather incredible – to me at any rate – upper-crust family. Ultimately she slotted into being part of our little antiques business. We got along from the start and had a great many laughs together, and I think Rachel loved that time with the stalls at Camden Lock every bit as much as Heather and I did.

Indeed, sometimes, usually when I'm learning my lines for a new production, which I still find so hard, I do dream of becoming an antiques dealer again. And maybe, even, not acting at all any more.

CHAPTER SEVENTEEN

❧

In 1981, there came another life-changing moment. I went into *Coronation Street* to play Alma Sedgwick. My first stint was for five weeks and I returned briefly the following year. The very first scene I had to do was playing opposite my heroine Pat Phoenix, who was, of course, the truly wonderful Elsie Tanner. The larger-than-life Elsie, with her almost film-star glamour and all that energy, reminded me in some ways of my mother. So, all in all, I was over-awed before I began. But it was worse than that. As the proprietor of the café I had to sack her. I was mortified.

The *Coronation Street* of the early eighties was very different to the one I went back to later. It was an old régime with a hierarchy. People had their own adopted seats in the Green Room, which is a kind of common room for actors, like specially revered regulars in an old-fashioned pub. You sat in the wrong seat at your peril.

When I arrived in the Street as a newcomer, it was extremely daunting to meet these people whom, in a way, I felt I already knew. They made me very nervous. I had a tendency to stare at the person I was working with, thinking, 'That's Pat Phoenix I'm saying these lines to. That's Elsie Tanner! Oh, my God!' It was quite overwhelming for someone as self-conscious as I am. The *Coronation Street* regulars in those days were rather like movie stars. And that's how they behaved. To me Pat Phoenix was Rita Hayworth, Doris Speed (Annie) was Phyllis Calvert, and Jean Alexander (Hilda) was Gracie Fields.

However, working with them was not like working with show-business pros at all. They had all been in the series for years and had total job security. This was unheard of in the business and quite unlike the way things are now in *Coronation Street* when the cast never know when or where the axe is going to fall. I was used to the kind of conversation which you normally got among show-business professionals, about whether or not you had seen the latest show in town, the quality of people's performances, and gossip about what various actors were up to. Within the Street conversation between the actors was much the same as you would get among the regulars of the Rovers.

'Are you going to Kendal's at lunchtime?'

'I've just seen these wonderful drapes in that new shop on Deansgate.'

Anne Kirkbride (Deirdre) once astonished me by meticulously applying little black dots onto silver wrapping paper. Apparently she wanted all her Christmas wrapping paper to match, and when the store ran out of the exact design she had chosen she decided to improvise. Anne has always been extremely industrious.

Every afternoon back then a huge tray of cakes and cream buns used to be delivered. I was amazed to watch Jack Howarth (Albert) fill his pockets with them every day. He'd trot out of Granada when he'd finished work with bulging pockets, looking as grim as ever. If anybody had bumped into him, cream buns would have spouted from every orifice.

I also discovered that in a soap people were inclined to ask you very odd questions, something I did not fully understand until I became a Street regular myself. Learning those lines every night and immersing yourself in your character within this long-running TV drama does something strange to the brain if you don't watch it.

I remember being rather surprised when Helen Worth (Gail) turned to me one day with a look of panic on her face. 'What's my home phone number?' she asked.

On another occasion I was walking down the corridor with Doris Speed when she suddenly asked, 'Could you tell me if I've got odd socks on, love?'

I looked down. 'Yes, you have,' I said. 'One's red and the other's blue.'

'Thought so,' she replied, and toddled on.

Coronation Street was a very different world for someone used to West End theatre. Newcomers were cannon fodder really. Their job was to feed the senior cast. I was well aware of this and developed a way of sliding in and out of scenes. I had an idea that if I wasn't noticed I might last longer. I was aware that almost all the leading characters back then were playing comedy, so I deliberately avoided that, even though it had always previously been my strength. Instead I disappeared into the shell from which Alma ultimately emerged as this quiet, sweet, gentle person whom I was then to become stuck with.

I particularly hated rehearsals, not least because they were held in a room with windows – which meant daylight. I've never been fond of daylight when I'm working. I prefer to be buried in the depths of a theatre basement somewhere. For me to rehearse in a bright room with windows, convinced that everyone was staring at me, was hell on wheels. In those days in *Coronation Street* we had what was called the 'tech run'. The words ran ice-cold water through your blood. This medieval torture was a rehearsal, a word seldom used now in soap. Indeed, you have to explain to younger actors in this kind of television what a rehearsal means. Tech run, when you rehearsed for camera in front of all the technicians and cast, took place every Wednesday at 2.00 p.m., and had its own weird dress code. The rule seemed to be that none of the assembled cast should ever look in any way like themselves. It was customary to dress up for the tech run, and it was really built up as a big occasion. Certainly it was unheard of to go in your jeans.

Pat Phoenix had amazing presence and wore the most extraordinary clothes. One tech-run day she came in dressed from head to foot in a white cowgirl outfit. She had on a big white Stetson, a white cowgirl jacket and suede skirt and white boots. Earlier in the day she had been wearing a frilly shirt and an A-line suit but that wasn't extreme enough for tech run, obviously. So she'd popped to Elite, Manchester's famous second-hand clothing shop, at lunchtime in order to acquire something suitably bizarre. Looking back on it perhaps the most extraordinary thing of all was that nobody paid any attention to Pat's Annie Oakley look. I also have this vivid memory of Lynne Perrie (Ivy) wearing a black-and-white evening dress, a hat and four-inch heels – all for a TV rehearsal in the middle of the day.

We all had to gather in the big rehearsal room. Normally we only rehearsed with the people we were in a scene with, and the rest of the cast would not be watching. But on tech-run day everybody watched everybody else, and it's always the opinions of my peers that I fear most. I am sure nobody did judge anybody else, we were all in the same state, but it just felt as if that was what was happening. I never slept at all the night before because I was always so nervous.

In spite of these various delusions of grandeur in the Street back then the working conditions were quite tricky. *Coronation Street* was not given its own home, Stage One, until 1990. Before that this huge show had to be squashed into Granada studios amidst whatever else was being made at the time.

This meant that nobody, not even the likes of Pat Phoenix and Doris Speed, could have their own dressing room. There were not enough to go round. Besides, they would all probably be needed for some other show when not being used by Street cast. So we shared dressing rooms and had to pack up all our stuff and take it home at the end of each working day, which was a real drag. The corridors were always full of people standing around chatting because the person with whom they were sharing their dressing room was trying to sleep. Even the Green Room was just a small crowded place off the rehearsal room where nobody had any space to themselves.

In retrospect though, particularly when compared with the way things are today, *Coronation Street* in 1981 was a doddle, an absolute doddle. The workload was pretty easy when there were only two shows a week. Back then, our working week didn't begin until Tuesday afternoon when there was a read-through, then rehearsals all day Wednesday, Thursday morning off, and in the studio on Thursday afternoon.

For me, one of the special joys of joining the Street was rekindling an old friendship with Tony Warren, the man who created *Coronation Street*. I had known Tony since we had shared the same agent, Dorothy McAusland, whose client I was during my early dancing years. I had last seen him as an aspiring performer prancing around at an audition entertaining all of us waiting in the wings. He didn't seem to have changed a bit.

During that first stint in the Street I stayed with my mother in Disley. She would bring me a bacon sandwich and a cup of tea in bed in the mornings, a time when I am never at my most aware, and while I was eating with one hand she would take the other and guide it while I sleepily signed cheques with which she could pay her gas and electricity bills. She was still running a hairdressing business of sorts. It was apparently failing to bring in as much money as she needed. That was where I continued to come in useful. I was also useful in impressing her remaining hairdressing clients. They all seemed to be *Coronation Street* fans.

It was, and still is, a big thing to go into the Street. But the viewing figures then were much greater than they are now, and with just four channels on the box *Coronation Street*'s share of the national TV audience was immense. Despite having played the lead in so many West End shows, in *Carry On Cleo* and all the other films and TV I had done, I was aware that the exposure you got in the Street far exceeded most other areas of show business.

It still makes me laugh when people tell me, as they do occasionally, that they never see *Coronation Street,* yet they know every single thing that's ever happened in it. Sometimes I think the Street has a lot in common with Margaret Thatcher. I suspect that many of the millions who 'never watched' *Coronation Street* might have been among the millions who claimed never to have voted for the Iron Lady.

That leads me quite nicely, I hope, onto Tony Williamson's *The Cabinet Mole* in which I played Mrs Thatcher. People tell me that I did rather a good impression of Maggie, which I find rather disconcerting. We toured with the show for several months but it was not a huge triumph and never made it into the West End. For me one of the most memorable aspects was that my friend Rachel from Camden Lock, who had a bit of a track record in the theatre both in small acting parts and backstage, became, with just a little bit of help from me, Assistant Stage Manager.

Now, Rachel is a very fine person, but I hope she will forgive me for confiding that she was, perhaps, not the finest ASM in the world. One of her jobs was to switch on a vacuum cleaner off stage so that the sound effect coincided with me appearing to use one on stage. I lost count of the number of times Rachel got it wrong and I would be vacuum cleaning away with no noise at all and then, just as I stopped to speak, she'd finally switch the thing on in the wings and everything I was trying to say would be drowned. I could have killed her.

But we had a tremendous amount of fun touring the country together. We took the opportunity to visit every junk shop and market we could get to, buying and selling voraciously like the devoted antiques dealers that we had become. Poor Rachel was always rushing to the dressing room to salvage something that we'd bought or talking the stagehands into collecting a huge painting for us, cleaning soil from the floor, where we'd tipped over a geranium that we'd bought in a wonderful Victorian urn. So, upon reflection, any shortcomings she had as an ASM were probably as much my fault as Rachel's.

It was during the tour of *The Cabinet Mole* that I returned for the first time in more than thirty years to St Anne's College where I had been so unhappy. We were driving across country and Rachel, whom I had told all about Bernie and the strange effect the place had had on me, suddenly suggested we should go there.

So we made a detour. And there was St Anne's, still a school, still standing like a little dolls' house in Clifton Drive. It must have been holiday time, because there were no pupils around. But the gates were open so I walked straight in and started poking about in the garden. A man came up, introduced himself as the headmaster and asked us what we were doing.

'I went to school here and this is just a sentimental visit,' I told him.

He offered to show us around. It was an unreal experience. Nothing had changed. Even the décor and the furnishings were pretty much the same, all the photographs going up the stairs, even the award boards with Bernie's name all over them. I even knew where the ink stains were on the desks. I felt so strange walking through that empty building. I'd always dreamed about it. I do that a lot still, dream about somewhere that has been important to me and go around and around the place inside my head. It was uncanny to find St Anne's just the same. For a brief moment it was as if I was reliving a part of my life which, apart from Bernie, had been so unhappy and yet had shaped so much of my life to come. As we left, the headmaster turned to me. 'You know, I sometimes feel as if I am the only man to have stepped foot in this building,' he said, 'and when I am here alone at night I know that I'm not really wanted.' He had heard all the stories about the old days at St Anne's. He had obviously picked up on the vibes of the place, which had so affected me as a child. I think that the relationship between Bernie and I could not have been what it was except in a place with this very particular atmosphere.

At about this time I changed my agent. Some time previously I had moved from Alec Graham to Julian Belfridge, a lovely man and an absolute top agent with extremely distinguished clients like Judi Dench and Maria Aitken. He expected all his clients to wait for the right, really good, prestigious job to come along. It was through Julian that I did *Early Struggles* for Stephen Frears. But if jobs of that calibre didn't come along, Julian just insisted that I wait until they did. I had to persuade

Julian that I should go into the Street – he'd ignored several approaches from Granada before that first five-week stint in 1981. I was still sending my mother money and helping Robin out and it wasn't just that I wanted to work, I needed work for Christ's sake. So I changed to Peter Charlesworth, also a very respected agent but one who was maybe a little more commercial than Julian.

At least that's the official version. There was another. Julian was a great racing man. He owned horses. We even flew to France together to watch Mill Reef run in the Prix de l'Arc de Triomphe and I still remember Julian throwing his hat over the winning post when Mill Reef won. However, he then tipped me five losers at Ascot. I ask you. Five losers from someone who claimed he had inside information. I sometimes think that was the real reason why I left.

Within just days of joining Peter, and very shortly after *The Cabinet Mole*, I was offered Michael Frayn's *Noises Off*, playing Dotty Ottley, which for me was an absolute joy because the play involves more action than words. As a dancer I felt it was made for me, but not everybody may have shared my opinion.

If it's done properly, and this production was, it's a notoriously difficult play to stage. *Noises Off* is quite ridiculously physical. The wings of the Savoy Theatre were like a set out of *Emergency Ward Ten*. People were always hurting themselves as they leapt about so we had a complete first-aid unit lined up. We had bandages, ice, arnica. We had everything at the ready.

I was in my element. I particularly loved the second act because there is virtually no speech in it at all, only movement. The actors have to be very fit, which I was, and my dancing training really clicked in. It was so wonderful for me to be at rehearsals and not be in a panic about learning my lines, while everyone else was getting panic stricken about the moves and writing them all down and trying to memorise them. I never have to write down moves. I'm there straight away. I am with movement the way the rest of the world is with words. It just comes quite naturally to me.

Shortly after *Noises Off* I went into *Stepping Out* at the Duke of York Theatre, and during the course of almost three years with the show my life changed forever. Two momentous things happened. The first was that my mother died. The second was that Heather and I came to the parting of the ways, and I met the woman with whom I was to spend the next fifteen years of my life.

My mother's death at the age of seventy-seven totally and utterly shattered me. It wasn't just that I lost her, it was the way it happened. She was still living in her house at Disley, with my sister Caroline, but had finally been persuaded to move to London, something she had been threatening to do forever. I was very pleased that she had made the decision to move because I was convinced she would be so much happier in London. She had found a place in Blackheath and was actually packing up the Disley house when she called me in between shows one Saturday and told me she had a pain in her chest.

'I'm sure it's indigestion,' she said.

I told her that I thought she should see a doctor in any case.

'No, it will be fine. I'm drinking hot peppermint,' she replied.

She just wouldn't budge and that was when we fought. Each year in *Stepping Out* we had a different company, and that was the last night of that year's run, and as usual on a last night, things were a bit fraught. I was in between shows trying to get ten minutes' sleep to keep up my energy, and I don't suppose I was at my most patient. Anyway, we rowed, and I shall always regret it. We hung up on each other, and we'd never ever done that even though we spoke to one another every day.

One of the worst things was that my sister Caroline was living with my mother at the time and when we fought I assumed that she was there with Mummy. It was only when Caroline called me a few minutes later, having by coincidence also just spoken on the phone to my mother, that I realised that she was actually in London and Mummy was alone.

I then had to go straight on stage and when I came off I didn't know whether to call her or not. If she had already gone to bed to get some rest it would be the worst thing I could do. I was uneasy though – with very good reason as it turned out. The next morning, a Sunday, my brother called to say that she had died. I screamed the place down. I didn't cry. I screamed. It wasn't just grief. It was frustration at the utter futility of so much of her life. She'd tried so hard to do all sorts of things, she'd been talking about moving to London for about as long as I could remember, and now, just as she was going to do it, she'd died. I sometimes think that although she wanted to live in London, the move, sorting out the house and everything, was just too much for her. Apparently she'd been watching snooker on TV, had an embolism, and died almost instantly. She hadn't called her doctor but my brother was alerted by a neighbour who noticed the curtains were still drawn and the milk hadn't been taken in. By the time he found her, there was nothing anyone could do. It was a terrible, terrible shock.

People had either worshipped my mother or were terrified of her. But nobody ever forgot her.

The very next day was the opening night of *Stepping Out* with the new company. I went ahead with the show. I don't think it occurred to me to do anything else. I remember that I told the director, Julia McKenzie, not to tell anyone else and somehow I got through it. I was on autopilot.

I had lost my best friend, my soulmate, this person who had been such an extraordinary presence in my life and who, it has always seemed to me, was responsible for everything that I became.

Naturally I never really considered just pulling out of *Stepping Out* and leaving them to get on with it. But every time it got to the parts of the show that always upset me I just disintegrated. Julia McKenzie was absolutely wonderful to me, however, and because of the nature of the role it fitted the part to be upset, so I think very few people were aware of the state I was in. Rachel, a good friend as ever, ran around giving me all the support she could, buying me bottles of Rescue Remedy and generally trying to look after me. Thanks mostly to her, I managed to do four shows before Caroline and I travelled up to Manchester together on the Thursday for Mummy's funeral.

It was the middle of that very severe winter of 1986 and there was a terrible snowstorm. We had an appalling train journey to Manchester that took most of the day. When we got there, having trudged through the snow for the last bit, the whole house was in chaos, half-packed and totally upside down. It was also freezing cold inside as well as out. So all Caroline and I could think of doing was to drink brandy and Benylin and then sleep together in the little bed in the spare room because we couldn't bear to use Mummy's room.

I don't think I have ever felt so desolate. Nothing was working properly, including the hot water, so we couldn't even have a proper wash before the funeral. I'd been so hysterical when I left London that I hadn't brought my credit cards with me and we didn't have enough cash to buy flowers. We ended up with a bunch of half dead daffodils which was all the local shop had that we could afford.

I had always dreaded my mother's death. But to have quarrelled with her the very last time that we spoke was something I would not have believed to be possible, and something I will never quite get over.

After I joined *Coronation Street*, Carolyn Reynolds, the producer, told me how well she remembered my mother. Carolyn had been a P.A. at Granada twenty years or so earlier when she met Mummy just once on a train and had had her ear bent about whatever I had been doing professionally at the time. One meeting. One train journey. I was not, however, a bit surprised that the memory of it was so clear for Carolyn. That was the effect my mother always had on people.

For myself? Well, she pushed me beyond all reason as a child, then she sent me away to a school I hated, and on occasions she drove me mad. But she was my very best friend until the day she died, and we never stopped laughing together. I enjoyed her company more than that of almost any other person I have known. When I really needed her she would invariably turn up, always out of breath, dressed in a Sherlock Holmes hat and that cloak, ready to spin into action like Supermum. I have never in my life met anyone remotely like her. I find it impossible to describe her in a way that she deserves. She was unique. She was my inspiration and my tormentor. She was my greatest ever fan. I shall never forget the way she used to strike a match when she came to see me in theatre so I would be able to see her face – nor the trouble this sometimes caused. Every time I go on stage I still look for her. And I know I always will.

I have no doubt that I owe her everything that I am.

As usual I buried my personal troubles in my work. In *Stepping Out* I played the dancing instructor Mavis, as portrayed by Lisa Minnelli in the Hollywood film. Once again it was a role that fitted me like a pair of old ballet shoes. I was overweight and out of shape after *The Cabinet Mole*. My eating disorders had disappeared and I had begun to put weight on easily. I hadn't danced for years, but the requirements of

Stepping Out forced me back into shape. I slimmed down quite quickly and found that the dancing came back to me as if my chorus-girl period had been yesterday. I loved *Stepping Out,* which was more than a little to do with Julia McKenzie who I think made a wonderful job of it.

It wasn't just my mother's death that was troubling me off stage, however. Heather had started to have the odd drink again, and although she assured me that she could handle it, I was terrified because of my experiences with Robin and his parents. She also showed signs of wanting more independence.

'Why don't you trot off to Bow Street, dear, for a couple of days,' she would say.

All of this came together, I think, and I know that I gave a very emotional performance in *Stepping Out*. I channelled all my feelings towards the audience. Then, while all this was happening I began to get letters from a southern European woman who had seen the show. She had picked up on the emotional outpouring and was interested in talking to me. I didn't reply for two reasons. Firstly I always ignore letters like that, and secondly my dyslexia makes it so difficult for me to read and properly understand people's letters, let alone reply.

Then just before Wimbledon one year there was a knock on my dressing-room door and in came this woman who had apparently tipped the stage-door man in order to be sure to get to see me. She told me that she was the person who had written to me. She was very jolly and extremely knowledgeable about tennis and what was going on at Wimbledon that year, which really interested me.

I was going out for dinner with some other cast members and it just seemed natural to ask her to join us. We all went for a meal round the corner to a little Italian restaurant. During the three years that I was in *Stepping Out* the cast varied considerably, but this was a particularly friendly bunch, and together with our unexpected visitor we had a lot of fun that night.

It certainly never occurred to me then that her interest in me was anything other than she had explained in her letters, just a fascination with what lay behind a stage performance. I didn't even consider in that restaurant that night whether or not she might be gay. I am always the last to guess, actually.

She returned home and the letters continued even though I still never responded. I remember she invited me to go on holiday with her, but in such a way that I didn't take it as a proposition. I suppose in retrospect I should have realised because people aren't often that direct, especially since I had consistently failed to respond – a tactic that usually makes people back off. She was extremely persistent. She continued to phone as well as to write, and then we met casually a couple more times when she was in England. As I've said before, persistence works with me. I have a track record of giving in.

But this was a rather strange one. I had an almost psychic experience. After *Stepping Out* finished in the West End we took it on tour and I had digs in Worthing right by the sea. I had bronchitis and didn't feel at all well although I carried on performing. One night after the show I was sitting up in bed watching *Prisoner Cell Block H*, eating fish and chips, when I heard an extraordinary commotion outside. Then I became aware of a Georgian rocking horse I had bought a few days earlier beginning to rock all on its own. It was the autumn of 1986 and the night of the big storm. I crawled out of bed and looked out of the window at an eerie scene. The wind was blowing ferociously, the whole front of the balcony to my room appeared to be falling off, but when I looked at the sea it was flat calm. It seemed like all hell had broken out, there was this piercing electric noise in the air, but no waves at all. I crawled back into bed with my Benylin, thinking I would be safe there, but my bed was right by the fireplace and in the morning it transpired that the chimney stack above my head was the only one left standing in the street.

It was some time in the middle of that dreadful night that I suddenly got an overpowering feeling that I must contact Helena my European friend. But I didn't even have a note of her phone number or address. She had always been the one who contacted me. So I rang my sister Caroline who happened to be staying at Bow Street and asked her if there were any letters from abroad. As usual there were. So I asked her to open one and she gave me a phone number from it. I could not, however, phone straight away as the UK was virtually without phone lines after that storm, but eventually I got through. I shall always remember that Helena said, 'It's funny that you rang. I was going to give you until the end of this week and that was going to be it.'

She arranged to come to England again, but still there was nothing overt between us. Indeed, she told me that she had contacts who had put on *Noises Off* in Europe and that she wanted to talk to me about the possibility of getting *Stepping Out* translated into other languages, and so she needed to see the show again. Ultimately she came to Coventry where she took one look at my digs, said she had never seen anywhere so terrible, and that she was going to book me into the hotel where she was staying. And it was there that she told me just how many times she had seen the show, I forget exactly but it was an awful lot, and that she was in love with me.

Heather and I were drifting apart, and I suppose I was susceptible. Also, Helena continued to be highly persistent. Looking back, everything she did was persistent, and rather brave too. It was an extraordinary thing to see someone on stage in a foreign country, decide that you were in love with that person, contrive a meeting, and ultimately tell her your feelings. It was even more extraordinary because Helena was married then, and had never had a gay relationship before. But then, that has never seemed so strange to me, of course, because as far as I am concerned relationships are about people, not sexuality, and I have never believed in labels.

But unfortunately, although Helena was still spending most of her time at home with her family, her persistence took the form of insisting that I should leave Heather. This was not really necessary because by this stage I was frequently being told to toddle off to Bow Street. Although Heather and I were having our difficulties, she still spelt home and structure to me. I had no desire to terminally destroy my little world for someone who continued to carefully maintain her own family structure in another country.

Helena phoned the mews constantly, still pushing, until I eventually moved myself back entirely to Bow Street. It was actually very hard for me to turn my back on the set-up I had with Heather, even though it was no longer what it had been. I always thought it was rather unfair of Helena to make me do it, because I am not a solitary creature. I am inclined to be depressed almost to the point of illness if I am left on my own too much.

She told me, of course, that she was leaving her husband to come to England to live with me. But she never did. Partly due to geography and partly due to her family commitments, we never properly lived together – she had homes on the Mediterranean and I had my London flat and the one I had bought in Manchester when I became a regular in *Coronation Street*. And although we were together for fifteen years I was never completely acknowledged as part of her life. It was many years before she told anybody in her extremely wealthy family about me.

Indeed, a number of family members and most of the friends she had before we met were never told. To them I have remained a shadowy figure, something which I have always found rather hurtful. But because of that, and out of respect for her wishes, even though in the UK our relationship became something of an open secret, she is therefore another one to whom I have given a fictional name.

In 1988, two years after I met Helena, I returned to *Coronation Street* and began what was to turn out to be a mammoth thirteen-year stint in the world's most popular soap. A whole new life opened up for me. Although partly because of the extraordinary exposure which the Street gives everyone who appears in it and partly because of Helena's personal set-up, I found myself in a very tricky situation. I had always been pretty open about relationships in the past. I was quickly to learn that this was no longer possible. For a *Coronation Street* regular every hiccup in their life is front-page news.

It had never really occurred to me that what I did or didn't do in my private life was any big deal. So although I was not open about my relationship with Helena, neither did I completely hide it. Apart from anything else, I was over fifty when I joined the Street. I didn't really consider that my sex life would still be of any great interest to anybody. I was apparently wrong. Very wrong. Even now I'm sixty-six the press are still interested.

Almost as soon as I returned to the Street I was hit by a double whammy. A producer I'd worked for years before, who had fallen on extremely bad times, decided to try to sell the story of Robin, Sally and me to the press. I could imagine all too well the lurid headlines. Wild sex orgies in Covent Garden, I suspect would have been the approach, rather than a truthful picture about desperately trying to sleep with a Yorkshire terrier on my head and loud snoring going on all around me.

Simultaneously another person who worked on the Street found out that I was sharing my life with a woman and tipped off the press. I would very much like to name this person – upon whose script I once noticed the scribbled phone numbers of the day and night desk of the *News of the World*, and whom I also on another occasion spotted writing down the numbers of all the actors' cars in the car park – but for legal reasons, I cannot. Suffice to say that this unsavoury creature, short of money, made a cottage industry out of selling stories to the national press. I have a feeling there is someone like this in most of the really high-profile shows where information is worth so much money, but I do think it's the lowest of the low.

The result of this double whammy was that I was pursued relentlessly by the press and only the sheer brilliance of Peter Charlesworth, who handled the whole thing for me, prevented some very unpleasant publicity. On one occasion a photographer took a picture of Helena and me saying goodbye at the gates to Granada in Manchester. Soon afterwards, there were a series of phone calls from the newspaper concerned threatening that this picture and an appropriate caption concerning my sexuality were destined for the front page. They had no evidence, but that didn't stop my heart sinking into my boots when challenged in such a way.

Another time there was a knock on my hotel bedroom door and a young woman who later told me she was a reporter working for a Sunday newspaper barged past me, looked around the room and pulled open the bathroom door, demanding 'Where is she?'

Then there was the reporter who rang me up and asked me directly, 'Are you a lesbian?'

'Only on Tuesday afternoons,' I replied.

People tell me I was quite good at dealing with the press through those *Coronation Street* years. I was actually terrified. There was a park in London, just by Lincoln's Inn Fields, where I used to go when things seemed particularly grim. Once I remember just sitting there and sobbing. Helena and I used to call it Paranoia Park. Maybe I was a bit paranoid. But, by God, I had reason to be. The pursuit was quite relentless.

On another occasion I was actually chased on board an aircraft when I was flying abroad to meet Helena for a holiday. Totally unaware that I had press company I went to the ladies' immediately upon landing, got talking to somebody and started trying to tidy myself up. I took so long that when I emerged all the luggage and all the immigration people had disappeared and I had managed to get myself locked in airside. There followed a few minutes of panic before a door opened and there stood a rather cross-looking Helena. She had apparently spotted me getting off the plane and so had known I was somewhere and had managed to persuade the airport officials to organise a search for me. We were then taken to the bowels of the earth beneath the airport to retrieve my suitcase and were shown out by a back door. Meanwhile, outside in the main arrivals hall, I later learned, stood a group of bewildered British press who couldn't understand where I had disappeared to.

Helena felt then that it was absolutely vital that nobody knew about her involvement with me, so I did my best to protect her. I was also protecting myself. But if it hadn't been for her side of things I may have been tempted to speak out, even while I was still in *Coronation Street*, because I quickly became so sick of the press intrusion. At the same time, however, I was pretty sure that if I had come out then I would have been sacked from the Street. When I went into the show, it was like going into a time warp forty years or so back. There were all kinds of prejudices that might seem unlikely in the show-business world, and I had no doubt about the prejudice against gay women. These kind of things are changing all the time. I am well aware that younger people, to their credit, in all walks of life are far more liberal-minded and sophisticated than their parents and grandparents.

But early on in the Street I felt the need to be so guarded that even if someone asked innocently what I had done over the weekend, I found myself in a dilemma. You could never ever use the term 'we' for a start. As time went by no doubt my relationship with Helena was known and indeed there were certain people like Barbara Knox (Rita), Sue Nichols (Audrey), Helen Worth (Gail) and John Savident (Fred) whom I trusted absolutely and was completely open with.

But having your life splashed on the front pages against your will and in as lurid as possible a way would have been something completely different. So every time anyone from the Granada press office phoned or came to see me my heart would stop. I thought it was ridiculous for somebody of my age, in what was then the latter end of the twentieth century, but I didn't know what to do except batten down the hatches. I had so often watched other Street stars walk into the Green Room at Granada knowing that everybody else in the room had read some unpleasant story about them in the Sunday papers, which had then been hidden somewhere. Indeed, I used to make a point of always ringing up any cast members in that situation because I was so aware of how dreadful they must feel.

I knew, you see, that if it were me, if what I then dreaded had happened to me and my sexuality had become lurid headlines at that stage in my life, that I just would not have been able to walk into the Green Room. It might sound silly, but that really is how I felt about it.

I made up my mind then, I think, that one day I would speak out for myself. I never wanted to live that kind of hole-in-corner life into which I seemed to be forced. I didn't like behaving as if I was ashamed of such an important part of my life. Because I wasn't. And that is one of the main reasons why I decided to write this book.

CHAPTER EIGHTEEN

❧

I have always thought that my return to *Coronation Street*, about six months after my mother had died, was probably down to Connie. I doubt the producers ever realised it, but I don't think they had a lot of choice when they signed me up to play Alma again. I swear to God that straight after her death, Mummy shot off to the casting agency in the sky to demand that I be reinstated. She was the original *Coronation Street* groupie, and throughout the years in between my five-week stint on the show and her death she bombarded Granada with phone calls begging them to bring Alma back. Each time she pretended to be somebody else, putting on a different voice, and telling them how brilliant I was.

I didn't know until, to my utter embarrassment, the then producer, Bill Podmore, sought me out while I was at Granada filming an episode of the Don Henderson detective series *Bulman,* to tell me about it.

'Please can you stop your mother phoning us,' he asked plaintively. She had got hold of his direct line from someone and was calling constantly. The truth was that I was so nebulous during that first brief stint that I doubt anybody noticed me. Naturally that didn't stop Mummy. I was horrified. I had this vision of her on the line putting on a funny accent and everybody in the *Corrie* office saying to each other, 'It's Amanda Barrie's mother again.'

Of course when I confronted her about it she was totally unabashed. 'It was just that we all thought you were so wonderful, darling,' she cooed – which really put me on red alert.

'What do you mean, "We all"?' I swiftly countered.

'Oh, just some of my ladies,' she replied.

It transpired that she had persuaded most of her hairdressing clients to join her in phoning the *Corrie* office about me. I doubt most of them had even seen me in the Street but that would not have bothered Mummy one bit. She also flatly refused to believe that Bill and his staff had any idea that she was the one doing the bulk of the phoning. 'They'd never have known it was me, dear,' she insisted. 'I put on all these different accents, you see . . .'

'But perhaps not quite as well as you thought,' I suggested mildly.

It made no difference what I said. My mother never ever gave up on anything. So I am quite sure that she would have continued her campaign in the afterlife.

She may, however, not have been quite so keen on my becoming a Street regular had she realised the treadmill the show was later to become when two episodes a week became first three and then four.

The hours were so demanding that we usually had to be in the studio at 7.00 a.m. for a make-up call, sometimes earlier, and quite often did not finish until 7.00 or 7.30 p.m. All too often, the body and brain were totally numb, you arrived at and left Granada in the dark, not seeing daylight at all. Mind you, it should be said that in Manchester it is frequently impossible to distinguish the two!

This numbness becomes increasingly stultifying as time passes. Being in a soap is like running a marathon in which nobody knows where the finishing line is. You become more and more tired, but somehow or other you just keep going. Each night you have to learn the next day's lines, which meant stuffing nine, ten or twenty-five scenes into your reluctant brain, all of which were inclined, unfortunately, to coagulate into one. Also, there was very little direction. There couldn't be. It wasn't the fault of any of our directors. There was just no time.

The early mornings were always the worst bit of the day. I would stagger out of bed at five and then begin the struggle to find my features, none of which seemed to be around at that hour. Anyone observing would also have noticed a sort of silent mouthing movement going on while I tried to get dressed and clean my teeth and so on. This was all part of the desperate process of remembering the next batch of lines.

Without the help of the redoubtable Sandra Gill who drove me in Manchester (being a theatre-land person whose home has always been in the centre of London I have never learned to drive) and looked after me generally while I was in the Street, I doubt I would ever have remembered anything, nor indeed got to the studio at all. Sandra would arrive at my flat, just a stone's throw away from the Granada studios, more or less as I got up in the morning. She would pour tea down my throat and go through the lines I had battled with the previous night with me. Invariably I felt as if I had learned one long blurred scene which then had somehow to be separated.

At the studio half-asleep creatures with their eyes stuck together who could not be recognised by anyone let alone half of the country would be creeping slowly and trance-like about the place. These blind moles would greet each other with conventional politeness.

'Hi, you all right?'

'Oh yes, I'm fine. You?'

'Yeah, fine.'

All of this, of course, was invariably a lie. But nobody ever admitted that there was anything wrong with them. They could be half dead from lack of sleep, bits of their bodies might be falling off. Bubonic plague, flu, whatever was wrong – they never admitted it.

The make-up girls were expected to resurrect us. Every day these poor creatures, radiating cheerfulness, genuine or otherwise, would endeavour to turn the walking dead not only into human beings, but into something actually vaguely recognisable as the stars of *Coronation Street*. Allegedly. At 7.00 a.m. on a wet winter's morning in Manchester there was, I can tell you, a very, very long way to go, as you grasped at tea, coffee, or indeed anything going which might keep your eyes open long enough for make-up to stick your eyelashes on.

A usual session also included various desperate pleas and laments along the lines of, 'Oh God! Can't you do anything with my eyes? My hair's gone funny again. I knew I shouldn't have washed it last night. Look at my fat face! I knew I shouldn't have eaten last night. Should I have surgery?'

There was, of course, no time to have plastic surgery, because there just isn't when you're in a soap, unless you do it yourself. So make-up simply had to do the best they could, a re-plastering job more or less, which, with only minor correction, had to last you all day, and was not helped because nobody ever seemed to get the temperature control right. The studio would get hotter and hotter as the day progressed, and more often than not half my make-up would detach itself from my skin, so by the time it came to my scene, I looked like Bette Davis in *Whatever*

Happened to Baby Jane? And my own home improvements, hastily layered on in the semi-darkness of my rabbit-hutch dressing room, didn't always help either.

My hair was a particularly vexed issue. Manchester's damp atmosphere turned it quite wild and it invariably refused to do anything I told it. One minute it stood on end and I looked like Tina Turner, the next minute it flattened itself and I was Adolf Hitler. It fought me from when I got up in the morning until seven at night, when, just as the day's work ended, it would start to behave.

Throughout everything, this strange mouthing continued, meaning, of course, that some kind of scene was being frantically rehearsed in a remote part of the brain. My dyslexia naturally made the constant learning task particularly difficult. But all soap actors suffer from a deep weariness that is quite apparent when you peer, bleary-eyed, into the equally bleary eyes of the person you are playing the first scene of the day with. Most of us at that stage could barely remember our own names or the name of our characters, let alone anything any more ambitious.

I have often wondered what people watching a highly dramatic and emotional scene on TV would have made of it had they watched it being shot first thing in the morning with the actors still wiping the sleep out of the corners of their eyes. We would also frequently be struggling with highly unsatisfactory costumes. And as the machinery of the day's filming began to crank into action you would hear desperate cries coming from the little rabbit hutches.

'I can't wear this with this!'

'She would never wear that to a funeral.'

'This skirt is nine years old and I can't get into it.'

I once did a scene with Johnny Briggs (Mike) in a pair of trousers that he hadn't worn for twenty years. They finished halfway down his shins, and I doubt he had grown. He looked like Norman Wisdom, and it was quite impossible to take him or anything that he had to say seriously.

It was certainly goodbye real world from the moment I entered Granada. From start to finish, *Coronation Street,* probably in common with all soaps today, is a miracle on celluloid.

Shortly after being glued together by the make-up department, the actors are on set with technicians all over them with sound booms, lighting men doing their stuff, and everyone trying to sort out the first shot of the day. There is no time to waste with a soap schedule so surprisingly quickly everything lurches into action and about ten minutes later, to our utter amazement, we are acting.

In my case, particularly during Alma's somewhat volatile relationship with Mike Baldwin, I was frequently screaming and shouting in some highly emotional turmoil. 'Mike! Don't lie to me! Don't lie to me! You saw her.'

Outbursts like that, of course, would be followed by tears and more tears which some people might think would be the most difficult thing of all. Not so. That was easy. I never needed chemical 'tear sticks' to make me cry. The pain of being awake at that time of the morning was always quite enough. Most of the time all that could really move any of us were the words everyone prayed to hear, the words dear to the hearts of all soap actors.

'We are checking that it's clear.'

Those words meant you'd managed it yet again – or hopefully you had. Unfortunately there was sometimes no respite even when you had managed to get through that first scene. All too often, just as you were about to breathe a sigh of relief, someone would call, 'Sorry, there was a shadow.'

I remember doing a scene with Roy Barraclough (Alec) in the Rovers early one morning when we had so many takes because of shadows, including the boom getting into one shot, that eventually he said, 'Go on. Why not give us the fan and the hare.' Indeed, sometimes I could almost imagine that a child was lurking somewhere deliberately making shadow puppets in the streams of light in order to cause us problems. Roy's remark resulted in a lot of laughs from the cast, and stony silence from the crew member responsible, who didn't find it funny at all. People under extreme stress tend to make jokes of that nature.

On those occasions when there was a mistake, panic was inclined to set in because you had frequently already used Tippex on your brain in order to get onto the next scene and it was no longer possible to remember the earlier one. Then those strange mouthing movements started again.

When one of those early morning scenes was cleared and subsequently sent out to the millions I often used to think it must have been done by some sort of out-of-body experience as I still wasn't awake. And I would always hope that the Great British Public watching these emotional scenes of us hitting each other and screaming and shouting would not judge we poor soap actors too harshly. I would actually have defied the great John Gielgud to shine in his first speech of the day in those conditions. Soap actors do it in spite of everything. I think probably fear is the spur.

Everybody in the Street is terrified of scenes in the Rovers, because they have to perform with the rest of the cast sitting in the booths waiting for their scenes. If you are the twit who can't get it right you feel that you're making an even bigger fool of yourself than usual. To have a dry or a fluff in the Rovers always turned me into jelly, and I think most people were the same. But once we were released from scenes like that we would all be so relieved to have got it over with that we would become reanimated and turn into rather chatty little people, going off to have coffee and smoke furtive cigs in hidden places.

In my case if I wasn't in the next scene I usually returned to my rabbit hutch and promptly fell asleep to be woken by calls of, 'Scene 17 in the Rovers, Amanda.' On some occasions I couldn't remember what day it was let alone which scene. So I would stagger downstairs and try to find anybody who was in the scene with me in order to do the mouthing out loud again. Then once more it was off into the studio.

To make matters worse, scenes are usually shot out of sequence, so one minute I might be screaming or crying, and the next I would have to be jolly in the corner shop. The shape of the day resembles the worst sort of package holiday. It can be hours of waiting followed by minutes of stark terror in the studio. You can seldom leave it, even if you actually have a very light day, because you are never quite sure when they are going to get to your scene. So the constant cry goes out to the production assistants, 'Will you get to me before lunch?'

They, like the make-up girls, have to display the patience of saints. From morning to night, they are asked,

'Am I next?

'Where are we up to?'

'Have they got to my bit yet?'

'Will they want me again today?'

The words 'me', 'my', and 'I', are constant.

They have to answer these questions from all forty members of the cast and as the day goes on their equanimity is stretched to breaking point.

When lunch is called it's a welcome respite for all, but may not be quite what the viewers would expect. Winter and summer the cast of *Coronation Street* eat from a catering truck, which is parked outside in the car park, always fifty or sixty yards away from the Granada building, just enough in Manchester weather to ensure that your hair, clothes and the remains of your equilibrium are all destroyed. The cast make the journey in all weathers, those wearing wigs clutching on to them while they climb the steps to the hatch from which lunch is served. Then, precariously carrying steak and chips on paper plates, they make their way back to the Green Room to eat. But balancing food on paper plates while struggling to keep on a wig means that you are extremely lucky to get there with your lunch intact. People usually grossly over-order to compensate for all the food that will have fallen off before reaching sanctuary.

In order to avoid this experience, whenever possible I got Sandra to whizz me back to my flat, invariably in an extremely elderly motor car. In contrast to Johnny Briggs' brand new Mercedes, or indeed almost any of the showroom-fresh models driven by most of the cast, Sandra drove a succession of old bangers including one in which we travelled around for some months that had been vandalised by an ex-lover who had poured four cans of vivid green paint over it. It looked like something out of *Sesame Street*. However, in spite of our dubious transportation we always seemed to make it home where we produced lunch at speed in the scant hour allowed. Unfortunately, during much of my time in *Coronation Street* daytime repeats of the show were broadcast in the Granada area, so if you switched on the TV in an attempt to allow your mind to escape the day, you would often be confronted with yet more *Corrie*.

It is strange what a large part food seems to play in producing a soap opera. Rather like animals caged up in the zoo, it's pretty much all soap actors think about. Helen Worth once said to me, 'I can't understand it, but as soon as I see Stage One I get hungry.'

Older members of the cast are invariably trying, usually unsuccess-fully, to avoid eating, so that they can get into their costumes. But temptation is everywhere. One ritual that has now ceased, due to cuts in spending at Granada although it's hard to believe this saved a great deal, was that we used to have delivered in the mornings a large chromium-plated tray covered in doilies and small sandwiches. These all tasted absolutely the same, but as the fillings were in different colours, presumably the contents were varied. In an effort not to pile on the pounds, we desperate actors would eat the insides only. So in the afternoon you would see us frenziedly searching through curly bits of white bread foraging for the odd bit of escaped corned beef or cheese. Eventually, increasingly desperate for sustenance, we usually ended up eating the stale bread too.

Throughout the day the Green Room is dotted with prostrate bodies, and some of the cast, particularly the younger members, will even lie on the floor. It was often more like an airport lounge on a particularly bad flight-delay day. At one point new chairs were brought in, very much like the kind of furniture one might find in an old people's home. In fact, the state of the actors sitting in these chairs reminded me of my visits to Denville Hall, the actors' rest home, to see aging thespians.

As each day mercifully approached its close, everyone's greatest dread was to be suddenly called for a scene they hadn't expected to do until the following morning. At this stage of total brain weariness you would be quite horrified at being faced with some big emotional scene at 7.00 p.m., and having to rush to get it in by a quarter past. Finally getting home at night brought scant relief. I would normally arrive back at my flat at about 7.30 – just in time to be faced with the Street on the box three working days out of five. And then I'd have to start learning those lines again.

On the very rare occasion when you felt strong enough to go out anywhere, in my case virtually only ever at weekends, you were so programmed to learn any words put in front of you that I was inclined to find myself trying to memorise the menus in restaurants.

In fact I did know the menu of Joe Allen's – the famous London theatrical restaurant just around the corner from my Covent Garden flat, which I'm inclined to refer to as my dining room – totally by heart. I regard the staff of Joe's, notably its celebrated pianist Jimmy, as my friends, which has always made the restaurant seem like an oasis to me. Joe's was the centre, really, of what little social life I could muster during my years in the Street. It was there that I got to know Barry Burnett, another greatly respected showbusiness agent. From the start he treated me like one of his clients and so I ultimately became one when I finally quit the Street and turned my whole life upside down. Barry always seemed to represent comfort – and, God knows, I needed it. Joe Allen's was, however, a relatively rare treat and invariably reminded me of how much I missed my Covent Garden home while I was forced to spend most of my time in Manchester.

There was one good thing about the heavy *Corrie* workload, though. Unlike the terrible nerves I suffered when I first went into the Street, I was hardly ever nervous during my second stint. As far as I know, neither was anyone else. We were all too tired.

And just in case any reader is still managing to nurture the belief that there may be anything remotely glamorous about being a star of *Coronation Street* I will relate one final story demonstrating the reality of life in this legendary soap.

A lavish reception and dinner was given at Manchester Civic Centre in 1995 to celebrate the show's thirty-fifth birthday. The cast was required to be on display, of course, and we all duly dressed up in our finery only to discover that the transport provided by Granada took the form of an elderly, none-too-clean, and slightly too small bus. So we set off for this rather grand occasion crammed sweatily together, some of us forced to stand and hang on to straps. Parts of this event were televised and anyone who watched it may be puzzled by my story as viewers saw us all emerging from shining limousines. The reality was that we were merely transferred briefly into the posh cars just for benefit of the cameras.

Arguably my greatest supporter through my *Coronation Street* years was the former deputy leader of the Labour party, Roy Hattersley, who hit the headlines in 1990 when he spoke at the Edinburgh Television Festival on the wonders of *Coronation Street* in general and, it must be said, Alma in particular. Roy was giving the first Annual Granada Lecture at the festival. There was no second one, but whether or not that had anything to do with one of the country's leading politicians declaring undying love for Alma I have no idea. He actually compared Alma with Tolstoy's Anna Karenina, which resulted in him being asked by a *Financial Times* journalist at the subsequent press conference if his 'post-structural analysis' was serious or ironic, and indeed, if he stood by that comparison.

More recently, in an article in *The Scotsman* headlined 'Ode to Alma', Roy Hattersley wrote:

Afraid of being accused of insufferable pretension I replied: 'Really, all I'm saying is that I fancy her.' I knew at once that my admission was a mistake.

Two days later Neil Kinnock, then leader of the Labour Party, asked me to his room for a pre lunch drink. As I walked in the door he held out his hand in congratulation.

'This,' he said, waving a copy of the *Daily Mirror*, 'is exactly the sort of down to earth publicity we need.'

Page five of the paper was dominated by a large picture of Amanda Barrie. Above it the headline proclaimed more or less, 'I fancy him too.' The actual words I have blocked from my mind. The story that followed the picture I was too embarrassed to read.

However I do recall that the incident provoked one of the classic moments of my relationship with Neil Kinnock. Having expressed a similar enthusiasm for Miss Barrie, he said that he had admired her ever since she had appeared as the eponymous heroine in *Carry On Cleo*. Noticing my look of surprise he added: 'Not that I ever saw the film.'

So it seems I had two very senior Labour Party admirers. I too can but cringe at publicly declaring that I fancied Roy Hattersley back, but it did seem the only polite thing to do at the time. When I subsequently met him at a special Granada screening of his lecture and later by chance in Joe Allen's, I did like him immensely and found him quite charismatic. It is definitely true that power attracts. After ceasing to be the Labour Party's deputy, Roy Hattersley wrote about television in several national newspapers and continued loyally to declare his devotion to me and to Alma. Frequently he suggested that he would like to be a knight on a white charger sweeping Alma off her feet and looking after her forever. When Mike betrayed Alma by spending a night with a prostitute while away at a sales conference, Roy quoted Paul Newman's remark about his absolute fidelity to Joanna Woodward. 'Why go out for a hamburger, when you can have steak at home . . .'

I was flattered by Roy Hattersley's attentions, and what he said about me in that Edinburgh Festival lecture actually gave me a tremendous boost at a rather tricky stage for me in *Coronation Street*. It was quite early on in my run in the show, a time when all *Corrie* actors are permanently convinced that they are about to be axed.

The majority of those writing for the Great British Press, however, appeared to remain consistently more interested in my sexuality than the quality of my performance as Alma. It therefore amused me enormously to know that while the tabloids were chasing me onto aircraft and door-stepping my home, there hung in the Royal Academy a seven-feet-high painting of me stark naked, by Maggi Hambling, one of Britain's leading artists. This particular oil painting was among Maggi's four entries for the prestigious Jerwood Prize, which she won that year. Earlier, I had been all over the Royal Academy's Summer Exhibition in watercolours painted by Maggi, which were all sold to people who had absolutely no idea that they had bought Alma.

I sat for Maggi frequently over a twelve-month period from around 1991 to 1992, during which time she produced a substantial series of nude paintings and drawings. Some, I have to admit, are quite raunchy, most of all probably the ones in which I am not entirely naked but wearing only fishnet tights and boots.

In view of that, had the identity of Maggi's latest muse, as she referred to me, been revealed our names would no doubt have been indelibly linked together by all the best tabloids.

I had always been a great admirer of Maggi's and had previously bought several of her paintings. Indeed, the first two I acquired I really couldn't afford and I had to raid my income tax money. That was in 1987 when I went to her exhibition at the Serpentine Gallery in Hyde Park, and met her for the first time. I had, however, seen her previously, on TV. George Melly presented a programme called *Gallery* in which various celebrities formed a panel and had to identify famous paintings. Maggi was one of the panel captains. In common, I should think, with most of her panellists, I found her quite terrifying. Indeed, she became famous for being so. Maggi didn't speak on TV, she barked at people. And they quaked. She later invited me to appear on the show and I was greatly relieved that it ended before I would no longer have reasonably been able to avoid taking part. She always wore what I referred to as her uniform, dinner jacket with a carnation in the lapel, white shirt, and any one of a selection of flamboyant bow ties. In those days, of course, she also had an amazing mane of hair, giving the illusion of her being some exotic creature out of another century. I always wondered if she had modelled herself on Beau Brummel or possibly Napoleon.

I was once nearly mown down by her when, innocently leaving the Tate Gallery one day, I collided with her in full flight. She was sweeping up the steps dressed in the upper half of her uniform over paint-spattered jeans and trainers, the whole ensemble topped off with a large black 'I am an artist' hat. She was, as usual, with her habitual cigarette, and, almost setting me alight at the same time as she brushed me aside, she didn't notice me or anyone else. We were, after all, there to notice her. As an actress I did note that it was a very grand entrance.

Meeting her properly was just as terrifying as I had anticipated. Having cavalierly committed myself to spending money I couldn't afford, I enquired of the woman running the exhibition if I could pay with three post-dated cheques.

'You'll have to ask Miss Hambling,' she replied, and immediately trotted off in search of her.

I was aware that I was turning bright red, and I didn't think I was actually capable of facing this exotic creature, the artist, but I had no choice. A few minutes later Maggi made another of her grand entrances – she never just walks into a room like an ordinary human being – this time homing in on me.

'Now, what is it you want?' she barked at me.

I blurted out my request.

To my great relief she agreed to my payment plan and then barked,

'It looks as if I am coming home with you,' a reference to the two works I had purchased.

I had chosen a self-portrait oil and the seminal drawing for her painting of the Minotaur, which was bought by the Tate, and which she always says she had modelled on herself.

'Remember this is an investment,' she told me modestly, as I proceeded to put myself in debt to the taxman.

It was some years later before I met her again, at Wimbledon when I was there with Helena. Maggi was kicking a cigarette machine that had obviously offended her in some way. The sight of this in the hallowed Members' Enclosure at the world's most famous tennis tournament was just hilarious. She was, of course, dressed in her uniform, in spite of it being a warm summer's day. Maggi does not allow her own special style to be influenced by considerations such as climate or the niceties of the tennis establishment and she was smoking what was apparently her last cigarette, hence her desperation to get more supplies.

'Oh Christ. It's Maggi Hambling,' I said.

Helena then insisted that I introduced myself and then introduce her. My fear of Miss Hambling had somehow gathered momentum over the years and I was rather reluctant to do so, but Helena was not someone to argue with. So I wobbled over to where the great artist was destroying this machine and forced myself to approach her. My mind then went completely blank, it seems, as I have no memory whatsoever of what transpired during the next few minutes. But Maggi later informed me that I was totally inarticulate and appeared to turn into a corkscrew intent on disappearing by winding myself into the floor.

Helena, however, promptly asked Maggi if she would like to meet the former tennis champion Maria Bueno, who was a friend of ours. Maggi was delighted and turned into a completely charming human being. Helena then invited Maggi, a keen tennis fan, to come to

Nottingham with us the following week to watch the Federation Cup – something I would never have dared do. Indeed, the very prospect of spending an entire day with her was quite beyond my comprehension.

However, once I became able to speak to her with any degree of normality, Maggi and I became instant friends. And I was soon to learn that although she appears so formidable and most certainly doesn't suffer fools gladly, underneath all that she is immensely kind and, quite simply, unending humour on legs. Our senses of humour gelled that day in Nottingham. I came to adore Maggi. We laugh together for England. She is also hugely talented and I was greatly flattered when she asked me to sit for her. I found it a quite extraordinary experience. For a start the whole process took place in total silence. Maggi never spoke when she was working – all you could hear was the sound of the charcoal crunching across the paper and snorting noises as she blew at the charcoal dust. I wasn't allowed to speak either, which for me, except of course when struck dumb by fear, is quite difficult. *Corrie* had yet to turn into a four-day a week nightmare so I usually had Mondays off and would sit for Maggi in the studio at her south London home every Monday from 9.00 a.m. until about 4.00 p.m. when I would limp off to catch a train to Manchester.

Anyone who thinks being an artist's model is glamorous has got it all wrong. Actually I think it may be even less glamorous than working on *Coronation Street*. I found that it had a lot in common with being a chorus girl, certainly in terms of physical endurance as you are forced to hold one position for hours on end, and also being told what to do in an arbitrary fashion. I do not think I could have got through it without my dancing training. At least I was used to aching muscles. In spite of all that, I loved every minute of it. I became totally caught up in the creative process. It was also quite therapeutic for me. In *Coronation Street* I was almost constantly wearing a pinny and serving meat pies and sausage and chips from behind the counter of Jim's Caf. In real life I do not think I had ever previously worn any kind of apron, and it was actually something of a relief for an old chorus girl to be back into those fishnet tights.

CHAPTER NINETEEN

❧

It's the laughter and the friendships made that I remember best and miss the most about *Coronation Street* and, in spite of the gruelling schedules, we managed plenty of that. I know actors always go on about laughter, but we are lucky enough to be in a profession that seems to produce more than its fair share of it.

Mind you, we were forced to make our own fun. One of the downsides of the show having had its own home for the last twelve years – Stage One, separate from the rest of Granada – is that its cast and crew are totally isolated. Stage One is a listed building and when it was adapted for the Street its façade could not be altered so there are no windows to the outside world at all. Therefore if you do not laugh you are inclined to go stir crazy. You do not see anybody except *Coronation Street* people and invited visitors. I remember once that the glove puppet Sooty, by then operated by Harry Corbett Junior, visited and we all made a huge fuss of him because he was the only pro we'd seen for ages.

Fortunately *Coronation Street* is known for the exceptional characters who have been the essence of the show from its inception. At worst it was an experience to work with some of them, and at best a huge privilege. In particular the Street has long been famous for its succession of daunting *grandes dames* of soap beginning at the very beginning with all-powerful doyennes like Pat Phoenix as Elsie Tanner and Violet Carson as battleaxe Ena Sharples. That tradition has continued with women like Julie Goodyear as Bet. It was as if Julie grew to the size of a giant within the Street. I used to reckon it must be something in the air wafting through Stage One. I always thought of *Coronation Street* as a garden in which certain plants take root and become quite exotic, growing to triple or quadruple the size of the others. The strange thing is that when they leave the Street they become normal size again.

Jill Summers, who played Phyllis, was another larger-than-life character, one of life's eccentrics and a real favourite of mine. She was a wonderful, strong north-country woman. Her son told me that when she was dying in hospital one of the nurses asked her if she would like a drop of brandy and she just shook her head weakly. Then the nurse offered Jill a cup of tea and got the same weak response, and finally a glass of water. Suddenly this voice from the bed said, 'It gets better, doesn't it?' Apparently those were her last words.

Bill Waddington (Percy) was famous for not being able to remember his lines, which was strange because he did one-man shows and was able to tell really long stories. He used to have his lines written on the inside of his cap so that when he took it off, there they were in front of him. Once we could still see the writing on his head where the biro had come off.

I am aware that *Coronation Street* is often regarded as a real place, and, indeed, even the cast sometimes call each other by their character names. Yet, of course, they are actors with invariably a very different lifestyle to the folk of Weatherfield. The Street is a place you imagine yourself being part of. Possibly its greatest strength has always been that it is one of those great TV places where people would like to go. What could be nicer than going down to the Rovers for a drink, with all those people you feel you know. It's probably hard for viewers to realise that the actors behind those people are often so far removed. Helen Worth and I always had a good chat and lots of laughs when we were doing scenes in the café, and once she suddenly remarked, 'The grouse haven't been frightfully good this year, have they?'

To hear that coming from Gail in her pinny was rather unexpected to say the least, particularly as she was shaking a chip pan at the time. But Helen is really a very sophisticated woman and a great foodie. Without doubt my happiest days in the Street were working with her in the café. In fact, when we had to have a row during one of our final scenes together there, after being told that our characters had to go their separate ways, we were so upset at the prospect of being parted that we both broke down and cried. We very nearly couldn't say our lines. I love Helen, and am very glad to say that she is one of the Street people I still see regularly.

Many other of the Street's stars are also not at all what you would expect. Eileen Derbyshire (Emily) is one of the funniest people I have ever met. She doesn't like being recognised or meeting fans or people she doesn't know. She puts on wonderful disguises. Once she wore Middle Eastern robes and a yashmak at Granada.

Liz Bradley, who as Maud was wheelchair-bound and a bit of a latter-day Ena, was very theatrical and lived rather grandly in a big house in Hampstead with swans at the bottom of her garden. But she adored being in the Street and it broke her heart to leave. However, she went straight on to portray Alan Bennett's mother in his play *The Lady In The Van*, with Maggie Smith in the title role. Sadly Liz died not long afterwards, and I still miss her a lot. But she did do so rather in the style that she had lived – while having a wonderful time in the south of France with her film-director son.

Then there is Sue Nichols, of course, who plays Audrey Roberts. When Alma moved into Audrey's house, Sue and I wanted to become a sort of double act, like *The Odd Couple*, and do lots of comedy together, but it just never seemed to happen. Not on screen anyway. Off screen we spent most of our time giggling in corridors. We are great friends and, a bit like Helen and me previously, were genuinely tearful when we were doing all Alma's death scenes because we knew we were really going to miss each other.

Speaking of comedy, I do think that the Street's Jack and Vera Duckworth, as portrayed by Bill Tarmey and Liz Dawn, are quite probably the best comic pairing since Morecambe and Wise. Just don't kid yourself that they are playing themselves. Bill is a gentle and attractive man, with none of Jack's vulgarity, who is multi-talented and also a much-acclaimed jazz singer with a string of records to his name. Liz is one of the best clothes horses I have ever seen and has seriously good taste, she works endlessly for charity, and is a successful businesswoman.

Johnny Briggs (Mike) is one of the few in the cast that I can think of who actually can resemble his character. I think it takes over a bit. Johnny can be very funny and very charming, and we always had a good time working together. But he only talked to me on set if we were doing scenes together. And if we had a quarrel as characters he would stop talking to me. I used to say, 'Johnny, it's not real you know.' But it was almost as if he forgot.

I shared more storylines with him than anyone in the Street I suppose. I always rather enjoyed working with Johnny because we came from the same kind of show-business background, we had both started very young, and we both like to run through our lines together repeatedly before each scene so that we could often do it in one take. One of my favourite episodes was in 1991 when Mike dumped Alma for another woman and I got to slash her duvet and cut up all of Mike's ties. I quite enjoyed that. But a rather more serious aspect of that storyline was Alma getting left alone for Christmas. She was very much a victim at the time, and I was staggered by how many people identified with what was happening to her. I received loads of letters about it. I could identify with it myself, because of the way I have always felt about being left alone. It was during that period that I came to like and appreciate the character I was playing, and allowed a lot of myself to come out in Alma – something I continued to do right up until I left the show.

Mike and Alma were reunited, of course, and their wedding day in 1992 is probably my most vivid memory of our working together. It was about the hottest day I can ever remember anywhere. We were on location in a registry office and the crew spent the entire day mopping us all down and trying to stop our make-up from melting.

The other *Corrie* man in my life as Alma was Bill Roache (Ken). I would imagine most people think he is very serious, but he isn't. He's a great giggler for a start, and he's very adventurous, qualifying as a Formula 2 racing driver not all that long ago. Bill is quite a man, and also extremely nice and extremely handsome. I have no idea how he manages to stay looking so young, but if he could bottle the formula he'd make a fortune.

I am also a great admirer of Barbara Knox (Rita), who is a real quality act and so under-used nowadays. If Rita had not become a Street regular I think she would have gone on to a spectacular career in the theatre. I saw her do a one-woman show in London's Barbican Theatre, with a one-hundred-piece orchestra, and she was absolutely breathtaking. I reckon her singing voice is every bit as good as that of her namesake Barbara Cooke.

Yet another *Corrie* actor with a great voice is John Savident (Fred) who has appeared in many top musicals including *Phantom of the Opera*. Once, when we had to spend an entire freezing rainy night on open moorland filming the exploits of the ill-fated staff of Freshco's who had been sent on an endurance trial weekend, John cheered us all up at four in the morning with a rousing rendition of 'The Lonely Goatherd' from *The Sound of Music*. Cold and wet as we were we all yodelled along with him. It must have been quite a spectacle. John and I together also led a rousing sing-song when we were forced to film the Freshco's siege all night long, three nights on the trot. This was because all the Freshco's scenes were shot in real supermarkets when they were closed. Usually that meant that we filmed on Sundays but because of the amount of footage given to the siege it couldn't all be completed in one day. So there we were again shivering together at four in the morning, this time sitting on a stone floor, right by, appropriately enough, the store's deep freezes.

Of course, we once more had with us that grand master of endurance, Freshco's bold leader and my very good friend Kevin Kennedy (Curly). To have been a Manchester City fan all your life, as I and my entire family know only too well, to have supported this thoroughly infuriating football team through all the ups and downs, trials and tribulations, not to mention abject misery, is a feat of endurance way beyond the capacity of most mere mortals. It takes a man of monumental spiritual fortitude to cope with the mockery and cruel taunts which follow Kevin through the streets of Manchester when he's trotting along carrying his little blue-and-white City bag and wearing his blue-and-white scarf. His is a special kind of courage.

During my time in the Street I suffered two serious health scares. Ten years ago I underwent a hysterectomy amid fears that I might have cancer. Then more recently I feared that I might be going blind.

The problems I was experiencing before my hysterectomy, which included bleeding so heavily it was as if I was haemorrhaging, turned out to be gynaecological. I have remained pretty well ever since, but I do very clearly remember my sheer terror. This made me particularly anxious about the effects on viewers of the way in which Alma, who of course died of cervical cancer, was written out of the Street.

I vividly recall waiting for the results of my tests, and how worried I was. My strongest feelings when I was acting out Alma's death was that if one woman stayed away from her doctor because of anything she'd seen in the show, then that would have been unforgivable. It seems that in the main, the opposite happened, and that the show made women more aware, but my own experiences did make me very anxious about the storyline.

Like many women, I think, I was aware for some time that something was very wrong before my problem was finally diagnosed. By and large it was fibroids that went wrong. I was given HRT treatment which caused my fibroids to more or less explode. There had been all kinds of minor signs, but at least two doctors and a gynaecologist said it was all nothing and put it down to the change of life. It turned out that I had these fibroids, non-malignant growths, in my womb, and by the time I was correctly diagnosed the operation was almost an emergency. I really was afraid that I had cancer and some of the tests came back borderline. I was just in a cold sweat all the time.

But the operation, thank God, was a success.

It went better than I could ever have expected, even though I ended up going into The Portland Hospital two days before the Grand National, which, naturally, infuriated me. Apparently my last words before I went under the anaesthetic were, 'Back Seagram.' I'd already put on a hefty bet myself, I came to just in time to see Seagram win and my bet paid my entire medical bill.

I walked down Marylebone High Street two days later and was working again within four weeks. My message to any woman having to face a hysterectomy is don't listen to the horror stories, ask lots of questions, and don't be fobbed off. The worst thing about the after effects of the op is something they never tell you – wind. There is often an enormous build up that causes your stomach to swell. In my case it was so bad that the nursing staff declared that there would probably eventually be a hurricane and that we should call it Alma! They were joking I think. But recently, in America, I learned that there was a hurricane on the way that had indeed, most appropriately, if a little late, been called Alma.

It was five years ago that I became afraid that I was going blind. I had a Retina Vein Occlusion, virtually overnight, in my left eye. It was a blockage in one of the channels that feeds the eye, sort of like having a kink in a hose. I woke up one day and I had a lot of black lines in front of my eye.

When I learned what was wrong I was wet through from head to foot from terror, because the same thing can happen to the other eye at any time. The treatment prescribed involved pints of blood being taken from my body and replaced with equal amounts of plasma. While still continuing to work in the Street, I underwent this treatment four times over a period of six weeks. The blessed Sandra ferried me to and from hospital in the latest of her succession of elderly vehicles and sat by my side throughout, trying to make jokes, and somehow or other got me back to Granada and usually more or less straight on set after each session. Thank God, my bad eye has partially repaired itself and the good one has so far not been affected.

It was strange. I backed a 100–1 horse called See Enough. When it won by five lengths, I decided it was an omen. I started talking to my eye. I called it Walter, and told it what it had to do. My specialist said on very rare occasions your eye can make itself another channel and if the channel points in the right direction it can start to correct itself. I used to lie there every night talking to Walter, and when I went back to see my specialist he said, 'Something's happening. Your eye is growing a new blood vessel and is beginning to empty.'

I think I experienced a minor miracle. I can still see, and I am eternally grateful for that gift.

Most importantly of all, my eyesight scare did not affect my ability to work, as I had feared that it might. I not only continued in the Street, but shortly afterwards was involved in one of my most testing storylines – physically as well as mentally, as it turned out. Alma was kidnapped by Don Brennan, played by Geoff Hinsliff. I had not really worked with Geoff before and discovered that not only was he a very good actor, he was also a very nice guy – which was all for the best considering the demands that were made of us. The storyline culminated in an hour-long special that mostly took place in Don's taxi.

In order for us to produce this extra-long episode as well as all the others, the filming had to be done at night in one week, working between 6.00 p.m. and dawn. We were also needed to be in the studio during the day, so the schedule was even more gruelling than usual, and the pressures were greater too. It was really important to get through all the scenes as efficiently as possible. But we were doing these highly charged emotional scenes in a motor car with a cameraman and a sound boom squashed in with us. I had to act terrified and burst into tears while looking at Geoff with a cameraman crawling all over him and a huge sound boom sticking up between his legs. We knew we just had to do it though, and I think we managed virtually every scene in one take. There was little margin for error but I don't think either of us fluffed once. Filming had to end promptly when dawn broke. It wasn't just daylight that was the problem, but the sound of bird song. The birds of Manchester became our biggest enemies that week.

The weather conspired to make things more difficult. It tipped down with rain too. There was one scene where Alma tried to run away from Don and I had to crawl up a steep, muddy hillside. Every time I tried to grab a sod of earth it seemed to come away in my hand and I slipped backwards. All the while I was virtually face to face with Margaret, a wonderfully stoic camerawoman on *Coronation Street*, who was lying there with me. We did ask each other once or twice in fairly colourful terms what exactly we were doing there. It should be said that the crew of *Coronation Street* must be about the best and most professional there has ever been. They have to be, with the schedules they are working to, and they never let you down.

The culmination of the kidnap sequence came with a sequence that really tested us all to the limits – particularly me. Looking back I think I must have been mad to let myself in for it but I did not realise quite what it was going to entail when I agreed to it. On screen Don was seen driving his car into the murky waters of Salford Quays, and then Alma was seen popping up, miraculously more or less unscathed.

In order to film this scene I underwent the most frightening ordeal of my acting career. I was told that it had been arranged for us to film in a police diving tank, and that I would merely be required to submerge myself briefly in the water while standing on a platform. We were driven to Liverpool to the place where police divers are trained. I could not believe what I saw. I had imagined the kind of neat sanitised tank generally used for these kind of scenes in major films. What I was faced with was an expanse of black water about the size of six Olympic swimming pools, 16 feet deep and covered in debris. I had to climb down two ladders tied together, the drop was too big for just one, and then, in the dark because the whole storyline took place at night, I had to walk out onto a kind of pipe just a few inches wide into the water. Because I was not likely to stay submerged for long enough without help, chains were fitted around my ankles to weight me down.

I must have been mad to go through with it. I just thought, 'Let's get on with it.' I had it in my head that if the water didn't kill me the crew probably would if we didn't get the shot done so that we could all go home. I was genuinely scared. But I did it. I shuffled out on this pipe and submerged myself in the water. That was the next shock. It was absolutely freezing. My heart had been nearly boiled in *Carry On Cleo*, and nearly deep frozen in *Coronation Street*. I almost passed out. But I did it. I plunged myself underwater and emerged as Alma escaping from Don's car – the only bit the viewers saw. The irony is that it was a night scene that happened so quickly, and I was in such a mess with my hair wet and glued to my head, that those watching probably thought they were seeing a stunt girl. I'm not at all sure that any stunt girl would have done it actually.

When I crawled up that ladder again I was taken into a caravan and rubbed down with towels, a reminder of my childhood experiences on Llandudno beach. Later that day I realised both my eyes had turned blood red, a side effect of being plunged into freezing water that nobody had told me about and which frightened me even more considering my recent scare with my sight. Thankfully all was well and I received a letter of thanks from Carolyn Reynolds, who was the producer then, and various other Granada executives. They expressed not only their gratitude but also their appreciation of my professionalism.

Sadly this all seemed to be forgotten in the months to come and I began to think that perhaps I no longer wished to remain a part of the world's most famous soap after all.

CHAPTER TWENTY

ॐ

All the cast, particularly the more long-standing members, are inclined to be sentimental about *Coronation Street*. It is, after all, an amazing show, the longest running TV drama in the world. Anyone would have to have a heart of stone to remain unmoved by the sheer privilege of being a part of it. Regardless of those schedules!

To this day there is a big Busy Lizzie plant which somebody put in the Green Room when the show started and it continues to survive. Everybody waters it and looks after it, and it's become symbolic to the cast over the years. In some ways I think many of us, albeit subconsciously, thought that as long as that plant was flourishing then all was well with *Coronation Street*.

Just before I left, Prince Charles visited the Street and it was decided the Green Room should be redecorated. Overnight our Busy Lizzie disappeared, causing considerable panic among the cast. It was Bill Roache who eventually found it. It had been put out with the rubbish and was pretty battered but once we'd cut it right back and made a big fuss over it, we managed to rescue it. The story of that plant is very significant to me. It should never have been thrown out like that. It was as if nobody cared and if nobody cares, goodness knows what might be thrown out on the rubbish tip next.

The whole concept of that royal visit was disturbing, particularly in view of Granada's well-publicised financial problems. The Green Room was pretty tattily furnished and always kind of messy, with plastic cups all over the place and so on. Suddenly it was given a complete revamp, smart new leather chairs were brought in, so that it ended up looking like an executive airport lounge rather than the package-holiday sort. It must have cost a fortune. The actors would have much preferred the money to have been ploughed back into the show, and I suspect that Prince Charles would probably have preferred to see the way actors really live. I am sure he would have been outraged about the plant.

I do believe that the Street has been betrayed in recent years as Granada has used its most successful programme to prop up all its other enterprises.

Coronation Street, sadly, has been bled almost dry. Its poor little heart has been torn out. I think of it as being like a listed building. All too many of the stones that have been hacked out made up the support walls. Of course you want and need some new extensions, maybe even a new wing, but if you take out too many of those supporting stones then you will destroy your building. That's what I fear might happen. I fear that *Coronation Street* may be destroyed. I believe, you see, that the Street belongs to the nation. In my opinion the company that makes it is just its caretaker, and that little word care is very important. The producers are just looking after it for the public. They should keep it safe. It's not just about money. It shouldn't just be business – not this show.

The problem is that those of us who love the Street, and I really think I can include the entire cast in this, are fighting money with emotion.

Around the time I left, there was considerable publicity about unrest among the show's stars who were told quite arbitrarily that their salaries would be cut when they signed their next contracts. This news, of course, coincided with the release of Granada's latest half-yearly financial report which revealed a huge fall in the company's profits. If the cast felt that any money saved was being put back into *Coronation Street* I suspect they wouldn't mind so much, but everybody believed it would be used to prop up the rest of the organisation at the expense of the Street. Certainly I hate the cast being represented as a bunch of money-grabbers. They are actually a great group of professionals. They have to be to cope with the sheer speed at which they have to work.

I think everybody who watches the Street regularly would agree that the show is not as good as it used to be. It can really be no other way now that there are four episodes a week, of course it was better when there were just two. It's sad really to think that the increase in episodes was purely a financially motivated decision. *Coronation Street* attracts massive amounts of advertising at top rates. More shows means more revenue – but there are bound to be drawbacks. How can actors who don't rehearse perform as well as they would if they did? Not only are there barely any rehearsals at all for the Street any more, but neither is there time to discuss the script with anyone. I didn't like that, and neither did anyone else. If you're in the Street it takes over your life, it becomes your life. All the cast want it to be the best it can be, and want to do the best they can themselves, but that's not so easy any more. I spoke out publicly on this issue right after I left the Street and I stand by everything that I said then. It is only someone who is out of the show who dares speak out. If you are in a soap it's tremendously difficult to make any kind of stand. If you speak up you may be the one to be sacked, and soap actors are like everyone else who has to work for a living. If you have a good, reasonably well-paid job, of course you are afraid of losing it.

There has been a lot of talk in the press about salaries, and again this year, at contract-renewal time, there has been publicity concerning trouble over more pay cuts. But it's only the biggest stars who earn anything approaching big money and even they only get a yearly contract. Wondering whether they'll be kept on is very hard for people who've given their career to *Coronation Street*, who've been in just this one show for most of their working lives.

I suspect that the earnings of the majority of Street actors is far less than most viewers would think. The sums of money bandied about in the tabloids are often far greater than the truth, and I have therefore decided to take what I think is the rare step of being honest about what I earned. Pay in *Coronation Street* is based on both how long you have been in the show and how many episodes you do – the episode rate, by the way, being exactly the same whether you are involved in a major storyline or merely ordering a round of drinks in the Rovers. My average annual salary was between £80,000 and £90,000. The most I ever earned in a year was just over £100,000 and the least about £70,000. Only a tiny handful of the really long-standing cast members earned more than this, and most of the younger actors earned considerably less. From our earnings, of course, we have to deduct agents' fees – usually a minimum of twelve and a half per cent nowadays – before tax. In my case, like many Street actors, my home remained in London so I was paying for a second apartment in Manchester and travelling costs between the two cities. I am not pleading poverty here, but I think it is important to point out that when it comes to *Coronation Street* wages we are most certainly not talking *Dallas* or *Dynasty*.

It wasn't just the financial side of things that became problematic for us Street actors. That was just the tip of the iceberg. The lack of communication in the Street was total at the time that I left. There was almost a barrier of communication. It was like the *Marie Celeste* – as if there was nobody and nothing out there. I suspect that Carolyn Reynolds, Granada's head of drama and a previous producer of the Street, who was brought in as acting producer at the end of 2001 replacing Jane McNaught, may have changed that. In my experience she was always very hands-on in her approach. But during my last two or three years in the show there wasn't enough feedback. I felt we were working in a vacuum.

The email culture hit *Coronation Street* in a big way, too. The executives weren't only not talking to the cast, they weren't talking to each other much from what I could see of it. People working in the same office would send emails to each other. There was a sense of distance about everything.

It is no secret that I did not enjoy a good relationship with Jane McNaught, and that is one of the reasons why I eventually decided to take the plunge and leave the show. I had a pretty strong feeling that I wasn't one of her favourite actors, so I was not optimistic about my future there. Obviously when you have a change in a producer of any programme they are bound to have their own preferences. Some producers take to you and some don't. That's perfectly natural and there's nothing more to say really, but I certainly did not want to be sacked and neither did I want to see any more of my friends sacked. If I had really wanted to stay, however, I would just have kept my head down and stuck it out. I have been in the entertainment business all my life. Nobody knows more than me how swiftly fortunes rise and fall and producers come and go – which is indeed exactly what has happened at Granada.

I did enjoy a strong professional relationship with previous Street producers. Bill Podmore was wonderful and really understood the Street, Mervyn Watson presided over one of the Street's finest periods, and Carolyn Reynolds was also great. If anyone can get the Street back on course it will be Carolyn. She was always around when I worked with her, and if she was particularly pleased with something you'd done, a difficult scene or a tricky stunt , she would always be quick to tell you. There'd be a phone call or a little note like the one she sent me following my 'short course in freezing to death' stunt during the Don Brennan storyline. Brian Parke was another good hands-on producer. He got blamed for a lot of the more unpopular changes in the Street, like getting rid of Derek, but actually that deed had been done before Brian took over, and I think he was very brave to take on the Street when he did.

Regardless of whoever might have been in charge I did feel that twenty years on and off in one show was quite long enough – even when that show is as special as *Coronation Street*. However, if I had been working with a producer I got on well with I would quite possibly still be muddling along in the Street, although in my heart I knew that I wanted to move on – so in a curious sort of way I am grateful to Jane McNaught because it is partly because of her that I was motivated to launch myself into the big, big world outside of Weatherfield again.

I do believe that the quality of the Street fell unavoidably during the years I was in the show. In the last chapter I tried to give a picture of what life in the Street is really like for the regular actors, and also to present the lighter, more amusing side of the relentless work schedule. But there is a serious aspect too.

It's lost some great writers. I don't know if that's down to money, I really have no idea. I do know that *Coronation Street* is Granada's flagship. The producers should be building it up, making it strong. Instead they are weakening it.

The axing of much loved classic characters like Derek, played by Peter Baldwin, is a typical example of the kind of unpopular arbitrary decision that has rocked the foundations of the Street. And the shortage of comic storylines of the sort Derek and his wife Mavis, so superbly played by Thelma Barlow, specialised in is a great loss. Even Jack and Vera can't do it all. I also think that getting rid of Don Brennan (Geoff Hinsliff) was a big mistake. Every soap needs its villains and Don developed into a really creepy one. To lose him after Alma's kidnap seemed to me to be a total waste.

The biggest problem that I had in all my years in the Street concerned the way in which Alma was finally written out. I considered it to be little more than a cynical attempt to win viewers regardless of the consequences. She died of cervical cancer in a manner I found immensely disturbing. Cancer touches all our lives. There can't be anyone who hasn't been affected. So if you take an issue like this and use it for entertainment you have to be very, very careful. From the moment I first learned what was going to happen I was extremely anxious about it. As Alma's illness and deterioration proceeded with such amazing speed I really did feel that I was being asked to take part in a cheap ratings ploy, and I didn't like it one bit.

From the moment the cancer storyline was disclosed I began to receive a huge daily mail bag of heart-rending letters. The one that really triggered off my anger over the cavalier way the issue was being treated came from a woman with two little kiddies, who was dying of cervical cancer. She wrote, 'Please, please, beg the producers not to do this story. Cancer is not something to be used for entertainment. I will probably not be able to watch much of Alma dying, I expect to die before you do, but my children watch the Street, and I do not want them to see this.'

I didn't reply, and I still feel guilty. But what could I say? That I didn't have control of the storyline? Why should this poor woman care? I didn't know what to do. I certainly couldn't send her a signed photograph, could I? That would have been really insulting. There was just no way I could get my dyslexic head around replying to that letter.

I have always been aware that a soap is different to any other kind of drama. I have already touched on this illusion of Weatherfield being a real place and certainly the characters become real to a lot of viewers. Therefore the responsibility on a soap is enormous, greater possibly than any other form of TV or cinema drama. I couldn't stand the fact that we were dealing with cancer in a way that might be considered irresponsible.

Both Sue Nichols and I were quite widely praised for the way in which we performed the scenes surrounding Alma's death and for the sensitivity we displayed. Both of us have been nominated for and won awards. Nonetheless, I was extremely uneasy throughout filming.

The very first time in my career that I have ever had rows over a script was over this storyline. I'd never done that before. I think I rowed every day with someone: the script editor, a storyliner, the director. It was the storyline editor, Di Burrows, who bore the brunt of my concern, and I actually felt very sorry for her. She always seemed to be the go-between, the person who had to deal with confrontation. She came to my farewell party and she said how sorry she was that we'd fallen out over the scripts. I thought that was very good of her, and we spent half the evening hugging each other.

It was actually in November 2000 that I resigned from *Coronation Street*. I had only recently renewed my contract but I was finally quite sure I would not wish to do so again. So I asked my agent, still Peter Charlesworth, to contact Granada and tell them so. I thought that it was only fair to do that and thus allow plenty of time for Alma to be written out in a suitable way. Very shortly afterwards I was approached by Di, who said that they were thinking of writing me a really spectacular ending, although she didn't say what. I quite liked the idea of going out with a bit of a bang, so I said I would sooner not just be waving goodbye out of a taxi, and they should do as they liked. There is no point in taking any other attitude. The storyliners always do what they want. The actors in the Street never have any input. The writers may once have talked to the cast but not any more. We were like children given their homework and told to get on with it. It was extremely rare for anybody to know in advance what was going to happen to their character. Usually we read it in the tabloids first.

A lot of the problems at the Street came about because the people in charge were inclined to treat members of the cast as if they were their characters, and not professional actors at all. The truth is that there was very little mutual respect.

So nobody ever discussed the cancer storyline with me at any stage. I learned about it because I heard it being muttered about by other people. That's another way you learn about things on the Street, from gossip among the cast, or maybe wardrobe, or make-up. It's like Chinese Whispers. I rang Di Burrows to try to find out if it was true, because I was worried about it at once. It was such an important issue to embark on in the name of entertainment. Di confirmed that Alma was going to die of cervical cancer. 'It's a very, very uplifting story,' she said.

It's true, of course, that cancer stories can be uplifting both in real life and in fiction, but not this one. I never found anything remotely uplifting about the Alma storyline, and I can't believe that anyone else could have done either. At the time, I had no idea how the storyline was going to be developed. Neither did I have any idea of the brief time span that was going to be allotted to Alma's illness and death. But I felt strongly that such a sequence of events must be represented with total accuracy and be absolutely medically correct and said so. I assumed,

naturally, that Alma would be given treatment, including chemotherapy, which, of course, more often than not involves hair loss. I
offered to shave my hair off. But Di said at once that there would be no
question of that. There couldn't be, given the speed with which Alma
was to depart. It didn't occur to me then that I would go so quickly –
after all, my existing contract with the Street did not run out until a
whole five months after my last appearance in the show. Part of my
reason for giving so much notice was so that Alma's exit, whatever form
it took, need not be rushed after she had been part of the Street for so
long. But nobody at Granada seemed to care about that. And, of course,
it was the speed of Alma's decline and death that I think were the worst
aspect.

Alma was summoned for a smear test after having first missed one
and then being the victim of a hospital blunder over a second one. A
biopsy was taken and the results were given to her virtually straight
away – an impossibility since this kind of biopsy involves developing a
culture over a minimum of four or five days. Then she was instantly
told by her consultant that her condition was terminal and that there
was little long-term point in her having treatment.

When I learned about that I was horrified. Cervical cancer takes
years to develop. No consultant would make a pronouncement as
quickly and as bluntly as that, and no woman would have reached that
stage without severe symptoms. I felt that it gave completely the wrong
message. I know that as the storyline developed a number of medical
experts spoke out against it which didn't surprise me one bit. I wasn't
the only one who felt that the storyline was a ratings ploy.

Alma was told that chemotherapy might prolong her life just a little,
but after only two sessions she refused any further treatment, which,
apart from anything else, I thought was totally out of character. I didn't
have a quarrel with Alma being written out in a sensational manner, but

the way the storyline developed was contrary to my personal beliefs. I believe in healing. I believe in miracles. I believe it to be a miracle that I can still see. Our own will and determination is a vital part of fighting illness. I don't think anybody should give up. Not ever. To give any other message in the name of entertainment has to be wrong.

The letters I received had a tremendous effect on me. I could so imagine some poor eight-year-old child sitting watching *Coronation Street*, knowing her mother was being treated for the same illness as Alma Halliwell. I didn't want them thinking, 'If there's no hope for Alma, then there's no hope for my mum.'

After all those years in *Coronation Street* I am recognised a great deal by the public and normally people just come bounding up to me. I like talking to fans, and I think that probably comes across. But after the cancer storyline started there was a noticeable change. It was as if people were a bit afraid to approach, unsure of what to say, just as you might be with someone in real life. I was particularly angry when one newspaper carried an article saying that I was 'thrilled' by the cancer storyline. Nothing could have been further from the truth. I found it all such a humbling experience. I found it presumptuous to act out this kind of death in a soap. It seemed almost sacrilegious to act out cancer pain.

But I do want to make it clear how I feel about that side of things. Actors can talk a lot of nonsense sometimes about how harrowing it is to act out sickness. I hate it when they say that they've suffered in a role. My attitude to that is, 'Come off it!' Acting that you have cancer is not a bit like having it, not a bit. I always get pleasure in acting out a scene with as good an actress as Sue Nichols. It is hardly a pleasure to have your best friend in real life tell you she has cancer.

I was so intent on putting right as many as possible of the mistakes I felt were being made that I insisted on changing some of the dialogue

– the kind of actor involvement that is certainly not encouraged on the *Coronation* Street set. They wanted Alma to keep saying that she was dying. Apart from anything else I don't think that is the way very sick people talk about it. I had never attempted to tinker with the script before but this was so important, I had to intervene.

There was one line I particularly remember refusing to say. The line was, 'They made me watch the TV monitor while they were scooping out bits of my body.'

Well, if that wouldn't put you off having a colposcopy, which is a very important procedure when they do a biopsy on a sample from the womb, I don't know what would. The fact that I know what it is like to be afraid that you have cancer did make me more aware of this. I know about the anxiety of waiting for test results. I also know what it feels like to have a dear friend tell you they are dying of cancer. There is nothing to say. One friend of mine had a brain tumour and suffered dreadfully. I didn't visit her or talk to her on the phone as much as I should have, something I now regret deeply, because I just couldn't. I couldn't bear her being so ill.

However, somewhat to my surprise there have been some positive results from the Alma storyline. I realised this when, just before Alma's death, I was asked by the Macmillan Trust, which sponsors specialist cancer nurses, to appear at a charity event where Prince Charles was guest of honour. They seemed to think that ultimately the storyline, in spite of its faults, might do some good. I understand, in fact, that the number of women going for smear tests may even have increased as a result. If true, then I also like to think that it might be at least partly because it became known how unhappy I was about the storyline, and certainly we did get some small changes made.

During my last weeks as Alma I was involved in a secondary storyline that also infuriated me. Alma became embroiled in a new romance and before her cancer was diagnosed was allegedly going to retreat to a cottage in the country with her lover. It was just impossible for me to accept that anyone could be told they have terminal cancer and die in six weeks and not have any symptoms worth mentioning. I flatly refused to do anything on screen that indicated that there was a sexual relationship between Alma and Frank. The prospect of her happily jumping into bed with someone under those circumstances I just found totally distasteful. I wouldn't even let them kiss. We ended up in one scene rubbing noses instead, which I think was my idea. Looking back that was one of the more ridiculous moments.

I did not take my decision to leave *Coronation Street* lightly. I have always known, however, that there was a world out there beyond Granada Television's Stage One, and I wanted very much to launch myself into it again.

I had started thinking that it was time to quit more than three years earlier. But I felt I was teetering on the edge of a diving board. I couldn't make myself jump. It wasn't just job security. It really was much more than that. A show like the Street becomes a way of life. It pulls you in. You get so that you feel you can't leave. However, I did have an instinct that the time was right for me to depart. I have always had the feeling that the Street has a mind of its own. When it runs out of storylines for you it's time to go. I also feel that soaps need younger characters nowadays. Alma really couldn't go on having all these romances, and there didn't seem anywhere else to go.

Nonetheless I did dither about leaving. I already wanted to go when I signed my final contract just before the show's fortieth birthday party, but we'd all done interviews and said marvellous things about the Street, and I felt I couldn't just hand my notice in straight away. It would have been so dishonest. That was when I decided to do what I hoped was the decent thing, which was for my then agent Peter Charlesworth to ring Granada and tell them that I wouldn't be signing again the following year.

I am acutely aware that millions of *Coronation Street* fans have followed the ups and downs of Alma Halliwell's life for twenty years. They've laughed with her and shared her joys and her sorrows. I know, too, that many of them wept for her passing. I was also deeply saddened to see the end of Alma. People are kind enough to tell me quite often that they miss her. Well, I miss her too.

There are, however, things I do not miss about the Street. I don't miss my Freshco's supermarket overall for a start. As a descendant of a family with a noble tradition in the rag trade I absolutely love good clothes. But there I was for years, married to Mike Baldwin who wore all those sharp suits, and I'd be sitting around in these dreadful ill-fitting overalls which, to make matters worse, seemed to burst open every time I moved, so we were always having to reshoot. Nobody ever seemed to be able to put that right. My overalls had a life of their own.

Nor do I miss all those train journeys between London and Manchester. My final winter in *Coronation Street,* from 2000 to 2001, when our entire rail service was terminally disrupted following that awful series of crashes, was quite horrendous. Every time I set off I expected to be found some weeks later as a skeleton in a siding at Watford Junction – having expired from lack of food and drink, because buffet cars became just a mirage during that period – by a cartoon figure of Richard Branson grinning like the Cheshire Cat from *Alice's Adventures in Wonderland.*

Also, of course, as a dyslexic I do not miss the torture of having to learn new lines every single night.

However, I do miss the camaraderie. The characters in a soap like the Street become a second family, as I believe they do for many viewers, particularly in an age when families are not what they were and so many people live alone. As an actor, the Street takes over your entire life, you have no time for anything else, so naturally it becomes very important – out of all proportion probably. I can be pretty cynical about most things, but when I stood on those cobbles looking at *Coronation Street* I rarely failed to feel a sense of enchantment, and I did always realise what a privilege it was to be there. One Christmas I remember being at a party at Granada with Tony Warren and we walked out onto that cobbled street together. It had been snowing, everything was covered in a thin white blanket.

'You can feel the magic of the Street, can't you?' I remarked.

'Oh yes,' replied Tony, the man who had created the show so many years before. 'I can always feel its magic.'

That is just how it is with *Coronation Street*.

I honestly do miss Alma, I think she was probably the better part of me. She was kind, she had good friends, and she was able to love people. She was fundamentally a good person. However, unlike me, she also knew when it was time to leave the party.

With her death a huge chapter of my somewhat varied life may have closed, but, although I do have my bus pass, I still look to the future. And even as I write I am aware of whole new chapters opening up.

EPILOGUE

ॐ

While in pantomime in Bradford last year I sat entranced in an Indian restaurant one night while I listened to my eight-year-old great-niece, Alex Broadbent, tell a joke – and quite a suggestive one it was, too, for a sweet little girl! She took the floor like an old pro and captivated everyone there. In a weird way it wasn't like hearing a child telling a joke. Alex, granddaughter of my brother Chris and his wife Edna, is already a performer. It seems to come naturally for her to size up her audience and go grab them. I was reminded so vividly of myself at that age that it almost hurt. If I had a pound for every time I stood up as a child and sang or danced for my supper, I wouldn't need a pension.

I have no idea whether or not Alex, or her sister Megan, who also shows talent in that direction, are likely to go into show business professionally or even if they would want to. Neither could I possibly have any idea what such a future might hold for them. Unlike me, of course, they would at least be able to keep their own names, should they ever launch themselves into the entertainment industry. Indeed, Broadbent is a more than respectable name for an actor nowadays, since Jim has found Hollywood glory.

Other than that I don't think the business has changed very much. This crazy profession, which has always been my driving force and responsible for so much of the roller-coaster ride of my personal life remains as volatile, as unpredictable, as wonderful, and as awful, as ever.

I do not know what the future holds for me any more than for Alex and Megan. It may even be presumptuous to assume I still have one at my age. But I know that I do. As life after Alma unfolds before me I have as many dreams as ever. Indeed, I wouldn't see much point in remaining alive if I could no longer dream.

When I quit *Coronation Street* I liked the idea of having at least a little more time off than previously, but things haven't worked out quite that way so far. I have already returned to TV as jailed con woman Bev in the popular series *Bad Girls*, set in a women's prison. Then there has been this book to write, and I have also returned to my theatrical roots, first of all in that Bradford pantomime, playing the wicked queen in *Snow White*, then in one of my all-time favourite plays, Alan Ayckbourn's *Absurd Person Singular* and finally in pantomime again this Christmas in Birmingham.

I was extremely nervous about going back on stage after the fifteen-year absence imposed by the Street, and, contrary to the usual misconception, I was more than pleased to initially return to the boards in pantomime, which is such a great British tradition. I couldn't think of a better way of finding my feet again after such a long time of only facing a camera. Television can put an actor out of touch with their audience.

Indeed, sometimes in a show like the Street, the whole process becomes so insular that, in spite of being aware of the enormous viewing figures, you almost forget that anyone is ever going to watch you apart from the crew. There can be few better ways of getting in touch again than through pantomime. *Snow White* was a great success. It was actually a revelation for me to play to capacity audiences for virtually every show, ten to twelve times a week for seven weeks, at the famous Alhambra, a huge theatre seating nearly 1,500. To my relief, I found that I loved every minute of it.

I was then delighted and flattered when the *Snow White* management, the highly successful Qdos led by Jon Conway and Nick Thomas, told me that they would like to choose a play to put on in Bournemouth especially with me in mind. It wasn't just that I liked the idea of spending the summer by the seaside. I jumped at the opportunity to work with Jon again, as he is the only producer I have encountered who seems able to perform most of the roles in his shows better than the performers he employs. We all watched in amazement in Bradford when he pretended to be a frog and hopped onto a ten-foot high rock on stage with no trouble at all. I was even more delighted when they took up my suggestion of *Absurd Person Singular* and when Alan Ayckbourn agreed to release it for an eight-week season. I played Marion Brewster-Wright, a role I have always loved, and was pleased to find that the play has stood the test of time magnificently. Our Bournemouth audiences seemed to love it.

This Christmas I played the genie in Aladdin at Birmingham's Hippodrome Theatre, home of the Birmingham Royal Ballet which, with a huage stage and the capacity to seat 1,800, is even bigger than The Alhambra and traditionally hosts Britain's premier panto. It was a privilege to play there.

I have also managed a holiday or two since leaving the Street, and find I am rather getting to enjoy them at last, although, in spite of my good intentions, I do seem to be doing my best to leave myself little time for them. I have already signed an option to appear in another series of *Bad Girls* next year.

The prospect of getting my dyslexic head around a new script continues to terrify me as much as ever, but I rarely seem able to resist taking up the challenge. The theatre, in particular, remains a magic place for me. The sheer joy of conquering that fear, walking out on stage and seeing an audience before me and knowing that, on a good night, I can make them believe in me, thrills me as much as ever.

Another source of joy to me is that I have rediscovered my family. The friendship of my sister Caroline, brother Chris, and sister-in-law Edna is extremely important to me. I have learned only recently just how much I can depend on all three of them for love and support.

I am also extremely proud of Chris's two sons, Adam, father of Alex and Megan, and Jamie, father of Dylan. Jamie is another Broadbent who is a natural performer, something I realised at once when I first heard him speak brilliantly at his brother's wedding when he was only a teenager. Jamie went on to work with Chris Evans, both on and off the air – he was 'Jamie the Student' – and now produces and presents his own radio show. I have kept very quiet about him until now so that he would not have to face being asked deeply tedious questions about his great-aunt in *Coronation Street*. Who knows, maybe his son Dylan will also prove to have inherited whatever those genes are that seem to give so many of us Broadbents the urge to entertain.

The other side of my personal life continues to be a roller-coaster. Helena and I are no longer together, and there is someone new in my life, but we are only beginning.

Nothing ever stands still for me. Just give me another few years, God, and there may be a whole new book . . .

INDEX

꒰꒱